You're Fifty—Now What?

OTHER BOOKS BY CHARLES R. SCHWAB

Charles Schwab's Guide to Financial Independence

How to Be Your Own Stockbroker

You're Fifty—Now What?

INVESTING FOR THE SECOND HALF OF YOUR LIFE

Charles R. Schwab

THREE RIVERS PRESS • NEW YORK

The information provided here is for general informational purposes only, and should not be considered an individualized recommendation or personalized investment advice. Although all reasonable efforts have been made to make sure that the information contained in this book is accurate as of the date of publication, the author and the publisher disclaim any liability with respect to the accuracy or timeliness of that information.

Published by Three Rivers Press, New York, New York.
Member of the Crown Publishing Group.

Random House, Inc. New York, Toronto, London, Sydney, Auckland
www.randomhouse.com

Originally published in hardcover in 2001 by Crown Publishers.

Printed in the United States of America

Library of Congress Cataloging-in-Publication Data

Schwab, Charles.
You're fifty—now what?: investing for the second half of your life/by Charles Schwab.—1st ed.
Includes bibliographical references and index.
1. Finance—Personal. 2. Investments.
HG179.S3343 2001
332.024′0564—dc21
00-058961

ISBN 0-609-80870-2

10 9 8 7 6 5 4 3 2

First Paperback Edition

To the employees of The Charles Schwab Corporation
around the world
for your commitment in acting
as the custodians of our customers' financial dreams.
You have my gratitude and my admiration
for all you do for our customers.

ACKNOWLEDGMENTS

One of the qualities that I most value is teamwork, and this book is a wonderful example of it. I have once again relied on the creativity and hard work of two individuals: Nicole Young had a vision for this book and her commitment has made that vision a reality, and Bo Caldwell articulated my investing philosophy and got it down on paper. With their grace and good humor, we have done it again. We're grateful to the Schwab Center for Investment Research, a division of my firm in which I take great pride, for their generous assistance.

CONTENTS

PROLOGUE

Dear Reader,

Think of sports: a football game, a round of golf, a tennis match, a basketball game. Or think of a play, or an opera. Now think of the halfway mark in that event—halftime, or the midpoint in the match, when things can look good or downright dismal. Or think of intermission, when everyone's in the foyer, talking about what will happen next. Everyone takes a breather, and the feeling in the air can be pretty electric, because everyone's wondering the same thing: *What's going to happen in the second half?*

We have a similar point in our lives, a sort of halftime, or intermission—a time when we find ourselves wondering about the second half. The age differs from person to person. For some it comes in their late forties; for others it's in their early fifties, or maybe it's a few years away from either of those. It's somewhere in what we hope will be the middle of our lives.

When we reach that age, we *feel* different. We may sense a change coming and we want to pause and to think about what we've accomplished, and what we still hope to do. It's a time when we've come to know ourselves well. We know who we are and who we aren't, what we like and what turns us off. We've suffered some losses, both business and personal, and there really is some truth to the cliché: We're not just older—we really are wiser.

And what that age represents, whether it's 47 or 57 or somewhere in between, is the beginning of the second half of our lives. It's a time to stop for a moment and ask a very basic but crucial question: *What do I want for the second half of my life?*

Maybe you know exactly what you want; you've had it all planned out for years. Or maybe you've never thought about it much; you just can't imagine yourself as "older." Or maybe you just want to keep doing what you're doing because you love what you do, and you don't plan to retire. I include myself in that category: I am fortunate in that I am passionate about my work, and I have no plans whatsoever to retire fully.

But I do think about what I want in this second half of my life. I want to give back some of what I've received. I want to pass on what I've learned about investing. I want to help my kids as they negotiate young adulthood and even middle age, and I want to cheer on my grandkids as they attempt new things. I want to support my favorite charities, and to spend more time on the things I care about most.

So what does all this have to do with investing? A lot. A sound investing strategy is what gives you the means and the courage to do what you want.

The issues involved in planning for the second half of your life may seem daunting. I've heard people say they can't wait to retire, but they can't imagine not having a paycheck and they don't know how and when to change their investments as they age. But it can be done. It *has* to be done, because while getting older isn't a bad thing, being unprepared for it is. And by not understanding the financial part of your future, you sabotage yourself and you limit your choices.

And that's what this book is about: helping you determine

what you can do now to improve the quality of the second half of your life. It's about spending some time on understanding where you are financially and where you want to go, so that the second half of your life can be as fulfilling as you hope it will be.

If you find the whole concept of financial planning intimidating or frightening, be assured that you're not alone. But also be assured that you can do this. Planning for your future isn't rocket science; it's simply a process that involves paying attention and sticking with it. You also need a road map, and that's what this book is. Little by little, chapter by chapter, you'll learn how to figure out what you're starting with, and how to estimate what you want to end up with. You'll learn how to choose the kinds of investments that are best suited to your needs and temperament, and you'll learn how to manage your portfolio in the second half of your life. None of this is magic; it just takes commitment.

So start today, maybe even right now. Take control of the second half of your life. Dream about it, wonder about it, think boldly about what you want. And take the first step, which is usually the hardest. Once you get started, the satisfaction you feel will keep you going. But don't delay in your preparations. The best is yet to come.

Sincerely,

Charles R. Schwab

Charles R. Schwab

I

Planning for the Financial Second Half of Your Life

1

Investing Strategies for the Second Half

I have a question for you, and it's simply this: *How much is enough?*

It's a tough question, and it's essentially the topic of just about every retirement book, article, or seminar. Everyone's trying to figure out how much they'll need, and all the experts are trying to tell you how to do it. So how much will you need? How much does it take? Will you have enough? *How much* is *enough?*

Chances are it's more than you think, thanks in part to some good news. We're living longer, for one thing. Today's 50-year-olds are a lot younger than the 50-year-olds of two generations ago. A lot of us will live to be 100. As a result, what we used to call retirement can last 30 or even 40 years. Not only that: We're healthier and therefore more active, so what we used to call our retirement years are a little more costly. And we have less help from the government—Social Security isn't what it used to be. So while a lot of people think that if they have $300,000 or $400,000 set aside for retirement, they're set for life, they're probably wrong. True, that's a lot of money; chances are that it's a lot more than your parents had. But in reality, it may not be enough.

So how much *will* it take to sustain the lifestyle you're picturing? There are some dangerous estimates out there. One number that's tossed around is 70%, meaning that in retirement you'll need 70% of your current income to live comfortably. That argument *seems* logical enough: a lot of costs will, after all, go down. If you're not working, you won't commute, you won't have to buy work clothes, and all those other work-related expenses will diminish.

But do the costs go down enough to justify a 30% reduction in income? I don't think so. A recent national news story mentioned a 58-year-old computer programmer who, when he retired, had heard that 70% estimate, but just had a feeling that it wasn't reliable. Instead he decided that he would need 100% of his pre-retirement income. Yes, he realized, there were costs that would go down—401(k) contributions, Medicare and Social Security taxes, commuting and other work-related expenses, for example—but he suspected that those savings would be more than offset by a whole laundry list of other expenses: medical care, travel and entertainment, eating out.

Many people have the same concerns. There are plenty of medical expenses for even healthy retirees, things that aren't covered by Medicare: prescription drugs, dental care, hearing aids, eye care. The house and car will still need maintenance, and it's common for retirees to find they can't or don't want to do as much of the work themselves, which means the added cost of hiring someone else to do work you used to do yourself. And a lot of retiring baby boomers are finding themselves part of the "sandwich generation." Retirement isn't their only financial concern; aging parents and the kids' college tuition—things that used to be almost mutually exclusive—are concerns as well.

To say that things have changed is putting it mildly, and retirement is at the top of that list. When all is said and done, a lot of people are finding that once they've looked carefully at the costs of retirement, the expenses are significant enough to warrant revising their master plan. They're thinking about working longer, or investing a little more each month. In short, if retirement has changed, then planning for retirement has to change as well. It's time to revise our assumptions and our plans. It's time for something new.

That's what this book is about: an investing strategy for the second half of your life that takes into account the changes we're seeing. It's a strategy that probably differs from what your parents did to plan for retirement, maybe drastically so. It's a strategy that may require a little more involvement than your parents' retirement planning did. And it's a strategy that is admittedly more aggressive than what you'll hear from a lot of the other experts out there.

But here's the thing: this is a strategy that can work, it's one I believe in, and it's one that I hope you'll at least consider. It's not complicated; I can sum it up in these six points:

1. Consider yourself an investor.
2. Invest for growth for the rest of your life.
3. Start with as aggressive an asset allocation model as you comfortably can.
4. Consider using a Core & Explore™ strategy for the stock portion of your portfolio.
5. After the age of 50, adjust your asset allocation and rebalance your portfolio every five years.
6. Devise a second-half income and expense strategy early on.

As you might guess, we'll be talking about all six of these strategies in the chapters that follow, and we'll build on them as we talk about the steps involved in developing a successful investing strategy for the second half of life. For now, let's start with an overview to set the stage and define our terms.

1. Consider Yourself an Investor

As many people have found, the second half of life is a great time to be a knowledgeable investor, and it's something that often happens naturally. In the second half of life, we often have a little more time to spend learning about investing and our investments. And because we understand the important role that sound financial planning plays in a rewarding second half of life, we become more involved.

I hope that that's true for you, and I want to encourage you to become, or to continue to be, a knowledgeable investor. Why? For your well-being. Financial security is one of the keys to a fulfilling life at any stage, but in the second half of your life it is mandatory. If you don't already know how to, learn how to invest wisely, and to monitor your investments, even if you end up hiring a financial advisor for the day-to-day management. The second half is a time to nurture your hopes and dreams; it's also a time to nurture and care for your investments, and to commit yourself and take action. The process doesn't take an advanced degree; it just takes attention.

And what happens when you do get involved? A lot. Little by little, you'll find yourself gaining financial competence that should lead to more financial independence.

Don't just be a spectator where the financial area of your life is concerned; be a participant. If you've let your partner handle the finances, now is the time to bring yourself up to speed, even if that person continues to make the day-to-day decisions. If you've never researched a stock, try it. Check out a mutual fund. Become educated, become informed. It will be worth your while.

One more thing: Many of us, perhaps even most of us, were taught as kids to be *savers,* an identity that a lot of parents worked hard to reinforce. And that's great. But if you're a saver through and through, don't let the saver part of you impede the development of the *investor* part of you. The difference? *Savers* expect predictable returns at regular intervals, and, above all, they count on their principal being safe. That's their number-one priority. An *investor,* on the other hand, is willing to accept some fluctuations in returns and to take some risk in terms of those returns, all in the interest of the possibility—I'd say the likelihood—of greater returns. Investors don't just want to save their money—they want to *make it grow.*

Part of being an investor is developing an investor's mindset: You know you're in this for the long term, so you don't panic at every drop in the market. If you don't have this detachment and patience at the outset, don't be discouraged. Those qualities can take a while to develop, but they do come.

2. Invest for Growth for the Rest of Your Life

What follows is advice you may not hear from other sources, but it's at the very heart of my investing strategy. Simply put, I strongly encourage you to invest at least some portion of your money—preferably a significant portion—in stocks and stock mutual funds for as long as you live. In other words, *never stop investing for growth.* The reason? In order for our money to outlive us, it has to outpace inflation. And to do that, it has to be invested for growth. According to the *Ibbotson 2000 Yearbook,* since 1926, large company stocks have outpaced inflation by an average of 8.0% per year (11.1% compound annual return for stocks less 3.1% average inflation).

In order for your money to outlive you, it must outpace inflation. I believe that to do that, it has to be invested for growth.

Let's back up for a moment. In the past, a lot of people (including, perhaps, your parents or grandparents) automatically shifted to a portfolio that was made up exclusively of bonds when they reached a certain age. The safety of principal was their priority, and anything that would help preserve that money was viewed as a potentially good investment. Social Security, pensions, and the dividends and interest from investments provided income, and the goal was to keep as much principal as possible intact so that it could be passed down to heirs.

That was a great idea, but the fact is that it just doesn't work anymore. First of all, to produce that much income, you have to invest in assets that produce high interest, and those investments usually do so at the cost of growth. And if you eliminate growth, then your capital isn't going to keep up with inflation, and you'll wind up in trouble. Remember, we're talking about the second half of your life, maybe 40 years or more, not a 15- or 20-year retirement. Thanks to longer life spans and better health, we face the very real possibility of outliving our money, which means that investing strategies for the second half need to change from what they used to be. And to my mind, the key point in a wise investing strategy for the second half is to invest for growth for the rest of your life.

Investing for growth after the age of 50 can seem risky. But to my mind, the far greater risk is investing too conservatively and outliving your money. Because of our increased life spans, it takes a little more planning to make sure your money outlives you. So I encourage you not to shift all of your money automatically into fixed-income and money market investments. It's wonderful to continue to grow at least some of your money for the rest of your life. By doing so, you help make certain that there will be enough for you, your heirs, and perhaps the charities of your choice.

This approach is admittedly more aggressive than traditional or even conventional wisdom, and while there are solid financial reasons for following it, there are other reasons as well. I like the *idea* of continuing to invest for growth because it's consistent with my view of the second half of life. Conventional wisdom seems to dictate that we slow down as we age. We're supposed to be less active, less interested as well as interesting, less vibrant. But that's just not what I picture.

To my mind, the second half of life doesn't mean less; it means *more.* It means more time, more choices, more breadth and depth, maybe more interests. And it means more growth. We never stop growing as individuals; we become wiser, kinder, more compassionate. It seems only natural to me to nurture that growth, to stretch and challenge ourselves as we age. And you owe it to yourself to nurture your investments as well, and to make certain that they continue to grow.

Over time, stocks have shown the greatest potential for long-term growth.

So how do you invest for growth? I consider investing in stocks to be investing for growth for the simple reason that a company is something that grows. When you invest in stock, you're buying shares of ownership of a company, something that's alive and growing. A year from now it might be 10% larger, and soon it can be 25% larger. If you're a shareholder in the company, your share of wealth is growing, too. Companies can even provide their own fuel. How? Instead of paying out all of its profits to shareholders (as dividends), a company can reinvest that money into itself. If a company pays out 100% of its earnings in dividends, it can't sustain growth. But what if it pays only 25% in dividends? Then 75% of the company's net income is plowed back into the growth of the company. *And that's fuel:* The company puts that money right back to work, so that it continues to compound, feeding the company, helping it to grow.

The long-term trend of the stock market in the United States has always been up. Over time, stocks have outperformed all other kinds of investments, including bonds, CDs, and U.S. government securities.

All of this makes stocks fundamentally different from all other investment alternatives, including money market funds, corporate bonds, CDs, government bonds, and real estate. Of the many investments available, it's my belief that stocks offer you the best potential for growth over time, and they can be a great solution for long-term investing despite their short-term volatility. History backs me up here: The long-term trend of the stock market in the United States has always been up, and over time, stocks have outperformed all other kinds of investments, including bonds, CDs, and U.S. government securities. Dr. Jeremy Siegel, professor of finance at the Wharton School, looked at stock market returns from 1802 to 2000 and found that the total returns on stocks outperformed all other assets. "One dollar invested and reinvested in stocks since 1802 would have accumulated to $10.2 million by the end of 2000," he says.

Investing doesn't stop when you retire; for many people, retirement is when they become truly knowledgeable investors. And that's wonderful. You've invested your whole life in your career and your family and your community and your future. Doesn't it make sense to continue to nurture those investments, to encourage growth for the rest of your life?

3. Start with as Aggressive an Asset Allocation Model as You Comfortably Can

I've just encouraged you to invest for growth for the rest of your life, meaning that you're wise to continue to invest in individual stocks or stock mutual funds throughout your life. The next question is *How much?* Am I suggesting that you invest solely in stocks? No. I'm suggesting a carefully chosen mix of investments, and the key to that mix lies in asset allocation, the process of deciding how much of your investing dollars to invest in each asset class—stocks, fixed income, and cash equivalents.

At least 90% of your long-term investment return variability is determined by asset allocation. Less than 10% of your return is determined by your choice of individual investments.

What do you think is the most important part of a successful investing strategy? The stocks you pick? The mutual-fund guru you find? Your timing? The size of your portfolio? Surprisingly enough, none of the above. Research tells us that at least 90% of your long-term investment return variability is determined by asset allocation, which means that less than 10% is determined by your choice of individual investments.[1] That tells me that your overall strategy is crucial, and that market timing and specific investment choices play a minor role at best.

[1]Gary P. Brinson, Brian D. Singer, and Gilbert L. Beebower, "Determinants of Portfolio Performance II: An Update," *Financial Analysts Journal,* May–June 1999, 40–48.

An easy way to think of asset allocation is as dividing up a pie that comprises your investing dollars—that is, all of your money. You want to divide that pie among the three major types of investments—stocks, fixed income, and cash equivalents—based on such factors as your age and your attitudes toward risk. I will say from the start that my approach to asset allocation is aggressive. Here's the bottom line: It's my belief that, ideally, you are wise to keep at least 50% of your portfolio in a diversified mix of stocks and stock mutual funds for as long as you live. If the notion of being at least 50% invested in stocks chills your very soul, I have to be honest: This may not be the approach—or the book, for that matter—for you.

What I'm talking about here goes beyond a specific investing style. I'm encouraging you to see the larger picture, and to aim toward the real goal: becoming what I call a sage investor, someone who is typically highly confident in the rest of his or her life, and is ready to become just as confident as an investor. This is something I've been thinking about for a long time, more than 15 years. A sage investor is very disciplined; he or she bases investing decisions not on emotions, but on information and analysis. A sage investor is comfortable with the risks that come with investing in stocks, someone who never loses sight of the big picture, which tells us that the long-term trend of the stock market in the United States has always been up, and that, over time, stocks have outperformed all other kinds of investments. Once you know this—once you really believe it and understand it—it's possible, at the age of 50 or 60, to invest the large majority of your portfolio, even 90%, in stocks, with only 10% of your portfolio in other types of investments, and to do so comfortably, with confidence and assurance. But if 90% feels too aggressive, don't give up. Cut back on your equity percentage to percentages that you're comfortable with.

One of the reasons that I'm encouraging you to choose an aggressive asset allocation model to start with is that, in my experience, investors often choose and stay with asset allocations that are too conservative. Sometimes they do so for the simple reason that they're very conservative at heart—it's almost part of their personality. But it can also be because they've come to believe in some exaggerated talk about the risks in the stock market, and they've become overly conservative investors simply because they've never understood the big picture. They're just afraid. That's where the sage investor comes in. Whatever position you take, whatever asset allocation model you adopt, make your choice with purpose and intent, and from a position of knowledge and information.

So, in Chapter 4, when you look at models for asset allocation, I encourage you to choose the most aggressive asset allocation model you're comfortable with. And remember that asset allocation is a dynamic process; chances are that you won't stay with your current percentages forever. But it's my belief that an aggressive approach is a good starting place for your future—and that's what this is all about.

4. Consider Using a Core & Explore™ Strategy for the Stock Portion of Your Portfolio

Once you decide on the mix of investments that you want, you can begin to look at how to invest in each class of investment: stocks, bonds, and cash equivalents. As I've said, it's my belief that to invest for growth, you need to invest a significant proportion of your portfolio in stocks. So where do you go from there? How do you choose? And do you use individual stocks or mutual funds? In Chapter 4 we'll talk about choosing specific investments, but let's start with what my firm calls a Core & Explore™ approach.

Including both index and actively managed mutual funds (rather than only one type of

fund or the other) in your portfolio reduces the risk of underperforming the market, and increases the potential for beating the market.

Core & Explore™ is an asset allocation strategy for the stock part of your portfolio, and it means that you use broad-based index funds (which are designed to track the performance of the total stock market) to form the focus—the Core portion of your portfolio—and actively managed mutual funds (which are managed by individuals who handpick the stocks and try to outperform total market returns using narrow selection approaches) or individual stocks for the remainder—the Explore portion in which you seek to maximize your upside potential. In other words, you include a combination of index and actively managed mutual funds.

Core & Explore™

Core = broad-based index funds

Explore = actively managed mutual funds or individual stocks

Result:

A better chance of beating the market and reduced risk of underperforming the market.

The rationale for that combination is simple: Research has shown that when your portfolio includes both broad-based index funds and actively managed funds (rather than only one type of fund or the other), you have a better chance of beating the market.[2] The index fund gives you the near certainty of tracking the return of an underlying index, which means that you're less likely to underperform the market, and it counterbalances the risk of actively managed funds. The actively managed funds let you aim toward trying to beat the market and improve your performance.

FOR BEGINNERS ONLY: STOCKS AND STOCK MUTUAL FUNDS

When you decide to invest in stocks, you can buy stocks individually, but an easier method is to buy them through a mutual fund, which pools the money of many investors and allows you to buy shares in 50 or even 100 companies with a low investment, often as low as $1,000. This approach is much simpler than trying to pick individual investments yourself. By investing in a mutual fund, you substantially increase your chance of a solid financial outcome. There's even something called a "fund of funds"; you can buy a mutual fund that is, in turn, made up of other individual mutual funds.

Generally speaking, there are two kinds of stock mutual funds: actively managed funds and index funds. Actively managed funds are those in which one or more dedicated individuals work their hardest to *outperform* the market by handpicking the stocks to include in the fund, trying to outguess the market. That isn't just challenging—it's very tough, and hard to do with any consistency over a long period. From 1991 to 2000, only 28% of actively managed large-cap funds were able to beat the S&P 500.

Broad-based index funds, on the other hand, don't try to outperform the market; they just try to track it. They're designed to track the returns of a specific index, which is a group of securities considered yardsticks of market behavior. The index fund simply moves in tandem with the index it's based on. Its gains and losses (minus annual expenses) parallel those of the index.

[2]Schwab Center for Investment Research.

With a broad-based index fund, you don't play the odds; you play the averages, which makes a world of difference. As an investment, an index fund gives you simplicity and consistency, low fees, and—perhaps most valuable—peace of mind. Index funds also provide diversification. With one broad-based index fund, you're investing in 500 or even 1,000 companies from a variety of industries or sectors, which helps you minimize the negative impact of a downturn in a specific sector. Index funds have low minimums and operating costs, and they don't charge load fees. They're also tax-efficient because they typically use a buy-and-hold strategy; this helps to minimize trading and research costs, which can drive up the expenses associated with actively managed funds, and they tend to keep capital gains distributions (which are taxable) down. These things work together to increase your after-tax rate of return, important stuff when you remember that taxes are the single largest drag on your return. They're good investments for both tax-deferred accounts, such as IRAs and 401(k)s, and currently taxable accounts as well.

5. After the Age of 50, Adjust Your Asset Allocation and Rebalance Your Portfolio Every Five Years

Say you try the approach I've outlined and, at 50, you adopt a fairly aggressive approach to asset allocation. What's next? Do you stay with that forever? No. Little by little, during your second half, you'll pull back and moderate the stock portion of your portfolio. Here's the how and why.

When you're in your prime wage-earning years—your 40s and 50s—investing 90% or even 100% of your portfolio in stocks makes sense, in my view. You still have income from your job, and you don't need income from your investments. But as you approach retirement, which I define as the time when you are totally dependent on your investments for your income, you are wise to gradually increase your fixed-income investments to protect your income sources from the inevitable periods of market volatility.

So at some point—perhaps when you're 55 or 60, but the decision will vary from person to person and will depend on their financial circumstances—I recommend that you begin reviewing your portfolio every five years to determine the most comfortable mix of growth versus fixed-income investments. You need to feel confident about the certainty of your income as you become totally dependent on investment income closer to retirement. You are always striving to find the perfect mix between growth and safety.

6. Devise a Second-Half Income and Expense Strategy Early On

The goal of any investing strategy for the second half is to make sure that your money outlives you, and a wise income and expense plan is an important part of that strategy. I have to add a word of caution here, though: Devising a sound plan for cash flow in the second half isn't easy, and it might just be the issue that worries and confuses people most about retirement. How do you replace your paycheck and create a new steady source of income? How do you know how much you can spend? How do you withdraw it? Do you take it from your IRA? From your regular brokerage account? And where does your pension fit in?

It's tricky stuff but critical, because you can have the smartest and most solid asset allocation and investing strategy on the block, but if you withdraw too much, too fast, you can do substantial damage to your second-half finances before you know it. You also need to be mindful of government regulations and taxes. Tax-advantaged retirement accounts like IRAs are great inventions, but there are strings attached, and those strings become only too noticeable when you're faced with the restrictions on withdrawing your money. In Chapter 5 we'll talk more about cash flow in the second half.

THE EFFECTS OF TAXES ON YOUR INVESTING DOLLARS

Remember that asset allocation statistic—*at least 90% of the fluctuation in your investment return is determined by the asset allocation you select, with less than 10% being determined by your choice of individual investments.* There's a sort of corollary to that, I believe, that is crucial to a successful investing strategy: Taxes are the single largest drag on your return. That's a sentence that you should commit to memory, because ignoring the tax implications of investing can dramatically lower the returns on your investments. The less you pay in taxes, the more you have to invest, so you're wise to plan ahead, particularly when rebalancing your portfolio. It's particularly important to consider taxes in your investing decisions in your taxable accounts, as opposed to your tax-advantaged accounts—government-sanctioned retirement plans such as IRAs, 401(k)s and 403(b)s, and Keoghs. Your returns in those tax-advantaged accounts won't be taxed until you retire, which means that tax efficiency doesn't have to be your main criterion for choosing investments. But in your currently taxable accounts (your regular brokerage accounts), tax implications are crucial. That's where you want investments that will maximize your after-tax returns.

Tax considerations are also important during the second half because of the tax restrictions on IRA withdrawals. The consequences of ignoring or being unfamiliar with those restrictions are considerable. Each year, somewhere around three million senior citizens pay tax penalties because they didn't follow those rules.

The Big Picture: Preparing Well for the Second Half

In Part 2, we'll look at several issues that may seem unrelated to investing, but are important second-half considerations. Keep in mind that while these may be issues that you need to consider, they may also apply to aging parents.

• ***Getting help if and when you need it.*** If your financial situation is more complex than average, or if you simply can't (or don't want to) find the time necessary for it, you may want to consider a financial advisor. (We'll discuss this in detail in Chapter 7.) But even if you do get help, it's still crucial that you educate yourself about your current situation, your future needs, and your choices. Making use of a financial advisor doesn't mean that you simply throw everything over the wall and let someone else take care of your life. It means that you're getting help, but you still ask questions, pay attention, and play an active role. You can't become fluent in a foreign language after a couple of classes; you take a lot of lessons, you practice, and you learn little by little. The same is true of managing your financial assets. Be patient—with yourself and with the process.

Sometimes we can need help on a much smaller scale. If you simply need more information than is in this book, I highly recommend Jane Bryant Quinn's *Making the Most of*

To My Women Readers

On the Importance of Financial Planning for Your Second Half

If you are a woman, it is essential that you pay close attention when it comes to planning for your second half. Because women outlive men by an average of seven years, and because divorce is so prevalent, it is very likely that women will spend their final years alone. One commonly cited statistic tells us that 90% of all women will be solely responsible for their financial well-being at some point.

Sobering thoughts, but there's more: Although there are more women in the workforce than at any other time in this country, on average women still earn less money than men. Recent studies show women making about 72 cents for every dollar a man makes. Women are also more likely to have their work years interrupted by childbearing or caring for family members, and they're less likely to have pensions or fully funded 401(k)s. And *that means that women often have less put aside for the second half, leading to what I consider an overdependence on Social Security. According to the Social Security Administration, nearly 75% of elderly unmarried women—including widows—get about half of their total income from Social Security. In comparison, unmarried elderly men receive 39% of their income from Social Security. And since women's pay rates have traditionally been lower, and thus they have contributed less over their work years, the amount of their monthly Social Security checks are less as well. The average monthly check for a retired woman runs about $600, while a man's is around $800.*

These statistics tell us that it is particularly crucial for you as a woman to deal with the financial issues of your life. The stakes are high, but there's good news, too: You can make a difference. By getting involved and by understanding your individual financial picture (or your family's), you can take action now to improve your second half.

Your Money (Simon & Schuster, 1997). It's a great personal finance book, a guide and reference book all in one.

• ***Making sure you're adequately insured.*** You may be wondering why a book on investing bothers to talk about various kinds of insurance. The reason is simple: You can have millions put away for retirement, but if you don't protect it through health, disability, and long-term-care insurance, it could be gone almost overnight. You know what health-care costs are like these days; a short hospital stay, not to mention loss of income due to disability, or the ongoing expense of long-term care, can do major damage to even a sizable portfolio. We'll talk about insurance in detail in Chapter 8.

• ***Preparing an estate plan.*** There's a dangerous myth to the effect that estate planning is only for the wealthy. The fact is that just about everyone can benefit—and substantially so—by creating some kind of estate plan. You may think your assets are too modest, or that you have plenty of time to plan for events that are still years away. But even if you have limited means or are just entering your peak money-earning years, a simple estate plan is essential. By preparing now for the future, you'll be doing both yourself and your family a favor. You can retain more of your assets, protect your estate, and leave a legacy for your family or the cause of your choice. Chapter 9 discusses estate planning and its two most common vehicles—wills and trusts—in more detail. Even though you will want to seek professional help from an experienced attorney and possibly a financial adviser or tax planner, it's wise to understand the basics before you do so.

• ***Charitable giving.*** What's the point of all this planning and investing? It's not to just pile up money. Money doesn't confer happiness as soon as you get it. It's not good or bad any more than a computer or a hammer or an oven is. It's a tool—a wonderful one, a powerful one, but only a tool. And a great use for that tool is charitable giving. I urge you to consider giving something back during your second half by contributing financially to the causes that are important to you. The old adage is true: You really do receive more than you give. Chapter 10 discusses charitable giving in more detail.

Paperwork Simplified

Every day you bring in the mail and find more stuff: statements, records, confirmation orders, more paper than you know what to do with. Don't let it get to you—you can toss a lot of it. Here's what you need to keep—permanently. (For a list that will help you keep track of important financial records, see Section 1 of the Appendix.)

• Your tax returns. *If you need copies of returns from previous years, you can get them (up to six years back) from the IRS—though it will cost you both time and money. You only need to keep the supporting documents for your tax returns (things like 1099s) for three years after you file. After that, you can be audited only if you've underreported your gross income by 25% or more, or if you're suspected of fraud.*

• Settlement sheets on any house closings. *Keep these documents along with records of remodeling and other improvements to your home.*

• Retirement plan records. *This includes records of contributions to retirement plans, as well as distributions, conversions, and rollovers.*

• Records of the purchase of securities you own. *This applies whether you bought the securities or received them as gifts. Keep these records for three years after you sell the securities.*

Source: Kiplinger's Personal Finance Magazine.

One last note before we move on: As you begin to formulate or revise your second-half plan, remember to hold it in an open palm. Be ready to alter it when necessary, or to even start again if you have to. The second half of life is at least as unpredictable as any other time, and all the planning and preparation in the world can't change that. We have to react and adapt to factors as diverse and unpredictable as our health, our nation's tax policy, and our economy, to name a few. It's entirely possible, maybe even likely, that you'll have to modify your strategy as the years go by. But don't let that dissuade you from being prepared. It's your future we're talking about. Don't leave more to chance than you have to.

Words to the Wise on Investing Strategies for the Second Half

• Everyone should consider "investor" an important and permanent part of their identity. If you don't already know how to, learn how to invest wisely, and to monitor your investments, even if you end up hiring a financial adviser for the day-to-day management.

• Thanks to longer life spans and healthier retirements, for our money to outlive us, we need to invest for growth for the rest of our lives. To do that, I believe that you're wise to include stocks (primarily in the form of mutual funds) as a minimum of 50% of your portfolio.

• Stocks are fundamentally different from all other investment alternatives. Of those alternatives, it's my belief that stocks offer the best potential for growth over time, and that they are a good solution for long-term investing.

• At least 90% of the variability in your investment return is determined by the asset allocation you select. Less than 10% is determined by your choice of individual investments.

• Start with as aggressive an asset allocation as you are comfortable with. Then, as your time frame shortens, you can pull back a little so that if there's a downturn in the market, you'll have more time to recoup whatever losses you suffer.

• The Core & Explore™ approach is a model for the stock portion of your portfolio. It means that you use stocks in the form of index funds to form the "core" of your portfolio, and actively managed mutual funds or individual stocks to explore market-beating possibilities. If you do this, the core of your portfolio has the near certainty of tracking the return of the underlying index, while the "explore" part can be trying to beat the market.

• Taxes are the single largest drag on your return, so it's critical to invest with tax efficiency in mind. Taxes are also a strong argument for a buy-and-hold approach to investing. If you don't sell stocks or mutual funds in your taxable accounts, you don't pay taxes on capital gains. By simply buying and holding, you keep the money that would otherwise go to taxes.

2

Adding Up What You Have

One of the first steps in financial planning for your future is knowing what you're starting with, for the simple reason that if you don't know what you've got, it's hard to know where you can go. What you have is a known quantity. It may take a little while to list and add up, but it's factual—there's no guesswork.

In this chapter you'll take stock of what you have accumulated, including investments and savings, your home, insurance policies, retirement plans—even possessions, if you like. In Chapter 3, during the process of calculating how much you'll need for the second half, you'll narrow that down to investments and savings, but for now it's helpful to look at the larger picture—in other words, to weigh your nest egg.

The worksheet at the end of this chapter will help you do that, both in terms of what you've invested and saved and, for many of you, how much your company has invested for you. If the idea of finding that out causes you some trepidation, be assured that you're not alone. It's possible that you'll find that you're better prepared than you thought; but I have to say that not once have I heard someone complain about having too much invested for retirement. There probably is no such thing. If you find that you're not as well prepared as you'd hoped, it's better to know that now and to work toward doing what you can than to hide your head in the sand. There's still time to put your money to work for you, and there's still time to invest for growth.

The Grasshopper and the Ants

Aesop's fable of the grasshopper and the ants concerns a happy-go-lucky but unprepared grasshopper who, rather than storing food for the winter, spends his time fiddling and making music, and before he knows it, the summer is gone and he has nothing to eat. The ants, on the other hand, have been busily working all summer, gathering grain and storing it for the winter. And they are quick to point out the grasshopper's mistake. They're long on advice, and short on help.

Aesop's moral to the familiar story is obvious—there's a time for work and a time for play—but there's an additional one in terms of finances. It's simply the fact that you don't have to be a person of extremes—all ant or all grasshopper—and that it's better, in fact, to be somewhere in the middle. In other words, you don't have to work at your financial plan with the seriousness and grimness of a drone. But neither should you ignore it.

If finances have never been your cup of tea, this next piece of advice may sound crazy, but just try it: Have some fun with this stuff. *You don't have to master it all in a day. If you give this some time and attention, you'll become more competent, and over time the process will become more fun. And if you find the process difficult or intimidating, tell yourself the same thing you'd say to your son or daughter or niece or nephew:* Go slowly. Take a break. Don't push yourself too hard. *And reassure yourself that you will get the hang of this. It's only a matter of time.*

In this chapter and the next one, you'll be encouraged to make estimates about your financial picture: how much you have put aside, how much it costs you to live, how much it will cost you to live ten or twenty years from now. As you do this, I have a very important piece of advice: *Relax.* You don't have to become your own financial planner overnight, and this isn't a test; it's just something worth doing. When you need an estimate of living expenses or income, the key word is *estimate,* and I really do mean *estimate.* At least when you're starting out, a ballpark figure will do. You don't have to dig through all those canceled checks or check stubs and count every dollar, every dime. Just come up with what you feel are realistic numbers. If you want to reexamine those numbers later, that's great. But as long as you're being realistic and honest with yourself about your spending and income, you'll be all right, and you'll be on your way to financial peace of mind.

Looking at What You've Got Financially

A nest egg is a natural or artificial egg left in a nest to induce a hen to continue laying there. In some ways, that's exactly what a retirement plan is: a start, something to encourage you to continue investing, both in your government-sanctioned plan and through other investments as well.

In this chapter, as you begin to look at what you're starting with, include only what you've already got: what you've invested and saved toward retirement, what your company has invested for you, and any other assets that you would consider selling. For now we'll exclude projected income—money that you will have, but that you don't yet—from Social Security and defined-benefit plans (company pensions, which are paid out to you after you retire). We'll consider money from those sources to be income, and we'll talk about those in the next chapter.

As you begin to compile a list of what you're starting with, it's helpful to think of your financial nest egg as parts of a whole:

Retirement Plans	Personal Assets
Employer-funded retirement plans	Investments
Self-funded retirement plans	Savings
	Insurance policies
	Real estate
	Collections

A lot of people find discussions that deal with money and the future intimidating and even unpleasant, and they end up avoiding the whole thing, barely glancing at the 401(k) and IRA statements that come in the mail. If you are unsure about what you're starting with, take heart: This can be done.

Start by getting organized. Get out those statements, make a list of what you've got. People who are recently widowed or divorced are often faced with this task in the middle of very stressful times, so count yourself lucky if you're *choosing* to do this, rather than *having* to. Set aside some time and promise yourself something enjoyable when you're done—a round of golf, a movie, a walk in the country, or a day at the beach. And know that you're doing the right thing for your future peace of mind.

Now, there are a lot of people who calculate what they have in terms of retirement on an almost weekly basis. They know exactly what they have and what it's worth right now, as well as what it was worth last year. If that's you, congratulations on your diligence, whether it came easily or was something that you had to develop.

But for better or worse, not everyone finds investing easy—so if you are among those who do, you may want to turn directly to the worksheet at the end of the chapter.

Retirement Plans 101: Learning the Ropes

IRAs, Keoghs, 401(k)s, 403(b)s—that's only the beginning of the list of retirement plans available today. They work differently, and they require varying levels of involvement by you, the employee or taxpayer. Some of these things might spring to mind immediately: that 401(k) you have at work, the mutual fund you've invested in. But maybe you have only a vague concept of what those investments are, and when they're available to you, and how much they're worth.

A lot of people would be hard-pressed to say what they have in terms of retirement plans. That's partly because retirement plans have become an industry unto themselves, which is good news and bad news. The good news is twofold. First, by definition, retirement plans allow you to invest your money and allow it to grow, tax-deferred, until you withdraw it, which is great. And, second, we have more choices in terms of ways to invest for the future—and some really wonderful choices at that—than ever in the past. The bad news is that the quantity and variety can be overwhelming. So before we go on, let's simplify.

When the Boss Helps Out . . . Employer-Sponsored Retirement Plans

First, two very general types of retirement plans exist: those offered and sponsored by the company that employs you, and those that you establish as an individual. We'll start with the company plans.

An employer-sponsored retirement plan doesn't preclude you from having an IRA as well. Retirement plans are one of the best and most efficient ways to invest, so be sure you're taking full advantage of them in every way you can.

The traditional word is *pension,* which, Webster's tells us, means "a fixed amount, other than wages, paid at regular intervals to a person or his surviving dependents in consideration of his past services, age, merit, poverty, injury or loss sustained, etc." If the word sounds old-fashioned to you, there's a reason for that: it's a word with a history—and a very American one at that. The first American pension plans were military pensions given by the members of the first colony of Plymouth in 1636. The first American corporation to offer a pension plan was American Express, in 1875.

These days the term "retirement plan" is used more widely than the word "pension," which has a more specific meaning. Statistics indicate that approximately two thirds of American workers are covered by some kind of company-sponsored retirement plan—a 401(k) or 403(b), for example. Of that number, an alarming number of people don't participate, which is, in my mind, a tragedy, because company-sponsored retirement plans are just about as good as it gets in terms of investing for your future, and those who don't take advantage of them are missing out on a great opportunity. The only problem is that you have to enroll, and although it's not anything complicated or time-consuming—it usually amounts to filling out a form—it is something, and somehow it keeps a lot of people away. If you're in that category, don't wait any longer. It's never too late, and you can remedy this today by going to your benefits office and doing the paperwork to get things going. (If you're unclear about the definitions of various retirement plans, see the following box. And see the cheat sheet later in this chapter for help in enrolling in a retirement plan.)

If you are fortunate enough to work for a company that grants stock options to employees, there is an important caveat: *Know and understand your stock option agreement well.* Let me explain. One of the intents of stock option offerings is to encourage employees to give their all and to remain with the company. If and when an employee retires, those are no longer valid considerations. As a result, in many companies, the time during which you can exercise your options after you retire is pretty limited. Worse, some companies even prevent you from exercising your options at all after you retire. This means it's crucial that you know the details of your stock option plan—especially its stock option exercise dates. A publicized case in point involved an executive of Bally Manufacturing Company, which makes such things as pinball and slot machines. The company offered this executive the option of buying one million shares of company stock. The option had a ten-year life, as long as the executive still worked for Bally, and if he retired, he could exercise the options for one year after retirement.

The executive retired on January 8 of 1993. On January 24 of 1994 he tried to exercise his options, but the company refused. Those 16 days cost him millions.

Obviously this is a place to pay close attention to the fine print. Be thoroughly familiar with your stock option agreement, and if you have questions, ask. Ignoring or breaking the rules can cost you substantially.

THE FINE PRINT ON RETIREMENT PLANS

Within the realm of employer-sponsored retirement plans, there are *qualified plans,* which are those that the employer defines and contributes to, in return for which the company receives some tax breaks, and *nonqualified plans,* which are those that the employer defines but doesn't contribute to, usually because, for one reason or another, the company doesn't qualify for the tax breaks mentioned above. Obviously a qualified plan is the icing on the cake, but either plan is a great deal, one you shouldn't pass up, because in each case, your money grows tax-deferred until you withdraw it.

A *defined-benefit plan* is one in which your employer alone funds your retirement plan—in other words, you don't contribute. The downside is that you don't have any choice in how or where the money is invested. The plan is open only to vested employees—those who've been employed for a certain number of years, typically somewhere between five and ten. How much you receive when you retire is calculated according to a formula that considers your salary and the length of your employment. That amount is usually calculated on a monthly basis, and you begin receiving checks in that amount when you retire (which is why we won't include this amount in this chapter's worksheet—it's income). As a result of today's job-hopping, this vesting period can be a problem; if you leave a company before you're vested, you can wind up with nothing in terms of retirement.

A *defined-contribution plan* is one in which you, your employer, or both of you contribute to your retirement account. Unlike defined benefit plans, defined contribution plans do allow you, the employee, to have some say in how and where your money is invested. In some of these plans, the employee is responsible for *all* of those decisions. These plans are popular to say the least; this category includes 401(k)s and 403(b)s. The big advantages are that you have control over your investments, and that you don't have to be vested to benefit from the plan. If and when you change jobs, you keep your contributions and potentially those of your employer as well. You can either roll your vested 401(k) balance into another retirement account, take it as a lump-sum distribution (usually with penalties, unless you're 59½ years old), or leave it where it is until you reach retirement age.

We're about to get to the words that count for you, some of the most common defined contribution plans.

401(k) plan. Its cryptic name comes from the number of a paragraph in the Internal Revenue Code, but despite that dull name, a 401(k) is something of an investing wonder. Your employer takes money directly from your salary—which means you don't pay taxes on it now—and places it in a tax-deferred retirement account—which means that you don't pay taxes on that money until you retire (or withdraw from the account). The decision about how and where the money is invested is usually yours. Employers often match your contributions, sometimes with as much as 50 cents for every dollar you contribute.

403(b) plan. Another dull tax-code name, but also another great deal. A 403(b) is basically a 401(k) in the world of charitable and nonprofit organizations, including educational institutions.

Your contribution is deducted directly from your salary before taxes, and your employer can contribute. But most employees participating in 403(b)s are allowed to contribute no more than 5% of their annual salary.

ESOP. An acronym for Employee Stock Ownership Plan. This is a plan in which you acquire your company's stock. Its pluses and minuses are pretty obvious; if you not only like but believe in your company, it's an appealing proposal. But if you have less than full confidence in your company, this is a worrisome plan. Another drawback is that you don't have much control. If an ESOP is your only retirement plan, you've put all your eggs in one basket—namely, your company. If you participate in an ESOP, be sure to participate in some other retirement plans as well (an IRA, for example) to diversify your holdings, so that you're not overly dependent on the success of one company.

You're on Your Own: Self-Funded Retirement Plans

Employer-sponsored retirement plans are great deals, and if you have one available to you, participate. But they're not the only retirement vehicles available. If your company doesn't offer a retirement plan, or if you're self-employed, you can still establish an individual plan and contribute to it yourself.

Even if you do have a retirement plan available through your company, I strongly encourage you to establish an Individual Retirement Account (IRA) as well. It's my feeling that it's just too good an offer to pass up. Taking full advantage of the retirement plans available to you is one of the keys to a sound investing plan.

An IRA is, to my mind, the retirement investment vehicle of choice, if you qualify. There are several types of IRAs.

With a traditional IRA, you qualify if you are employed, or if your spouse is. You can then contribute $3,000 a year to that account, and the money grows tax-deferred until you withdraw it, which you are allowed to do after the age of 59½. You have control in terms of what you invest the money in; it's my feeling that a broad-based index fund is often a good

Cheat Sheet for a Visit to the Benefits Office

If you find you're unclear about what is being offered or what you've signed up for in terms of an employer-sponsored retirement plan, go to your benefits office and learn the following:

1. The name of the plan being offered, and a simple description of it.

2. Whether or not you're required to pay fees to participate in the plan.

3. Whether or not you have a choice in terms of how and where your money is invested. If you do have a choice, find out (a) what those choices are, and see if there is printed information available, and (b) whether or not you can make changes, and, if so, whether there is a charge.

4. The maximum you can invest in the program annually.

5. Whether the company contributes to the plan, and if so, how much.

6. Past performance of the plan's investments.

7. If you leave the company, what happens to your money; whether you can take it with you, and whether there are penalties for doing so.

You might also find out whether or not that money can be automatically deducted from your paycheck. This is called an Automatic Investment Plan, or AIP, and it's my method of choice. It falls in the category of paying yourself first, and it's by far the easiest and most efficient way to invest regularly.

choice. You want this money to grow, and to allow it to take advantage of compound growth for as long as possible.

A Roth IRA is a relatively new type of IRA that is aimed at providing benefits to a broad segment of the population. If you qualify, this is the IRA that I like. A Roth IRA offers more flexibility than a traditional IRA. Earnings can accumulate tax-free as long as the account is open, and there are a variety of ways to withdraw funds without penalty. Whether or not you are eligible to contribute to a Roth IRA depends largely on income. In very general terms, it's designed for single investors whose annual income is less than $110,000 and for married investors (filing jointly) whose combined annual income is less than $160,000. If you already have a traditional IRA, it may be possible to convert it to a Roth IRA.

Good news: Beginning in 2002, investors over the age of 50 can contribute an additional $500 per year into their IRA *and* 401(k) due to the new "catch-up" provision of recent tax legislation. In 2003, the catch-up amount will be $1,000 per IRA and 401(k).

A SEP-IRA (Simplified Employee Pension) is an alternative for those who are self-employed or own a small business with employees. You can fund a SEP-IRA each tax year, although annual contributions are not required. Contributions may be made until your tax filing deadline, including extensions. The plan allows you to contribute up to 15% or $24,000, whichever is less. The withdrawal rules are the same as those for traditional IRAs.

When you set up your IRA, you name a beneficiary, the person to whom that account will go in the event of your death. Be sure you name someone—if you don't, the assets in that account will simply be part of your estate. Also be sure that the beneficiary is current—in the event of a divorce or death, you may want to change beneficiaries. Finally, it's wise also to name a secondary beneficiary in case your first beneficiary predeceases you.

Finally, an EIRA (Educational IRA) is a trust or custodial account established to help pay the education expenses of a child, grandchild, or other designated beneficiary who is a minor. The EIRA is managed by the person establishing the account (the parent or guardian, for example). Eligible contributions to EIRAs are not deductible. Amounts deposited in the account grow tax-free until distributed, and the child won't owe tax on any withdrawal from the account if the child's qualified education expenses at an eligible educational institution for the year equal or exceed the amount of the withdrawal. Eligibility to make EIRA contributions depends on the income, not on the relationship to the child. Married taxpayers filing jointly with earnings of $220,000 or less, and single taxpayers with earnings of $110,000 or less, are eligible to contribute to EIRAs. Contributions are limited to $2,000 per child. One caution, though: an EIRA may limit other types of financial aid available to a child.

Contributing to any of these types of IRAs is, in many ways, long-term investing at its best. I'd even go so far as to say that for many people, most of their investing dollars should be in retirement accounts. The combination of deferred taxes (or no taxes at all, in the case of a Roth IRA) and compound growth has incredible power to make your nest egg grow. My own IRA is a case in point. Since 1982, I've contributed $2,000 a year and invested primarily in index funds. In that time I've contributed $40,000—but as of April 2001, the value of the account is $161,707, thanks to the power of compounding.

THE FINE PRINT ON IRAS

There are several different types of IRAs: traditional IRAs, rollover IRAs, education IRAs, and Roth IRAs. See the Glossary for more information on each of these.

SEP: An acronym meaning Simplified Employee Pension. SEPs are an alternative for those who are self-employed or own a small business with employees. The plan is aptly named, because SEPs are easy to administer and maintain, which makes them very popular with the owners of small businesses because the employees manage their own accounts. The employer doesn't have to administer the program; he or she only has to contribute.

Keogh plan: Named for Eugene Keogh, a U.S. representative from Brooklyn who sponsored the legislation that established the plan in 1962, the term refers to retirement plans for those who are self-employed. Strictly speaking, there really isn't a "Keogh plan" anymore; the term is used to refer to retirement plans established by small businesses and self-employed individuals. Like employer-sponsored plans, Keoghs can be defined-benefit or defined-contribution, and there are four kinds of Keoghs available.

Keoghs are not for the faint of heart. The issues can get pretty complex, particularly determining how much to pay each year—so complex that if you establish a Keogh, you're required by law to consult with an actuary each year to review your plan and calculate how much you have to contribute in the following year to meet your projected payout at the end of your employment road. You have to submit a copy of the actuary's report with your tax return. But if you are self-employed, it's worth checking out because you may be permitted greater deductible contributions under a qualified plan.

Before you begin looking at your personal assets, take some time to examine your retirement accounts and to find out the current value of each account or plan. You can do this by looking at your most recent printed statement for each plan or account. You probably receive these statements in the mail on a quarterly basis. You may also be able to check the value of each account on the Internet. Many people have their money in various brokerage firms, banks, and mutual fund companies, and receive statements from each of those places each month.

Personally, I find that simpler is often better where

finances are concerned, and at my company we've worked to do just that: simplify. You can do it all with one company: invest in hundreds of mutual funds and stocks, have checks and a debit card, all at one place—and all on one statement. Consolidating your paperwork with one firm can go a long way toward simplifying your life.

Getting Closer to Home: Personal Assets

Once you know what you have in terms of retirement plans, you can get a little closer to home and look at your personal investments and other assets.

For most people, this part's easier than dealing with retirement plans. We're usually more familiar with our personal assets. That said, a lot of people let their partners take care of this part of their lives. If that applies to you, I strongly encourage you to get involved now—and to understand your financial picture.

Once again, assemble the paperwork, if you have to—bank statements, brokerage statements, mortgage statements—so that you can fill out the worksheet that follows, or you can do it online on *retirement tools* at **www.schwab.com.** You'll need information on the following:

- ***Investments.*** These are investments you've made outside of any retirement accounts. Include mutual funds, individual stocks, bonds, and cash-equivalent investments such as CDs and money market accounts. You'll need the current market value of each of these, available on your most recent statement.
- ***Savings.*** Leave out investments for now—we'll include them below. Include here only traditional cash savings accounts. For each, you'll need the account balance shown on your most recent bank statement.
- ***Life insurance policies.*** You'll need to know the cash

value of each policy. You can learn this by calling the insurance company. As a side note—but an important one—if you haven't considered life insurance, this is the time to do it. If you have dependents, life insurance can be crucial. It's the best hedge against the risk of premature death in a family. Inexpensive term life insurance will protect your family against the hardships that result from a premature death, and it's something that every conscientious parent and partner should consider. Make sure you know the difference between term and permanent life insurance (to be discussed in Chapter 8). Term insurance can be one-tenth the cost per $1,000 of coverage. I have a preference for low-cost term insurance.

• ***Home equity—if you're considering moving.*** If you own your primary residence (a home or condominium), and you might consider scaling down by moving somewhere smaller or less expensive, you should know the current market value of your home. On the worksheet, you can subtract your current mortgage and the approximate selling costs. You can learn the current market value by doing some comparison shopping through the paper, by asking a neighbor, by getting help from a realtor, or by visiting a Web site that performs this service.

Doing the numbers for your home equity is relatively easy, but behind the how-much-is-it-worth question is a more complicated and important one: Do you *want* to move? Where to live is one of the biggest issues for people in the second half of their lives. It's a question that deserves some thought, so if you haven't decided, don't hurry. If you're even considering it, you may want to do the numbers and include the value of your equity in brackets, just so you know.

• ***Other real estate.*** If you own other real estate, the same applies: Find out the current market value, and give some thought to whether or not it's time to sell.

• ***Possessions.*** This category is up to you. If you have valuable collections, you may want to think about whether or not you'd want to sell them at some point. If you'd never consider it, don't include them here. If the idea seems possible, include their fair market value—what you could sell them for, not what they're worth.

Doing the Numbers

As you fill out the worksheet that follows (or as you do something similar online), remember the grasshopper and the ants: Don't be extreme in either direction. Just make a list, and estimate, to the best of your knowledge, the value of each item on the list. Do some homework later on if you need to; for now, just get started. The level of detail is up to you; what's important is to include a reasonable estimate of the big things so that you'll have an accurate estimate of what you're starting with. If you're part of a couple, you will probably want to consider your partner's assets as well as your own.

You'll use some of the information in this worksheet in the worksheets in Chapter 3. You'll also use this information in Chapter 9, on estate planning.

WORKSHEET 1

How Much Have You Got?

Item	**Approximate Value**
PART 1. RETIREMENT PLANS	
Employer-sponsored defined contribution plans	
401(k)	$700,000
403(b)	________
ESOP	________
Self-funded retirement plans	
IRAs	
Traditional IRA	42,000
Rollover IRA	________

Roth IRA ____________

Education IRA ____________

SEP ____________

Keogh ____________

Part 2. Personal Assets

Bank accounts (checking and savings)—the balance in each account: $____________

Investments (other than retirement plans)—for each, the current market value:

Mutual funds ____________

Individual stocks ____________

Bonds ____________

Cash equivalents (for example, CDs and money market accounts) ____________

Life insurance (call insurance company to determine cash value) ____________

Home equity (current market value) (only if you would consider selling—current market value less your current mortgage and estimated selling costs) ____________

Other real estate (current market value less current mortgage and selling costs) ____________

Business partnership interests ____________

Personal property (replacement value of jewelry, autos, household furnishings, etc.) ____________

Collectibles—current market value:

Jewelry ____________

Precious metals ____________

Fine art ____________

Other collectibles ____________

Annuities, trusts, or other assets ____________

Total value of retirement and personal assets: **$____________**

WORDS TO THE WISE ON ADDING UP WHAT YOU HAVE

• It's helpful to think of what you have in terms of (a) retirement plans and (b) personal assets.

• What you've saved is not a mystery. It may take some time to find the paperwork and add things up, but it can be done. You can probably find the information you need on the Internet—or you can use the quarterly or monthly statements you receive from your retirement plans, brokerage firms, and banks.

• Include only what you've already got: what you've invested and saved toward retirement, what your company has saved for you, and any other assets that you can count in the plus column as you get older. For now, exclude projected income—money that you will have, but that you don't yet—from sources such as Social Security.

• Remember that even if you have an employer-sponsored retirement plan, you can have some type of IRA as well. Be sure to take full advantage of all of the retirement plans available to you.

3

Estimating How Much You'll Need for the Second Half

You've given some thought to how you want to spend your second half, and you've taken stock of what you have. Now for the real questions: How much will you need? *How much is enough?*

Chances are that it's more than you think. Life is unpredictable, which is why you try to invest as much as you can and to aim toward investing too much rather than not enough. Today, the time of life we used to call retirement is lasting longer. The average 50-year-old American's life expectancy is around 83 to 86 years, but that's simply the average—a lot of us can hope for even longer lives. The age of 65 could soon be the start of middle age. All of which means that the second half of your life will probably last longer—and therefore cost more—than that of any previous generation.

A Rough Estimate of How Much You'll Need

To start with, I'd like to show you an easy way to come up with a rough estimate of how much you'll need for your second half. The worksheets in this chapter will show you a pretty precise method—this is just to get you an idea of what we're talking about.

To do this, first think about how much you'll need to live on in your second half, based on what you need now. Use a percentage of your gross annual income as a basis. A typical number for this is 80% to 100%, meaning that you will need between 80% and 100% of your gross annual income per year in your second half to enjoy your current lifestyle. If you think your expenses will decrease in the second half, use a percentage close to 80%. Some people use estimates as low as 70% to 75%, but I'm wary of such a low number. On the other hand, maybe you're planning on being more active than ever—traveling more, entertaining, indulging yourself—then the percentage you use might be 100% or more. It all depends on you.

So take a moment to imagine what you hope to do, and estimate what it will cost, compared with what it costs you to live now. Decide on a percentage that represents what you feel is a realistic estimate. Then do the math, and you'll have an idea of how much it will cost you to live in the second half.

	Your Information	Example
Current gross annual income	$ 160,000	$ 100,000
multiplied by the percentage you estimate you'll need for the second half	X 90 %	X 80%
equals how much you'll need per year in the second half	= $ 144,000	= $ 80,000

Now you can use that number to come up with a rough estimate of how much you'll need to have invested when you stop receiving a paycheck. To do this, you use what I call the guideline of 230K, which goes like this: *For every $1,000 you'll need each month, you should have at least $230,000 invested when you stop working.* Remember to use what I call a "total valuation approach" when looking at your investments. This means including *all* of your investments—those in your regular brokerage account as well as your IRA, your 401(k), and any other pension plans that you might have. Also, this guideline applies to a moderately aggressive asset allocation; if your asset allocation is more conservative, you'll need to use a higher number than 230K.

Here's how to use this guideline. You have an idea of how much you'll need on an *annual* basis. Divide that number by 12 to get a *monthly* amount. Then divide that number by 1,000, and multiply the result by 230,000, like so:

	Your Information	Example
Annual income needed for second half	$______	$ 80,000
Divide annual income by 12 to get monthly amount	$______	$ 6,666
Divide monthly amount by 1,000 and round up	______	6.7
Multiply result by 230,000 to get an estimate of the grand total you'll need to have invested for your second half	$______	$ 1,541,000

That amount ($1,541,000 in our example) is the rough estimate of how much you'll need for your second half, which, for the purposes of these estimates, I'm calling 40 years. Why 40 years? The traditional way to estimate the length of retirement is to use a life expectancy chart. But it's entirely possible that you know yourself better than the tables do, and this is not a time to underestimate. You want your money to outlive you, not the other way around. Nobody wants to worry about money in their late eighties. And maybe you're even hoping to quit working at 50. So I suggest that you think of your second half as lasting 40 years.

What's compelling about this 230K guideline is that because it's based on research that factors in historical inflation rates, the number you come up with is indexed for inflation. For example, if you need $5,000 per month (before taxes), you'll need to have 5 × 230,000 invested moderately aggressively when you retire to expect $5,000 per month. Ten years later, the $5,000 per month will have grown to keep pace with inflation. At 4% inflation, $5,000 would need to be $7,401. This means the $1,000 per month increment adjusts for inflation each year so your standard of living and buying power don't diminish due to higher prices. (For details and charts that document the research behind the guideline of 230K, see Section 4 of the Appendix.)

A More Precise Estimate of How Much You'll Need

The guideline of 230K is great for rough estimates, but you may want to get more precise. The four worksheets in this chapter will help you do that; they are designed to guide you through estimating how much you'll need for your second half. Before you start, a few suggestions:

A. The worksheets here aren't rocket science. They're fairly straightforward and will probably take less than an hour to do, so even if you don't consider yourself the worksheet type, I urge you to try them. Once you've done them, you'll know where you stand, and how much you'll need to invest to meet your second-half goal. Even if you're planning on using the professional help of a financial advisor (which we'll discuss in Chapter 7), I still encourage you to go through the steps in this chapter.

B. "Estimate" is the key word. Don't get bogged down in trying to come up with these numbers. Just make informed and realistic estimates, and keep going.

C. You might want to photocopy the blank worksheets so that you can do the calculations for more than one scenario, and so that you'll have blank copies in the future.

D. Before you start, you might want to have the financial records you'll need at hand. These include your most recent statements from your brokerage and bank accounts, any pension and IRA statements, and information about your current expenses.

1. Estimating How Much Annual Income You'll Need in the Second Half

The first step is to come up with an estimate of how much income you'll need each year in the second half (meaning when you're no longer working full-time). To start, you'll need to estimate how much it will cost you to live. The following worksheet lists the expenses that most people will face per month and per year. Fill in what you expect to spend on each of these things during the second half, using today's dollars (you don't have to figure in inflation right now—that will come). For each category, try to use the average amount you'll spend each year for most of your second half. Once you've done that, you can do some simple calculations to figure in taxes. The notes that follow the worksheet may help you in doing the estimates.

WORKSHEET 1

How Much Income Will You Need?

Part 1. Estimating Your Second-Half Expenses

Category	Your Information		Example*
	Monthly Amount	*Annual Amount*	*Annual Amount*
1. Housing (mortgage or rent)	$________	________	________
2. Property taxes	$________	________	4,500
3. Travel and entertainment	$________	________	12,000
4. Utilities	$________	________	3,900
5. Insurance (life, health, home, auto, etc.)	$________	________	10,000
6. Transportation (e.g., subway, gas, parking, auto upkeep, etc.)	$________	________	3,000
7. Durable goods (e.g., furniture, art, home remodels, etc.)	$________	________	3,600
8. Health-care expenses (not covered by insurance)	$________	________	1,800
9. Education	$________	________	500
10. Food	$________	________	6,600
11. Clothing	$________	________	3,000
12. Personal care	$________	________	900

13. Alimony/child support	$______	______	—
14. Other	$______	______	10,000
15. Estimated expense: (does not include taxes) Sum of Lines 1–14	**$**______	______	59,800

*The numbers in this column give a theoretical example for a working couple who are both 50 years old and hope to retire at 60 and live to be 90. Because of their concern about the long-term plans for Social Security, this couple wanted to see how close they were to their goal without counting on Social Security income. Based on their risk tolerance and time horizon, this couple estimated a 10% rate of return while they were working and 8% once they had stopped.

Part 2. Estimating How Much Income You'll Need

The number in Line 15 gives you your estimated annual after-tax expenses in the second half. Next you need to convert this into an annual pre-tax number, which you'll use to estimate your future needs based on your current tax bracket. (For tax rate tables, see Section 2 of the Appendix.)

	Your Information	**Example**
16. Effective federal tax rate during your second half	______	0.28
17. Tax factor (subtract Line 16 from 100)	______	0.72
18. Estimated annual income needed (divide Line 15 by Line 17)	**$**______	83,056

Notes for Worksheet 1

• ***Expenses that often decrease in the second half*** include several things. Housing costs, for example, can be lower because people often move to less expensive homes in the second half. You may even pay off your mortgage and eliminate that expense altogether. (See the sidebar "To Sell or Not to Sell Your Home" in this chapter.) Life insurance payments usually decrease or end altogether, as do job-related expenses (such as commuting costs, business clothes, cleaning, and business dinners) if you stop working. Even if you do continue to work part-time, you may spend less money doing it.

• ***Education costs.*** Traditionally, education costs were eliminated by the time people retired because parents had finished paying for their kids' educations by then. But times have changed, and college expenses may be a very real part of your second half. If so, include them.

• ***Health care expenses*** may rise, in terms of both insurance and care. Be sure you're adequately insured in terms of health, disability, long-term care, and life insurance. See Chapter 8 for more information.

• ***Travel and entertainment expenses*** can be difficult to estimate, and vary tremendously. Maybe you'll be going to the movies more often, or spending more time on the golf course, or traveling to those places you've always daydreamed about.

• ***Other expenses*** can include any additional expenses not covered in the categories above. As a result of what we call the "sandwich generation," referring to those who are responsible for aging parents, you may have additional expenses that are significant. If so, be sure to include them.

• ***Include state taxes in your estimates.*** Because state tax rates vary so widely, these worksheets do not figure in state taxes. If you do want to include your state taxes, add your state tax rate to your federal tax rate on Line 17 on page 52, using this formula:

Federal tax rate + state tax rate – (federal tax rate × state tax rate)

Example: $.28 + .07 - (.28 \times .07)$
$= .35 - (.02)$
$= .33$

• ***The tax factor*** is intended to help you make a rough estimate of your federal income tax during your second half. It cannot take into account many factors that will affect your tax bill, including state taxes, future tax law changes, capital gains tax, alternative minimum tax, and the taxability of pensions and Social Security. Contact a tax advisor for help in making an accurate tax estimate.

2. Determining Your Grand Total: Your Investing Goal for the Second Half

By "grand total," I mean the total assets you'll need for your second half, based on the estimated annual expenses that you came up with in Worksheet 1. This worksheet takes into account the number of years you have until your second half, as well as the number of years you expect your second half to last. It also figures in the income that you expect to be receiving.

WORKSHEET 2

What Is Your Total Second-Half Asset Goal?

Years Until Your Second Half	Your Information	Example
1. At what age do you plan to stop working? (Couples should enter the retirement age of the partner who will stop working first.)	______	60
2. How old are you now? (Couples should enter the *current age* of the partner who will stop working first.)	______	50
3. Years until you stop working (subtract Line 2 from Line 1)	______	10

Years in Your Second Half

4. What is your life expectancy? ________ ___90___
(I suggest using a life expectancy of at least 90 years.*)

Life Expectancy (nearest whole number)

Age	Male	Female	Age	Male	Female	Age	Male	Female
1	86	87	34	84	86	67	84	87
2	86	87	35	84	86	68	84	87
3	86	87	36	84	86	69	85	87
4	86	87	37	84	86	70	85	87
5	86	87	38	83	86	71	85	88
6	86	87	39	83	86	72	85	88
7	85	87	40	83	86	73	86	88
8	85	87	41	83	86	74	86	88
9	85	87	42	83	86	75	86	89
10	85	87	43	83	86	76	87	89
11	85	87	44	83	86	77	87	89
12	85	87	45	83	86	78	87	89
13	85	87	46	83	86	79	88	90
14	85	87	47	83	86	80	88	90
15	85	87	48	83	86	81	89	91
16	85	87	49	83	86	82	89	91
17	85	87	50	83	86	83	90	91
18	85	87	51	83	86	84	90	92
19	85	87	52	83	86	85	91	92
20	84	87	53	83	86	86	92	93
21	84	86	54	83	86	87	92	93
22	84	86	55	83	86	88	93	94
23	84	86	56	83	86	89	94	95
24	84	86	57	83	86	90	94	95
25	84	86	58	83	86	91	95	96
26	84	86	59	83	86	92	96	96
27	84	86	60	83	86	93	96	97
28	84	86	61	83	86	94	97	98
29	84	86	62	83	86	95	98	99
30	84	86	63	83	86	96	99	99
31	84	86	64	83	86	97	100	100
32	84	86	65	84	87	98	100	101
33	84	86	66	84	87	99	101	102
						100	102	102

*Life expectancies calculated using the generational UP94 Mortality Table updated to 2000 by American Academy of Actuaries.

5. At what age do you plan to stop working? ________ ___60___
(Couples should enter the age of the younger partner when he or she will stop working.)

6. Years in your second half (subtract Line 5 from Line 4) ________ ___30___

Sources of second-half income—annual amounts

7. Social Security (For a rough estimate, use $1,000 a month if you're working, and $1,500 for couples with a nonworking spouse. For more detailed estimates, see Section 3 of the Appendix.)	$________	—
8. Income from pension or other defined benefit plan (If you opt for periodic payments as opposed to a lump sum, both of which are discussed in Chapter 5, you'll receive a fixed amount on a regular basis. You can learn the amount of the check you'll receive from your employer's plan manager. Do not include withdrawals from your IRA, 401(k), or other defined contribution plans.)	$________	13,000
9. Other annual income (e.g., from a job, trust, or rental property. Include only additional annual income that you expect to receive throughout your second half.)	$________	3,000
10. Estimated annual second-half income (sum of Lines 7, 8, and 9)	$________	16,000
11. Total annual income needed in the second half (from Line 18 on Worksheet 1)	$________	83,056
12. Estimated additional investment income (subtract Line 10 from Line 11)	$________	67,056

Investment assets needed when you start your second half

13. Inflation adjustment factor (see Table 1, below) ________ 1.4
14. Estimated inflation-adjusted additional income needed (multiply Line 12 by Line 13) $________ 93,878
15. Income-to-assets factor (see Table 2, below) ________ 17.0
16. **Second-half asset goal** (Line 14 × Line 15) **$**________ 1,595,926

Table 1
Inflation Adjustment Factor

The inflation adjustment factor helps calculate the future value of $1, assuming a 3.5% rate of inflation over a certain period of time. (Remember that in the real world, inflation rates can vary from year to year.) This factor represents how much more something that costs $1 today will cost in a specified number of years. If you are in between years, I suggest choosing a longer time frame, which will give you a more conservative estimate.

YEARS UNTIL RETIREMENT
(See Line 3 of Worksheet 2)

	1	5	10	15	20	25	30	35
INFLATION FACTOR	1.0	1.2	1.4	1.7	2.0	2.4	2.8	3.3

Table 2
Income-to-Assets Factor

The income-to-assets factor helps you to project the assets you'll need to generate the income you desire. It represents the number of dollars in assets you will need to cover each dollar of expense you anticipate in the first year of your second half. The factor you choose should be based on how long you expect your second half to last, and the return you expect to generate from your portfolio during your second half. If you are in between years, I suggest choosing a longer time frame, which will give you a more conservative estimate.

EXPECTED ANNUAL RATE OF RETURN DURING RETIREMENT
(See The Investor Profile Questionnaire in Section 5 of the Appendix)

EXPECTED YEARS IN RETIREMENT (See Line 6 of Worksheet 2, page 55)	5%	6%	7%	8%	9%	10%	11%	12%
10	9.4	9.0	8.6	8.3	8.0	7.7	7.4	7.1
15	13.5	12.7	11.9	11.2	10.6	10.0	9.5	9.0
20	17.4	16.0	14.7	13.6	12.6	11.7	11.0	10.3
25	21.0	18.9	17.1	15.5	14.2	13.0	12.0	11.1
30	24.4	21.5	19.0	17.0	15.3	13.9	12.7	11.7
35	27.5	23.7	20.7	18.2	16.2	14.6	13.2	12.0
40	30.4	25.7	22.1	19.2	16.9	15.1	13.5	12.3
45	33.0	27.5	23.3	20.0	17.5	15.4	13.8	12.4

This table assumes the following:

1. The income-to-assets factor represents the present value of an annuity (i.e., a sum of money paid yearly or at other regular intervals) estimated at the selected return rate.
2. This table assumes a constant annual rate of return. In reality, return rates will vary from year to year, causing fluctuation in the value of your portfolio and resulting potential income stream.
3. This table adjusts the return rates for an assumed 3.5% inflation rate.
4. In calculating the income-to-assets factor, these calculations assume that you will spend your last dollar on the last day of your life.

3. Estimating How Much You Might Have in the Future

To estimate the amount of money you may have when you start your second half, you need to consider your current assets and your estimated expected rate of return over time. Your estimated rate of return depends on how aggressively you invest. If you don't know your rate of return, you can determine one that suits your investing style by completing the Investor Profile Questionnaire in Section 5 of the Appendix. It will suggest an asset allocation model designed to meet your needs, and it will show you historical rates of returns that correspond with that asset allocation model.

WORKSHEET 3

How Much Money Will You Have When You Begin Your Second Half?

Current Financial Investment Balances	**Your Information**	**Example**
1. IRA accounts (current value)	$________	72,000
2. Employer-sponsored plans (current value of 401(k), 403(b), SEP-IRA, etc.)	$________	282,000
3. Other accounts (current value of regular brokerage accounts, money market accounts, etc.)	$________	118,000
4. Total current balance (sum of Lines 1, 2, and 3)	$________	472,000
5. Compound growth of your current balance (insert factor from Table 3, page 61)	$________	2.6

6. Estimated value when you stop working, not including taxes or transaction costs (multiply Line 4 by Line 5)	$________	1,227,200

Additional annual contributions while you're still working

7. IRA accounts (annual contribution amount)	$________	—
8. Employer-sponsored plans (annual contributions made by you and your employer to a 401(k), 403(b), SEP-IRA, etc.)	$________	13,000
9. Other accounts (annual investment amount in regular brokerage accounts and money market accounts, etc.)	$________	6,000
10. Total annual contributions in today's dollars (sum of Lines 7, 8, and 9)	$________	19,000
11. Compound growth of your annual contributions (insert factor from Table 4, page 62)	$________	15.9
12. Estimated value when you stop working, not including taxes or transaction costs (multiply Line 10 by Line 11)	$________	302,100

Other assets that will be available to you when you start your second half (e.g., sale of property, inheritances, etc.)

13. Estimated value when you stop working	$________	—

Total value of your second-half portfolio

14. Estimated assets when you stop working (sum of Lines 6, 12, and 13) $________ 1,529,300

Table 3
Compound Growth of Your Current Balance

The compound growth factor helps calculate the future value of a dollar invested at a particular point in time and for a specific expected growth rate. It tells you how much you could have at the end of the selected time period if you invest $1 at the rate indicated. If you are in between years, I suggest using a shorter time frame, which will give you a more conservative estimate.

EXPECTED ANNUAL INVESTMENT RATE OF RETURN PRIOR TO RETIREMENT

YEARS UNTIL RETIREMENT (See Line 3 of Worksheet 2)	5%	6%	7%	8%	9%	10%	11%	12%	13%	14%
1	1.1	1.1	1.1	1.1	1.1	1.1	1.1	1.1	1.1	1.1
2	1.1	1.1	1.1	1.2	1.2	1.2	1.2	1.3	1.3	1.3
3	1.2	1.2	1.2	1.3	1.3	1.3	1.4	1.4	1.4	1.5
4	1.2	1.3	1.3	1.4	1.4	1.5	1.5	1.6	1.6	1.7
5	1.3	1.3	1.4	1.5	1.5	1.6	1.7	1.8	1.8	1.9
10	1.6	1.8	2.0	2.2	2.4	2.6	2.8	3.1	3.4	3.7
15	2.1	2.4	2.8	3.2	3.6	4.2	4.8	5.5	6.3	7.1
20	2.7	3.2	3.9	4.7	5.6	6.7	8.1	9.6	11.5	13.7
25	3.4	4.3	5.4	6.8	8.6	10.8	13.6	17.0	21.2	26.5
30	4.3	5.7	7.6	10.1	13.3	17.4	22.9	30.0	39.1	51.0
35	5.5	7.7	10.7	14.8	20.4	28.1	38.6	52.8	72.1	98.1

Table 4
Compound Growth of Your Annual Contributions While You're Still Working

The annual contributions compound growth factor helps you calculate how much you'll have if you invest $1 at the end of each year for a selected number of years and at a selected rate of return. If you are in between years, I suggest using a shorter time frame, which will result in a more conservative estimate. This table assumes you invest the same amount each year.

EXPECTED ANNUAL INVESTMENT RATE OF RETURN PRIOR TO RETIREMENT*

YEARS UNTIL RETIREMENT (See Line 3 of Worksheet 2)	5%	6%	7%	8%	9%	10%	11%	12%	13%	14%
1	1.0	1.0	1.0	1.0	1.0	1.0	1.0	1.0	1.0	1.0
2	2.1	2.1	2.1	2.1	2.1	2.1	2.1	2.1	2.1	2.1
3	3.2	3.2	3.2	3.2	3.3	3.3	3.3	3.4	3.4	3.4
4	4.3	4.4	4.4	4.5	4.6	4.6	4.7	4.8	4.8	4.9
5	5.5	5.6	5.8	5.9	6.0	6.1	6.2	6.4	6.5	6.6
10	12.6	13.2	13.8	14.5	15.2	15.9	16.7	17.5	18.4	19.3
15	21.6	23.3	25.1	27.2	29.4	31.8	34.4	37.3	40.4	43.8
20	33.1	36.8	41.0	45.8	51.2	57.3	64.2	72.1	80.9	91.0
25	47.7	54.9	63.2	73.1	84.7	98.3	114.4	133.3	155.6	181.9
30	66.4	79.1	94.5	113.3	136.3	164.5	199.0	241.3	293.2	356.8
35	90.3	111.4	138.2	172.3	215.7	271.0	341.6	431.7	546.7	693.6

* This assumes you invest the same amount each year.

4. Seeing Where You Stand

With the figures from Worksheets 1 through 3, you can now see where you stand—in other words, you can get an idea of whether your assets will meet your second-half needs—or, if you'll be short, just how far short. If there is a shortfall, it's better to know it now, so that you can take action to help increase your assets to meet your estimated needs.

WORKSHEET 4

How Close Are You to Your Second-Half Goal?

Second-Half Surplus or Shortfall	Your Information	Example
1. Estimated assets when you stop working (insert value from Worksheet 3, Line 14, page 61)	$________	1,529,300
2. Second-half asset goal (assets needed to meet expenses) (insert value from Worksheet 2, Line 16, page 57)	$________	1,595,926
3. Potential second-half surplus (+) or shortfall (–) (subtract Line 2 from Line 1)	$________	–66,626

5. Seeing How Much You'll Need to Invest Each Month to Reach Your Goal

That number above is the *total* you'll need to invest between now and when you stop working. If you want to break that down further, you can use the tables below to calculate how much you'll need to invest each month to reach that goal. To use the tables, first choose the one that represents your pre-tax rate of return. I encourage you to be conservative. Even though the market has achieved a 10% average return over the past 75 years, when you plan for your second half, go low. I'd use only an 8% pre-tax average return, in part because a second-half portfolio becomes, over time, more diversified with fixed income.

Once you've found your projected rate of return, find the number of years you have to invest (the time between now and when you want to retire, or age 59½); then, in that column, find the amount closest to the estimate of what you need to invest from Line 3 in Worksheet 4. The number in the left-hand column is your monthly investment.

Monthly Investment Estimates

8% AVERAGE ANNUAL RETURN

Monthly investment	5 years	10 years	15 years	20 years	25 years
$200	14,683	36,257	67,957	114,534	182,973
$300	22,024	54,385	101,935	171,802	274,459
$400	29,366	72,514	135,913	229,069	365,945
$500	36,707	90,642	169,892	286,336	457,432
$600	44,049	108,771	203,870	343,603	548,918
$700	51,390	126,899	237,848	400,870	640,405
$800	58,731	145,028	271,827	458,137	731,891
$900	66,073	163,156	305,805	515,405	823,377
$1,000	73,414	181,285	339,783	572,672	914,864

10% AVERAGE ANNUAL RETURN

Monthly investment	5 years	10 years	15 years	20 years	25 years
$200	15,434	40,292	80,324	144,797	248,632
$300	23,152	60,437	120,486	217,196	372,948
$400	30,869	80,583	160,649	289,595	497,264
$500	38,586	100,729	200,811	361,993	621,580
$600	46,303	120,875	240,973	434,392	745,896
$700	54,020	141,020	281,135	506,791	870,212
$800	61,737	161,166	321,297	579,189	994,528
$900	69,445	181,312	361,459	651,588	1,118,844
$1,000	77,172	201,458	401,621	723,987	1,243,160

12% AVERAGE ANNUAL RETURN

Monthly investment	5 years	10 years	15 years	20 years	25 years
$200	16,221	44,807	95,186	183,972	340,442
$300	24,331	67,211	142,780	275,958	510,663
$400	32,441	89,614	190,373	367,943	680,884
$500	40,552	112,018	237,966	459,929	851,105
$600	48,662	134,422	285,559	551,915	1,021,325
$700	56,773	156,825	333,152	643,901	1,191,546
$800	64,883	179,229	380,745	735,887	1,361,767
$900	72,993	201,632	428,339	827,873	1,531,988
$1,000	81,104	224,036	475,932	919,858	1,702,209

Monthly investment to reach your second-half goal: $________

HOW AVERAGES LIE

Place one hand on a hot stove, and the other on a slab of dry ice. Any statistician will tell you that on average you are comfortable—but of course you know it's not so. The market's average returns hide very long periods of both very weak and very strong performance. What's more, averages are derived from past returns, but future returns are unlikely to mirror the past exactly. Naïvely relying on "average" numbers without considering the market's wide variations can lead to disaster.

Imagine that you retired in 1972. You had $500,000 invested in equities and planned to withdraw 8% each year for income. From 1973 to 1974 the market dropped 50%, and you made your withdrawals as expected. In just two short years, you were down more than 60%. Your remaining capital was about $200,000, so depleted that it could never recover under the weight of your planned annual $40,000 withdrawals—which, after the disaster, amounted to 20% of the remaining capital!

Investors must assess both the probability and the potential consequences of their strategies. Given the possibility of market crashes, the wide variation of investment returns in the short term, and the consequences of failure, retirees must adopt strategies with the highest probability of success. They will want to build in a little extra padding for safety. The market neither knows nor cares whether you have retired. It can go down at any time, and stay there for several years. This situation leads to Armstrong's Law of Averages: *Don't expect to ever see an average year.* From this profound axiom we can derive the corollary: *Don't expect retirement to be a long string of average years.**

*Frank Armstrong, C.F.P., is president and founder of Managed Account Services Inc., Registered Investment Advisor (**www.fee-only-advisor.com**) and the author of *Investment Strategies for the 21st Century.*

THE THIEF IN THE NIGHT CALLED INFLATION

It's a topic that inspires one-liners galore. Despite the jokes, inflation is a very serious matter. Look at all the attention we give it. Not only do we measure it as a percentage (4% or 6%, for example); we classify it according to its severity. *Mild inflation* occurs when the price level—an average of all prices—rises from 2% to 4%. *Moderate inflation* refers to an inflation rate of 5% to 9%. *Severe infla-*

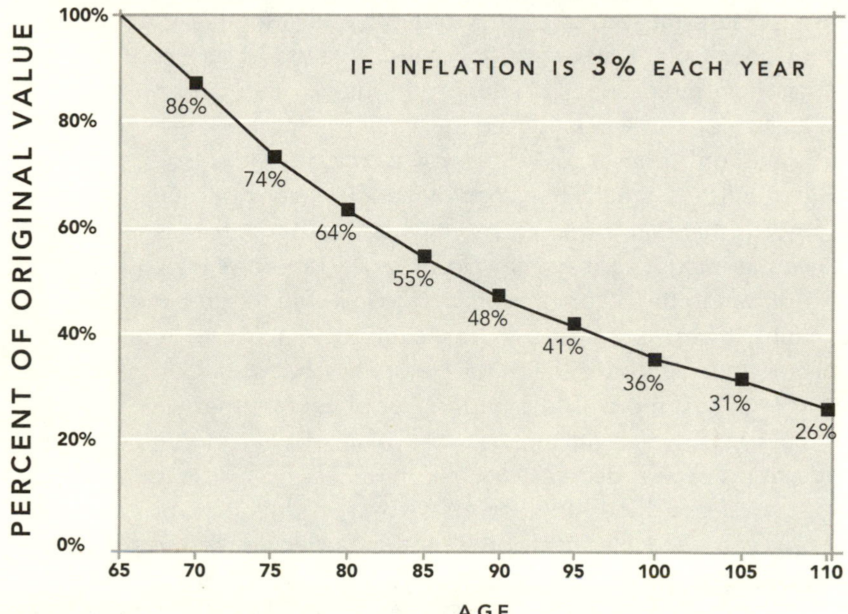

*Ron Gebhardtsbauer, American Academy of Actuaries.

tion—or "double-digit inflation"—refers to an inflation rate of 10% or higher. *Hyperinflation* is out-of-control inflation that ruins a country's economy; an example from the twentieth century is Germany just after the end of World War I, in 1918. Money loses its value, and often people turn to barter rather than relying on currency.

Closer to home, along with taxes, inflation is one of the major forces working against you as you work toward your investing goals. One way to think about inflation is as an additional tax. If inflation is at 4%, imagine that you have a 4% annual tax (in addition to real taxes) on your savings and investments. Even during periods of relatively low inflation, it's a thief in the night, a slow leak that never lets up, and if you ignore it, you'll regret it. Your money will lose its purchasing power without your spending a dime. And it gets worse over time because inflation compounds every year. At an annual inflation rate of 3%, prices will double in 24 years. At 4% inflation per year, inflation doubles prices in just 18 years.*

*Schwab Center for Investment Research.

Everyone knows that, simply put, inflation means that things cost more this year than they did last year. Whether it's a bottle of Coca-Cola, a sleeve of golf balls, a gallon of gas, or a carton of chow mein—not to mention things like cars and homes—it costs more now than it used to.

Not only does it cost more now than it did—it'll also cost more in the future than it does now. Inflation never goes away, which means that things will cost more when you begin that second half you're imagining than they do now. And prices will continue to rise during the 30 or 40 years that follow. Meals, groceries, vacations, travel, leisure activities—everything will cost more. Just how much more remains to be seen. That's half of inflation: Things cost more. The other half is, of course, that your money buys less, which means that the value of your money, or purchasing power, decreases.

It's a good idea to know how to figure inflation for yourself. Say you want to invest for something specific: Ten years from now, you hope to travel around the world, and you want to have $20,000 set aside for the trip. But that's 20,000 of today's dollars. How do you know how much you'll need in ten years? Like so:

1. Estimate the number of years to your goal: ________
2. Determine the current cost of that goal: $________
3. Enter your inflation factor from the table below, which assumes a 4% rate of inflation: ________

Years to your goal	Inflation factor
5	1.22
10	1.48
15	1.80
20	2.19
25	2.67

4. Multiply item 2 by item 3 to find your inflation-adjusted investment goal: $________

So what do you do with this thief in the night? You fight back by doing what you can to help your money earn more than what inflation is taking away. You have to invest at a rate of return that exceeds inflation, which isn't hard to do, once you pay attention. If inflation is at 4%, you want your rate of return to be at least 5%, and preferably higher, because inflation isn't your only enemy—you've got to factor in taxes as well. Chances are that a bank savings account won't give you a high enough return—the interest rate on bank savings accounts is typically around 2%.

What does do it? Stocks. From 1926 to 2000, U.S. stocks had average returns of approximately 11%, while the average inflation rate was 3%. Good companies can adjust for inflation; they can change their prices or cut their costs to compensate for it. Bank-paid interest and bonds will often match or do a little better than inflation, but companies have the ability to change their pricing and stay ahead of it, one of the many reasons that stocks are, in my view, the investment vehicle of choice, before and during your second half.

Recap: How Did You Do?

There, you've done it: You've gone through the process of figuring out what you'll need. You know what you've already put aside, and you know what you'll need to add to that to make your plans a reality. It's not a difficult process, as you know, but it can be a little nerve-racking, partly because of all the unknowns, and partly because it deals with the future, where anything can happen. But congratulations are in order because you're on your way. Take heart—with time, this will become easier. My suggestion is that you go through these steps every couple of years.

So how does your estimate look to you? Is it possible? Is it completely impossible? Somewhere in between? If it's in the ballpark of possibility, congratulations. You really are on your way. Keep working to put your plan into action as soon as possible.

But what if your shortfall is substantial? It's not uncommon for people to go through this process and find that what they'd hoped for simply isn't possible. If you're in that position, that doesn't mean you have to throw everything out and forget all this. Please don't. It just means you have to do a little revising.

Variability Analysis

As I write this, new technology-driven tools are becoming available so that individual investors can take advantage of a method that has been used for years by actuarials at big pension plans. These tools allow you to see lots of different scenarios instead of basing your future outcome on one estimated average rate of return. The computer program simulates different market environments based on the holdings in your portfolio and sketches a range of possibilities that you may face, from very optimistic to very pessimistic. It tells you the probability that your actual portfolio as it is constructed now will grow to whatever wealth objective you specify. If you're the kind of person who likes to see the big picture of possible outcomes, I think you'll find a variability analysis program fascinating. It should be available from your brokerage firm.

BUILDING A FINANCIAL SAFETY NET

Your "safety net" is the minimum amount of money it takes you to live. I'm talking about a very pared-down lifestyle here, and the intent is not that that's what you'll do; the intent is that once you come up with an estimate for that kind of life, you'll have a bottom line for how much you need. Once you reach that amount, other things are negotiable. It's a safety net for the balancing act that we're calling the second half.

To calculate the amount you need for your safety net, estimate what you would need for the categories listed below, and only those. Leave out the extras—vacations, meals out, new clothing, and entertainment—and use only the bare minimum you can get by on. Once you know your annual total, you're wise to go through the steps in this chapter twice—once with your safety net estimates, and again with your ideal second half in mind.

Expense	**Minimum amount needed per month**
Housing	$________
Food	________
Telephone	________
Utilities	________
Transportation	________
Insurance	________
Monthly total:	$________

Total annual expenses for safety net: $________
(Monthly total × 12)

If You've Come Up Short: Contingency Planning

Maybe you've faithfully and carefully done the worksheets in this chapter and the results are far from what you'd hoped. If so, take heart, and don't give up on your plans for your second half, or on your investing plans, even if you know in your heart that you haven't done enough. Get started and work with what you have. This is a place where every little bit counts. Yes, it's entirely possible that you should have started a long time ago, and that your expectations have been unrealistic. But start now. Figure out what you can do, and do it.

Revising Your Plan

Think of your life as a work of art. Our first impulses are rarely perfect, and if your estimates just aren't possible, there are several things you can do. If your estimate is out of whack, it may be time to reconsider some things. Chances are that you're motivated to cut back on your expenses and invest more now than you thought you could.

To Sell or Not to Sell Your Home

Where to live is one of the biggest decisions people face in the second half. Should you stay in the same house? If you sell, should you buy a less expensive place and invest the difference? Should you sell at all?

There are a lot of arguments for owning your own home, whether you keep the one you've got, or sell it and buy something less expensive. For one, it's a safety net. In the event of severe inflation, real estate is one of the few investments that could do better than stocks.

If you do stay in your home, the next question is whether or not to pay off the mortgage. One argument for not doing so is that owning a home is a good hedge against inflation. If the interest rate on your mortgage is less than what your stocks are earning, you're probably better off keeping the mortgage. The flip side is that your mortgage is most probably your largest single expense, and by paying off your home you lower your monthly expenses significantly. For proof, try eliminating the cost of your mortgage from the safety net expenses above. You may be surprised at the difference.

Paying off the mortgage is wise when both of the following are true: the interest rate you're paying on your mortgage is higher than the rate of return on your investments (e.g., a 9% mortgage interest rate, and a 7% rate of return on your investments); and you have less than five years to go on the mortgage.

Finally, as always, there are tax considerations. Thanks to the Taxpayer Relief Act of 1997, you can exclude from your income up to $250,000 ($500,000 for joint filers) of gain realized on the sale or exchange of a residence. The exclusion applies to only one sale or exchange every two years, and you must have owned and occupied the residence as your principal residence for an aggregate of at least two of the five years before the sale or exchange. The two years of ownership and use do not have to be *continuous. If you fail to meet this requirement as a result of some unforeseen circumstance (a change of employment, for example), you can still exclude a fraction of the $250,000 or $500,000. This legislation replaces the old rule that specified a one-time exclusion of $125,000 for those 55 and older.*

As a start, go back to the beginning. Return to Step 1, where you estimated how much it will cost you to live in the second half, and think about the assumptions on which you based those estimates. Ask yourself where you might realistically cut back. Look at the timing you were considering; if you were planning on early retirement, you could postpone it and consider working longer, or at least weigh the advantages. Working just a few more years may have a considerable impact on both the amount of money you can invest for the future and the amount of money you'll need. Look at where you planned on living, both location and type of home. Do some what-ifs: What if you lived in a less expensive or smaller town? What if you owned one car rather than two? What if you bought a smaller home and reduced your mortgage payments? What if you could increase your income through part-time work, or a home business?

You can also try to put more money aside now, especially by maximizing your annual contributions to both tax-advantaged and currently taxable accounts. And you can reexamine the rate of return you used in your calculations, if you're willing to assume more risk and revise your asset allocation. We'll talk more about this in Chapter 4.

Finding Money to Invest

Now it's time to get practical. Two pretty simple things you can do are to cut back on what you spend, and to lighten your load in terms of possessions. Remember when you were a kid and there was something you really, really wanted? Maybe you'd do anything to earn money toward that goal: You'd wash the car, look for quarters in the sofa, ask your parents for additional odd jobs, babysit like crazy, collect bottles and haul them to the market to sell (my personal favorite). This time the goal is bigger, and yes, you're older. But if you can recapture some of that energy and enthusiasm, it will serve you well.

Cutting Back and Getting Ahead

Think of your grandmother, or your grandfather, or an aunt or an uncle, or maybe it was your own parents—some frugal soul who truly knew the value of a dollar, and demonstrated respect and caution and wisdom in the way he or she dealt with money. There's a lot to be said for the old-fashioned habit of simply living beneath your means and investing the difference.

But we're not living in a very simple time, and the idea of investing now so you'll have more later can get lost in the shuffle of the good life of here and now. Just paying a little more attention to what you spend your money on can be very educational.

What follows is a laundry list of ways to cut back on your spending and get ahead on your investing. Maybe some of these ideas will serve you well; or maybe they'll lead to other ideas that will work even better.

- Start by looking at your cash flow—how much money you have coming in, and where it's going. If your spending is equal to or greater than what you're making, it's time to cut back and get your spending under control.
- Keep track of where your money goes. To do this, you have to get more detailed about your monthly expenses. There may be places where you're spending more than you realize, and certainly more than you intend to. Keep a list of everything you spend for at least a week; a month is better.

Include checks, credit cards, debit cards, and cash. Chances are you'll be amazed at where your money goes.

• Once you know where your money is going, consider cutting back on the personal extras, the little luxuries like the midmorning latte, weekly manicures, the deli lunch (instead of bringing your own). Use your library card instead of buying every new best-seller. Those items seem harmless, but they add up. Get rid of a few, and adding to your nest egg may be easier than you think. For example, would you consider skipping the cream cheese on your morning bagel for $7,000? How about skipping the popcorn at the movies for $11,000? If you cut back on the little extras of life, you may not see a difference right away, but they do add up, especially when you invest the money.

Adding Up the Extras

The extra you go without . . .	. . . saves you this much per year . . .	. . . and this much in 20 years (invested at 10%)
A bagel ($1.00) 3 days a week vs. a bagel with cream cheese ($1.75)	*$117.00*	*$7,371.29*
A carton of premium ice cream ($4.99) once a week vs. store brand ($2.49)	*$130.00*	*$8,190.32*
A movie once a week ($7.00) vs. a movie with popcorn ($10.50)	*$182.00*	*$11,466.45*
A regular coffee ($1.10) 5 days a week vs. a specialty coffee drink ($2.75)	*$429.00*	*$27,028.07*
Premium cable ($75.00 monthly charge) vs. regular cable ($30.00 monthly charge)	*$540.00*	*$34,021.35*

Pizza delivery once a week ($18.00) vs. store-bought ($5.99)	*$624.52*	*$39,346.32*
Dinner out once a week ($33.00) vs. dinner out with appetizers and dessert ($46.00)	*$676.00*	*$42,589.69*

You may want to pass these numbers along to someone just starting out. Imagine what these number would be with 40 years of compound growth!

• Take a credit check. Do you have too many credit cards? Consider getting rid of all but the essential ones, or use cash for all but major purchases. Most people seem to spend less when using cash.

• Once you've analyzed your spending patterns, develop a budget. This is a place for discipline, and that discipline can take you a long way.

• Look for ways to reduce fixed expenses such as your mortgage payments (by refinancing, if you can get a lower interest rate) and your insurance payments (by doing some comparison shopping for lower rates).

• Go bargain-hunting online. There are many online sites that are great consumer resources for finding the best deal for just about anything. As a start, you might look at Consumer World (**www.consumerworld.org**), a public-service Web site that provides information on over 2,000 of the most useful online consumer resources. For example, you can find reviews of specific products, last-minute travel bargains, guidance on filing a consumer complaint, and low mortgage and credit rates.

• Look at your withholding tax to see if too much is being withheld. If your income will drop this year, if you'll be receiving a tax refund this year, or if your deductibles will rise substantially this year, it may be wise to decrease your withholding, then invest the additional take-home pay.

• If you own your own business, look at your business expenses in the same way. You may be able to cut back on labor, rent, insurance, or other business expenses.

• Finally, when you do cut back, don't spend the extra money. *Invest it.* You start by depositing it to your brokerage account rather than your savings or checking account. Learn to think of your brokerage account as a holding place for money that you want to invest.

• Make investing a habit, and—even better—an automatic one, if you can, by using electronic funds transfer from your checking account or paycheck to your brokerage account (or you can sign up for an automatic investment plan), and by using dollar cost averaging (see the box below).

MAKE INVESTING A HABIT: DOLLAR COST AVERAGING

Successful investing is a little like a successful exercise program, in that doing it regularly—even if it doesn't feel like very much—is the key. Recent research has shown that people who exercise regularly, even if it's just a 20-minute walk every day, are often in better shape than those who exercise hard once or twice a week.

Same with investing. Investing a few times a year is certainly better than nothing, but there's a better way: a systematic method known as dollar cost averaging, which simply means investing the same amount of money at regular intervals. The most common way to do this is to set aside a fixed amount of money to invest every month. (This gets even easier if you do it through an automatic investment plan, so that your funds are transferred electronically, which means you don't even have to write a check.) It could be $100, it could be $500, it could be more or less whatever you can afford.

The advantage of investing through a set dollar amount rather than a set number of shares is that you buy more shares when the prices are low, and fewer shares when the prices rise. The result?

You may just be able to lower your average cost per share—and you stop worrying about market timing and trying to figure out when it's time to buy, when it's time to sell, two questions that are always hard to answer. You also don't worry as much when the market goes down, because that simply means you're acquiring more shares of stock. And though the method requires discipline—you can't just stop investing if the market goes down—it can be worth the effort. (Remember, however, that periodic investment plans like this do not assure a profit and do not protect against loss in declining markets. Since the plan involves continuous investment in securities regardless of fluctuating price levels of such securities, you should consider your financial ability to continue your purchases through periods of low price levels before deciding to invest this way.)

The table below shows how it works over a five-month period.

	Regular Investment	Share Price	Shares Acquired
	$400	$10	40
	$400	$8	50
	$400	$5	80
	$400	$8	50
	$400	$10	40
total	$2,000		260

Total investment: $2,000

Average cost per share ($2,000/260 shares): $7.69

Lightening Your Load

A lot of people are simplifying these days. They're finding that less truly is more, and they're unloading possessions and complications and cost from their lives. It's worth a thought, at least. An example is a car. People often go from two cars to one, and they find they're happier. If the kids are grown, and public transportation is good, it's worth considering.

Simplifying can do things for your spirit as well as your

brokerage account. The second half of your life is a time—an opportunity, really—to examine your life and, in doing so, your values. For a lot of people, "things" become less important as they age, and it's often natural to shed some of our material possessions. Maybe the painting or sculpture you loved 30 years ago doesn't give you the joy it used to. Maybe you use the sailboat only a couple of times a year. Maybe it's time to take a good look at your surroundings.

So look around, literally. Consider lightening your load. Get up and walk around your house and see if there are things you'd be happier without. Look in the garage, the basement, the attic, the nooks and crannies of storage, and think about which of your possessions you might want to liquidate in order to increase the cash you have available to invest. This doesn't mean you have to get rid of everything you own, and the idea isn't to tighten your belt and feel deprived. The idea is to loosen up and let go of some of those things you're holding on to needlessly, things you may not even need or like anymore. If you think they might bring in some money, consider having them appraised, find out where and how to sell them, hold a garage sale if all else fails—and then invest the money for growth. And if you have possessions that have more sentimental value than monetary, pass them on to friends or family or someone else who can put them to use. You don't have to do it all in a day; a lot of people make paring down a part of their lives. Sometimes living simply is living at its best.

Putting the Money to Work

Once you've found more money, don't lose it. Sounds obvious, right? But "losing it" means doing anything with it other than investing it. Don't just deposit it into your checking account. Deposit it into your brokerage account and put it to work for you by taking advantage of the snowball effect called compound growth.

Say you have a garage sale and you make $500, a nice little windfall. If you deposit that $500 in your checking account, yes, you'll pay some bills or you'll have a little extra that month, or maybe you'll buy something new or eat out a few times extra. Then the $500 is gone and you're back where you started, with that found money lost again. A few years from now you'll remember the garage sale, but you probably won't remember what you did with the money.

But look what happens if you invest it. Say you take that same $500 and invest it in an index fund, where your dividends are reinvested. In a year (based on historical performance), that $500 can grow to $550, and a year after that it might be $605. But look down the road a little: Five years from now it's $805, and ten years from now it's $1,297, all because of compound growth. So even if it's $100, put it to work, because one of the great facts of compound growth is that every little bit counts.

Words to the Wise on Estimating How Much You'll Need for the Second Half

• Chances are that the amount you'll need to have saved for your second half will surprise you. This is definitely a time to err on the conservative side, and to aim toward saving too much rather than not enough.

• Don't worry about the unknowns and uncertainties in your estimations. Just make informed and realistic estimates, and keep going.

• When you need an estimate of living expenses or income, the key word is estimate*—a ballpark figure will do. You don't have to count every dollar, every dime. Simply start with what you believe are realistic numbers.*

• To get a rough estimate of how much you'll need annually in your second half, you can use a percentage of your current annual income. The rule of thumb is 75%, meaning that 75% of your current annual income will allow you to continue living at your current lifestyle in the future. I suggest using 90% of your current annual income.

• To get a more detailed estimate of how much it will take you to live, estimate your expenses individually by using your current expenses as a base, then adjusting them according to whether you believe they'll increase or decrease in the second half.

• It's also wise to figure out the minimum amount it will take you to live in the second half—your safety net. This number gives you a bottom line, and represents how much you'll need to live. To calculate your safety net, estimate what you would need for only housing, food, telephone, utilities, insurance, and transportation. Leave out the extras.

• The most common types of income in the second half are Social Security payments and income from employer-sponsored defined-benefit plans. Other possible sources of income include royalties and rental income from real estate properties.

• An easy way to estimate how long your second half will be is to assume a life span of 90 years (or even 100), then subtract the age at which you'll start your second half from 90 or 100.

• *Averages lie. Over time it becomes more dangerous to base your investing strategy on averages. "Average" means 50% of the time you fall short of your goal, and 50% of the time you do better.*

• *Along with taxes, inflation is one of the major forces working against your investing goals. If inflation is at 4%, imagine that you have a 4% annual tax (in addition to real taxes) on both your savings and investments.*

• *From 1926 to 2000, U.S. stocks had average returns of approximately 11%, while the average inflation rate was 3%. Good companies can adjust for inflation; they can change their prices or cut their costs to compensate for it.*

• *If you find that your estimate for how much you have to save just isn't realistic, it may be time to reconsider some of your assumptions and to redo some numbers. Perhaps you can cut back on your expenses, so that you can be investing more now than you thought. Or maybe it's time to reexamine your vision of your second half and look for places to compromise.*

• *The biggest potential areas for compromise are time and lifestyle. Look at the timing you were considering; if you were planning on early retirement, you could postpone it and consider working longer, or at least weigh the advantages. Look at where you planned on living, both location and type of home or condominium. Look at the expenses you estimated, and the income as well, and do some what-ifs.*

• *There are a lot of arguments for owning your own home, whether you keep the one you've got, or sell it and buy a smaller place. In the event of severe inflation, real estate is one of the few investments that could do better than stocks.*

• *There are also strong arguments for paying off the mortgage. Doing so will significantly lower your monthly expenses, often by as much as one-half.*

• *Make investing a habit, and—even better—an automatic one, if you can, by using electronic funds transfer from your checking account or paycheck to your brokerage account (or you can sign up for an automatic investment plan) and by using dollar cost averaging, a systematic method of investing in which you invest a fixed amount of money at regular intervals.*

• Repeat the steps in this chapter every couple of years so that your plan reflects any major changes in your personal circumstances, as well as in the economy. A year from now you may have a more accurate estimate for some of those variables. And you may have a different inflation rate to deal with. The good news is that the process gets easier. It's also crucial. This is very definitely a place where you want to stay ahead of the game.

4

Choosing Investments for the Second Half

I'm a big fan of simplifying when you can. Think of buying a car—say you're looking for a first car for your daughter or son, or your niece or nephew. Do you set off on Saturday morning and look at every car on every lot? Of course not. Before you've even left the house, you've narrowed your search considerably. In other words, you've simplified the task. Maybe you want to buy American, maybe you're a big fan of Japanese or German cars. Your price range rules certain things out, as do safety factors, size, model, and make, all of which means that if you give the matter some thought, it can be pretty uncomplicated. That's the beauty of simplifying: It saves time.

Choosing investments can be a fairly straightforward process, and it's something you can take one step at a time. We'll start with the heart of the matter: asset allocation.

First Things First: A Second-Half Approach to Asset Allocation

Before you can decide on specific investments, you need a master plan—a strategy for how to divide your investing dollars among the three classes of investments: stocks, bonds, and cash equivalents. That strategy is called asset allocation.

Pie charts are an easy way to visualize asset allocation. The five pie charts that follow show five different approaches to asset allocation, ranging from the most aggressive (the most heavily invested in stocks) to the most conservative (the least invested in stocks). The approaches they illustrate are based on diversification—allocating your investing dollars among different types of investments. But they all have one thing in common: They all include stocks. You know the reason: In order for your money to outlive you, you need to invest for growth for the rest of your life.

ASSET ALLOCATION PIE CHARTS

For each approach, here is how I suggest that you set up your portfolio:

1. Very Aggressive Plan

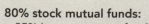

5% cash equivalents in money market funds

0% bonds or bond mutual funds

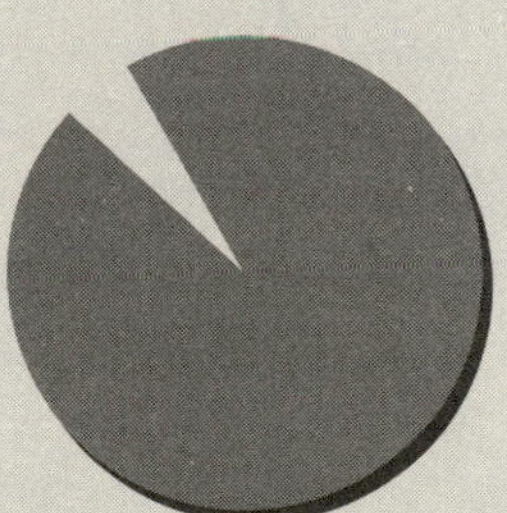

95% stock mutual funds:
40% large-company funds, mostly in broad-based index funds
25% small-company index or actively managed funds
30% international funds, mostly in actively managed funds

2. Moderately Aggressive Plan

5% cash equivalents in money market funds

15% bonds or bond mutual funds

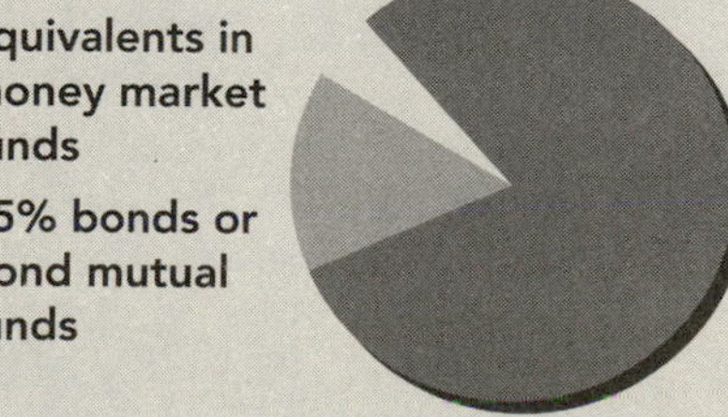

80% stock mutual funds:
35% large-company funds, mostly in broad-based index funds
20% small-company index or actively managed funds
25% international funds, mostly in actively managed funds

3. Moderate Plan

10% cash equivalents in money market funds, Treasury bills, short-term CDs

30% bonds or bond mutual funds

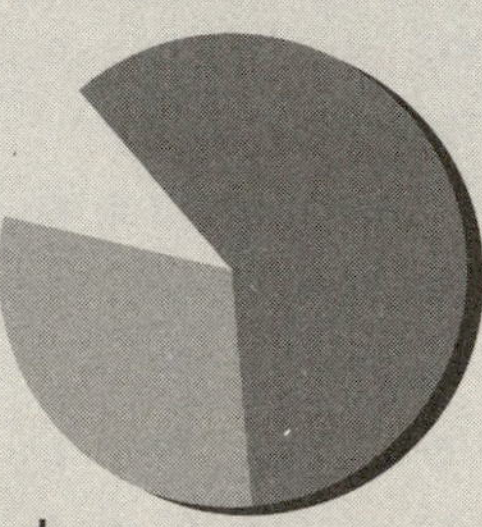

60% stock mutual funds:
30% large-company funds, mostly in broad-based index funds
15% small-company index or actively managed funds
15% international funds, mostly in actively managed funds

4. Moderately Conservative Plan

Note: I don't recommend this plan for anyone under 80. In this model, you're not invested for growth enough to prevent you from outliving your money.

15% cash equivalents in money market funds, Treasury bills, short-term CDs

45% bonds or bond mutual funds

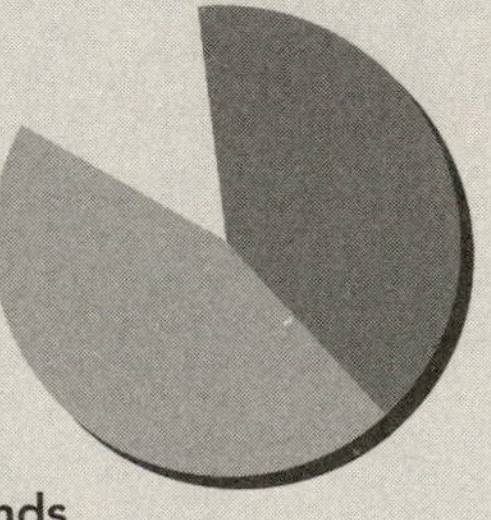

40% stock mutual funds:
20% large-company funds, mostly in broad-based index funds
10% small-company index or actively managed funds
10% international funds, mostly in actively managed funds

5. Conservative Plan

Note: I don't recommend this plan for anyone under 80. In this model, you're not invested for growth enough to prevent you from outliving your money.

25% cash equivalents in money market funds, Treasury bills, short-term CDs

55% bonds or bond mutual funds

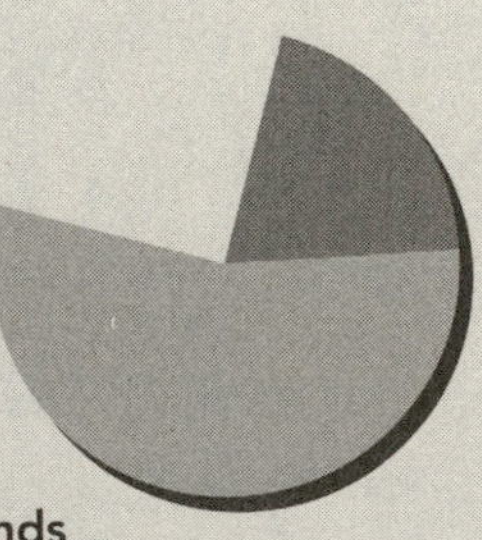

20% stock mutual funds:
15% large-company funds, mostly in broad-based index funds
5% international funds, mostly in actively managed funds

Note: For those of you willing spend the time and energy to research and track individual stocks, they can be used in place of stock mutual funds. My personal preference is to use mutual funds as the core portion of my portfolio.

For Beginners Only

If you haven't developed an asset allocation strategy, don't panic—but don't put it off. Now is the time. See the Investor Profile Questionnaire in Section 5 of the Appendix or on the Web in the Smart Investor tab *at* **www.schwab.com.** *It will help you to match your needs and situation with one of the pie charts.*

Your asset allocation may already be in line with one of these pie charts. (To determine what your current asset allocation is, see the box on page 89.) If it is, you may want to look at whether or not that's where you want to be. And remember that a common mistake is staying with an asset allocation that's too conservative. As you look at the pie charts, remember the following:

- ***Include all of your investing dollars—your entire portfolio—when deciding on asset allocation.*** Your "entire portfolio" means everything: the investments you have in retirement accounts as well as regular brokerage accounts. Be sure to include the money in your checking and savings accounts as well—count them in the cash-equivalent part of your pie chart. If you don't, you may end up overly weighted toward cash.

Investing at Its Simplest: Asset Allocation Funds

An asset allocation fund is a mutual fund that can mirror a specific asset allocation pie chart. It usually includes a mix of stocks, bonds, and cash equivalents to meet a specific growth objective, so that with one investment you diversify not only within investment classes, but among them. Over time the fund manager professionally reallocates the fund's assets, based on changing market conditions, so that your asset allocation doesn't fluctuate by an inordinate amount, despite the market's fluctuations. Aside from hiring a financial advisor to manage your investments, using an asset allocation fund is as simple and efficient as investing gets.

- ***Consider pension and Social Security income.*** If you expect the income from your pension and Social Security to go a long way toward meeting your income needs, you may want to consider a little more risk in your asset allocation—in other words, you can include a higher percentage of stocks than you otherwise might—because you won't be depending solely on your investments for your income.
- ***Remember that asset allocation is dynamic.*** Those pie charts aren't just models for today. They're a road map, really, for the asset allocations you'll move through in your second half. Over time, as you cut back on work and begin to withdraw money from your accounts, you'll probably adjust your asset allocation percentages and gradually alter the proportions of stocks to bonds. I suggest that you reexamine your asset allocation every five years, at a minimum, and alter it as needed. So for now, choose what you're comfortable with, and remember that this isn't a lifelong decision.
- ***Don't assume more risk than you're comfortable with.*** Fear and anxiety can reach a point where the risk you've assumed just isn't worth it. If investment worries are keeping you up at night, you should consider modifying your investment plan, by decreasing your risk to a point where you're comfortable. Life is too short to lose sleep over this. You have to be comfortable with the asset allocation plan you choose. Otherwise it's like buying clothes that don't fit: You'll have something to wear, but you'll never be comfortable.

Keep in mind that risk/reward is a thin line; you don't want to choose an asset allocation that's going to keep you up at night, but you don't want to let fear run your investing life, either. And remember that the other side of risk is reward. If you can afford to be more aggressively allocated, your money has more potential to grow.

SEEING WHERE YOU STAND: DETERMINING YOUR CURRENT ASSET ALLOCATION

You'll need to know what your current asset allocation is so that you can compare it to the pie charts on pages 85–86. Maybe you'll be happy with what you've got, but it's worth examining. As you look at this, remember to look at your asset allocation for your entire portfolio—all of your money and investments—not just your IRA or your regular brokerage account. Remember to include cash in bank checking and savings accounts as well.

If you're unsure about what your current asset allocation is, the easiest way to find out is by going online. Your brokerage firm's Web site should be able to give you this information in a few seconds. Or you can figure it out yourself by following these steps:

1. *Find out what the current market value of each of your investments is.* You can use the value shown in your most recent brokerage statement, or you can go online.
2. *Total the value for each class of investment—stocks, fixed income, and cash equivalents.* Be sure to consider all of your money—investments in tax-deferred accounts and regular accounts, in 401(k)s or 403(b)s, and in savings and checking accounts. The money in retirement accounts can seem as though it's separate from the rest of your investments, but it's not. It's all your money, all part of your nest egg, and you have to think of all those parts as a whole. If you're married or part of a domestic partnership, you should look at both portfolios. The second half should be, after all, a joint venture.
3. *Once you have the market value for each investment class, calculate the percentage of your portfolio that each class represents.* For example, suppose your portfolio contains stocks and

stock mutual funds worth $150,000, and bonds and bond mutual funds worth $50,000, and that your portfolio is worth a total of $200,000. You can then calculate percentages:

Investment Class	Current Value	% of Whole
Stocks and stock mutual funds:	$150,000	75%
Bonds and bond mutual funds:	$50,000	25%
Total value of portfolio:	$200,000	100%

Those percentages tell you your current asset allocation.

Choosing Investments

Once you've chosen a model for asset allocation, you can begin to look at the specific kinds of investments for each piece of the pie. To my mind, this is a place to simplify. The reason? Visit your favorite bookstore and you'll find a huge number of books on investing, some of them staggeringly detailed. There are whole books on choosing stocks, on picking mutual funds, on investing in bonds. But who has time to read all that? So let's simplify. I've been an investor for more than 40 years, and as a result I have some preferences, and what follows are my investing recommendations. They're not complicated, they're not overly long. This is not an exhaustive list of every investment available. It's not even close. Instead, I've narrowed things down to include only what I recommend. It's a simple approach to what should be a fairly simple endeavor.

To that end, these are the investments that I prefer:

Stock mutual funds are, to my mind, the core of a solid investment strategy, and I encourage you to use the Core and Explore™ strategy for the stock portion of your portfolio. In my opinion, index and actively managed funds are the tool of choice for both building your nest egg and generating income through dividends and capital gains. Investing in individual stocks is very appealing, but because choosing solid stocks can be tough—unless you're an experienced investor who does the necessary homework—I suggest you allocate no more than 10% of your investing dollars to individual stocks.

Five-year Treasury notes and tax-exempt municipal bonds are the fixed-income type of investments that I like. They can add stability to a portfolio, and they generate income.

Money market mutual funds are the cash-equivalent investment that I like. They're a great investment for cash reserves that you'll need in 6 to 12 months, and as a parking place for cash between investments.

FOR BEGINNERS ONLY: INVESTMENT BASICS

In very general terms, investments fall into three categories: stocks, bonds, and cash equivalents. Stocks represent ownership of shares in a company, and are, because of the growth I've talked about earlier, by far my investment of choice. Historically they've been a great hedge against inflation; in fact, over the long term, stocks have beat inflation by around 7% a year. Bonds are like IOUs from a corporation or a municipal or federal government: You loan the borrower some money, and in return, the borrower promises to return the full amount on a specific date and pay you interest in the meantime. That sounds like a good deal, but I'm wary of bonds for two reasons. First, they don't grow—you're paid interest, but your principal remains the same. In other words, you're putting safety over growth. Second, they don't protect you from inflation, which stocks can do. Despite those factors, however, bonds are often appealing to more conservative investors. Cash-equivalent investments, the third type of investment, are investments that you can easily convert into cash, such as money market mutual funds, Treasury bills, and certificates of deposit. I view them as a place to keep emergency funds, money you know you'll need within a year or two, and cash that you'll soon be investing, a sort of parking lot for cash. A money market mutual fund is, in my view, the best of these, followed by Treasury bills.

Each of these types of investment offers a particular kind of return and involves particular risks. Stocks, for example, historically offer higher returns on your initial investment—in other words, generally speaking, they have greater potential for producing wealth than bonds and cash equivalents. Risk refers to what you're putting on the line in the investment. The biggest risk, the worst possible outcome for investors, is, of course, losing the money they invested, and the very thought of it instills such fear that entire financial industries have been built upon counteracting that risk. Banks and savings and loans advertise savings accounts and CDs as "risk free," while government bond brokers promote risk-free Treasury securities. But loss of capital is only one type of risk; what about the loss of purchasing power through inflation? That's another kind of risk, and a very serious one. A savings account may eliminate market risk, meaning that you probably won't lose the money you deposit in it, but with respect to the purchasing power of your money, savings accounts are almost as risky as you can get. An interest rate of 2% just doesn't keep pace with inflation. Treasury bonds are free from default risk, but not from inflation risk or market risk or yearly taxes.

To my mind, the whole concept of risk is often misunderstood, and to an extent, stocks have taken a bad rap where risk is concerned. As I said above, there are many kinds of risk, and there's some element of risk in every type of investment, which means that there really is no such thing as a "risk-free" investment. In a way, that's good news because it means that you can stop trying to eliminate all risk. For better or worse, risk is part of the deal, just as it's part of life.

And as far as stocks are concerned, it's entirely possible that the more you know, the less you'll worry about risk. It's often true that what people label as risk is simply a discomfort or anxiety having to do with lack of experience or lack of knowledge. It's my experience that as you learn about investing and as you gain experience, the risk factor will bother you less. Knowledge is empowering.

So relax. You don't have to eliminate risk. You just have to deal with it, and that's a fairly simple three-part harmony. First, you have to educate yourself, and as you do, you'll become more objective and less afraid. Second, once you're educated, you can look at how much risk—real risk, not perceived risk—you can tolerate, based on who you are. Once you know which kind of risk you most want to minimize, you'll be better able to choose the right investments for your situation. And, third, you have to keep your balance, which means maintaining a balanced portfolio by diversifying among types of investments. By holding part of your portfolio in stocks and part in bonds, you don't avoid the risk of stocks or bonds, but you cut their effect. And you double your sources of return.

Building the Stock Portion of Your Portfolio with the Core & Explore™ Approach

In Chapter 1 we talked about using a Core & Explore™ approach for the stock portion of your portfolio—that is, using a broad-based index fund for the Core portion, and adding actively managed funds for the Explore portion. The index funds track a specific index; the actively managed funds give you the opportunity to outperform the market, and to therefore raise your investment return. You might choose funds that are weighted toward specific market segments, or in emerging markets, for example.

Once you've chosen a model for asset allocation, the next step is to decide on the percentages of index and actively managed funds to include. To do this, you need to understand how these funds are categorized. In general terms, both index funds and actively managed funds are categorized by size (large-cap and small-cap) and whether they are domestic (they invest only in U.S. companies in this country) or international (they invest in companies outside of the U.S.). According to research, actively managed funds add the most value to a portfolio in the small-cap and international asset classes, which means including a higher percentage of them than of large-cap funds. Explore portion funds intended to maximize upside potential were less effective in the large-cap area, which is why our model uses 60% to 70% for small-cap and international Explore portion funds and only 20% for large-cap. From 1991 to 2000, only 28% of actively managed large-cap funds beat their benchmark index. But in that same period, 59% of actively managed small-cap funds beat their benchmarks, and 73% of actively managed international funds beat theirs.[1] Looking ahead, the percentages below are what I recommend:

Component	Large-cap stock funds	Small-cap stock funds	International stock funds
Core	80% index funds	40% index funds	30% index funds
Explore	20% actively managed funds	60% actively managed funds	70% actively managed funds

These percentages are guidelines, and they may not be right for everyone. For example, a more conservative investor might include a higher percentage of index funds (perhaps even 100%), while a more aggressive investor might include a higher percentage of actively managed funds.

Let's look at an example of what these dollar amounts might be. Suppose an investor had $50,000 to invest. Let's say this investor has 95% of his money in stock mutual funds and 5% in cash equivalents. The cash portion would be $2,500. Here's how the remaining $47,500 would be divided between index and actively managed funds according to the strategy above.

[1]Schwab Center for Investment Research® with data provided by Morningstar, Inc.

Type of Fund	Total % for This Class of Fund	Equivalent $ Amount	% for Core/Explore	Equivalent $ Amount
Large-cap	40%	$20,000	80%/20%	$16,000/$4,000
Small-cap	25%	$12,500	40%/60%	$5,000/$7,500
International	30%	$15,000	30%/70%	$4,500/$10,500

FOR BEGINNERS ONLY: TYPES OF STOCK MUTUAL FUNDS

Both index and actively managed funds are categorized by several factors including the size of the companies they invest in (large or small), the style of the funds (growth versus value, for example), and whether the companies are domestic (those that invest within the U.S.) or international (those that invest outside of the U.S.):

- *Domestic stock funds* invest chiefly in stocks issued by U.S. companies. They are classified according to size and goals. Size is measured by companies' median market capitalization. Large-cap funds invest in companies with median market capitalizations in the top 5% of the largest 5,000 domestic companies, mid-cap funds invest in companies with median market capitalizations in the next 15%, and small-cap funds invest in companies with median market capitalizations in the remaining 80%. The investing style of mutual funds is classified as *growth, value,* and *blend.*

  Growth funds invest in companies that are seeking rapid growth in earnings, sales, or return on equity.

  Value funds invest in companies whose assets are considered undervalued, or in companies that have turnaround opportunities, with lower price-to-earning ratios.

  Blend funds invest in a combination of stocks and include both growth and value stocks, or stocks that fall between the growth and value categories.

- *International stock funds* invest outside of the U.S.:

  World funds invest in securities issued throughout the world, including the U.S.

  Foreign funds invest in developed markets outside the U.S.

How Many Funds?

Once you have percentages, you can begin to look at how many individual funds you want. As you might guess, choosing the best number of funds is a balancing act. Including only one fund in each asset class might give you a better chance of beating the market by a lot, but it also exposes you to the risk of significantly underperforming it. The key, of course, is diversification. But you don't want to go too high; including ten funds seems to preclude outperforming the market, or to at least make it pretty unlikely. Just as when you choose an asset allocation pie chart, you're trying to reduce risk but maximize your potential for high returns.

Let's look first at index funds. I suggest including one broad-based index fund for each asset class—in other words, one small-cap index fund, one international index fund, and one large-cap index fund.

Now for actively managed funds. If you already own an index fund in an asset class, I'd be wary of owning more than an additional two active funds in that asset class. The reason is that you've already achieved diversification within that asset class with the index fund. If you buy several more actively managed funds, your active funds, as a group, are so spread out that they could very well start to perform just like an index fund, but at active-management fees. In addition you've dramatically added to your record-keeping requirements. (Remember my suggestions about simplifying your life?)

To summarize, build a core with one broad-based index fund in the large-cap, small-cap, and international category.

Add to these funds, at most, an additional two actively managed funds in each equity asset class. Throw in a bond fund and a money market fund and you're done.

Choosing Index Funds

My preference for an index fund is one based on a broad-based index, meaning one that includes a large portion of the market, rather than being too specific. For example, the Schwab 1000 Index® includes the 1,000 largest publicly traded U.S. companies as measured by the market capitalization (the worth of a company's publicly traded stock) of those companies (excluding investment companies), and it represents about 89% of the U.S. stock market's value. The S&P 500 (its full name is Standard & Poor's Composite Index of 500 Stocks) is a well-known index. As its name implies, it includes only 500 companies, and it accounts for around 82% of the market value of the U.S. stock market.

As I see it, a broad-based index fund is one of the most useful and efficient investments around. If you really don't want to spend a lot of time in research and trading, you could even consider investing only in a broad-based, tax-efficient index fund, a sort of all-Core approach. It's investing at its simplest, but in my view it's a solid approach for the long term.

Make sure you're familiar with the underlying index for any index fund you're considering. Most index fund investors are looking for a fund that represents the general market, so they expect a fund's underlying index to represent broad stock market averages. But you may want a more specific index, such as small companies with more-aggressive growth potential. There are a variety of indexes to choose from, and more are being created all the time to address new goals. You should know, however, that the farther a fund moves from the general market, the more it begins to resemble an actively managed mutual fund, which may mean higher fees and greater risk.

Further, I suggest that you look for funds specifically devoted to long-term capital growth without excessive risk. As you look at performance charts, remember that the funds with the best long-term records have rarely appeared among the top performers in any one year. Unless you're an experienced investor with special knowledge of individual industries, avoid sector funds, which invest solely in one industry or a narrow range of related industries. Funds available through large mutual fund families are usually good choices. Reputable investment firms offer a good selection of funds and a customer service network that will make fund investing easier. Both are especially important if you intend to use switch privileges to move your money among the funds in a family of funds.

Choosing Actively Managed Funds

Choosing an actively managed mutual fund is similar to buying a house. If you set out to find the right one by checking out everything in town from the humblest shack to the poshest mansion, you'd throw in the towel pretty fast. But you don't do that, of course; you have certain criteria that narrow your search dramatically. Selecting actively managed mutual funds is a similar process. First you develop a list of criteria; then, and only then, do you go shopping. Doing this on the Web is easy.

Your list of criteria is crucial in the world of mutual funds; as of this writing, there are more than 8,000 funds available, so do your homework. The following are some guidelines to start:

1. Consider only no-load mutual funds. A load is a commission or sales fee. A no-load fund is one in which you pay no sales charge on the purchase or sale of shares; you can buy no-load funds directly from the fund company or a "fund supermarket." A load fund, on the other hand, includes a sales charge when you buy shares (called a front-end load) or sell them (a back-end load). A low-load charges about 3%. A regular load is about 4¾% to 6%.

Mutual Fund Shopping Made Easy

If you find yourself drawn to funds from several mutual funds companies, which I often do, there's an easy way to invest in them—through what's come to be called a "mutual fund supermarket." This is a sort of one-stop shopping for mutual funds, in which one brokerage firm makes available hundreds of no-load mutual funds from different fund families. There is usually no transaction fee; there may or may not be a fee for opening an account. Perhaps the biggest plus is that you get all your fund reports on one statement. You can buy and sell funds from different companies through the same brokerage firm without paying any more than you'd pay if you bought the fund directly from the fund company. If you use a supermarket offered by a broker, you can buy and sell individual stocks and bonds as well.

You should, however, be aware that in general, funds traded through a supermarket are typically subject to short-term redemption fees. Such fees are usually around 0.75% of the principal. They apply to redemptions made within 180 days of the time you purchased the fund.

A load is a commission, plain and simple, and it's a big chunk out of your capital, whether it's charged up front or as a back-end charge. So by simply considering only no-load funds—where all of your money is invested in the fund—you avoid paying commissions to the salesperson. Making sure that you don't buy load funds is one thing you can do to keep your costs down. You can't control the economy; you can't control the cost of the fund itself. But you can control whether or not you pay this extra fee. A fee table in the beginning of the prospectus will list the fund's loads, if there are any.

It's easy to spot a no-load fund in the mutual fund table. The initials "NL" appear in the offer price column, which means that the fund can be bought and sold at the price in the NAV (net asset value) column. That said, there may be situations in which a load fund makes sense in order to meet certain unique objectives for a portfolio.

Mutual funds are traded based on their net asset value (NAV), which represents the total value of the fund, less expenses, divided by the number of outstanding shares. Funds with an offer price identical to the NAV are either no-load or funds with a back-end load (sometimes referred to as a contingent deferred sales charge). Many funds also impose a short-term redemption fee because they want to discourage investors from actively trading the fund. If you're not sure, ask your broker whether a fund is a no-load or not.

2. Examine mutual fund expenses carefully. Unfortunately, loads aren't the only fees to watch out for. You should also check for management fees, 12(b)-1 fees, and other expenses, which you'll find listed along with any loads in the fee table at the beginning of the fund's prospectus. All of these fees can affect your return substantially. For example, although operating expenses are usually lower percentages than loads (typically between 0.5% and 1.75% of a fund's total assets), they are assessed annually. They add up, and they can become substantial over time—and as your assets grow. If a fund's expenses are higher than average for its category, it should be because that fund has a greater potential for above-average returns. And because a fund's expenses are always deducted from its total return, if all else is equal, a lower-cost fund might be a better value over time.

When you look at costs and compare them among funds, make sure you're comparing apples to apples. For example, compare only funds in the same peer group, and look at the average for that category. Don't compare a fund in one category with a fund in another. You should also be aware that some types of stock funds simply cost more than fixed-income or money market funds. It's important for small-cap funds to research companies for which there is less publicly available information, so their expenses can be a little high, as can those of funds in emerging markets, thanks to the extensive—and expensive—research required in countries where reliable financial information is scarce. To find the expenses for a fund, you can access Morningstar's data online at **www.morningstar.com;** by mail at 225 West Wacker Drive, Chicago, IL 60606; or by phone at 800-735-0700. Schwab's Mutual Fund Select List™ is another good resource, as is Schwab's Mutual Fund OneSource Online Web site at **www.schwab.com.**

For more information, see "Sales charges and fees" in Section 6 of the Appendix, "Reading the Fine Print: What to Look for in a Mutual Fund Prospectus and an Annual Report." Section 7 of the Appendix gives a comparison of mutual fund costs.

3. Consider only funds listed in financial publications such as* The Wall Street Journal, Barron's, *and major daily newspapers. Why? Because you want to be able to check on the fund's performance and track record easily. These publications list the per-share net asset value of mutual funds, and sometimes the historical performance records of funds as well.

4. Choose funds with steady performance and a solid track record. You want a fund that has a good performance record, not only for this year but over the life of the fund. As you look at a fund's performance over time, make sure it's steady in up-and-down markets. Look for median funds, i.e., those with steady (versus volatile) records in good markets and bad. Historically, I've paid particular attention to the last five years because it seems to me that three years is often the length of a cycle; there's usually been an up and a down market in that time, so by looking at five years of returns, you can see how the fund has performed in both kinds of markets. That said, the last five years (1995–2000) have been highly unusual, so you may want to look at the returns for the last ten years for a more realistic view.

Performance records are less critical for index funds because we can calculate what that performance is for the last 100 years—it tracks its underlying index. Of course, past performance cannot guarantee future results.

5. Read the prospectus carefully. Once you find a fund that you're interested in, phone or go online to contact the mutual fund company or your brokerage firm and ask for a prospectus, which is a legal statement that describes the objective of a specific investment. Every mutual fund is required to publish a prospectus and to give investors a copy, free of charge. The prospectus lists the fund's goals, restrictions, advisors, and fees, and you should read it carefully before you invest. You should look for three key pieces of information: the detailed statement of the fund's investment policies; an account of the kinds of transactions the fund may execute and the types of securities it can buy or sell; and a statement of the costs associated with buying the fund's shares and maintaining the investments. The prospectus must also detail the fund's investment policies, and it must say whether or not the fund has a sales load or charge. (For more detailed information on reading a prospectus, see Section 6 of the Appendix.)

6. Don't buy a mutual fund in a regular account during the fourth quarter without doing some homework. You may be hit with a distribution that you'll have to pay taxes on, even if you've owned the fund for only a few weeks or months. Mutual fund companies usually distribute any capital gains and dividends at the end of the fund's fiscal year (typically October), and you pay taxes on those distributions even if you reinvest them, and even if you've only owned the fund for a few weeks or months. So find out the fund's annual distribution date (called the "ex-dividend date"), and hold off on investing until after that date. (This applies only to regular accounts. If you're buying the fund in a retirement account, any taxes will be deferred.)

Individual Stocks: The Icing on the Cake

When you invest in a company's stock, you own a part of that company, and your money is a vote of confidence for that company. You're putting your money where your mouth is, and saying, "I believe in this company." And once you own stock in a company, you feel differently about the company.

A lot of people approach investing in stocks as something that they have to get right—they think they have to pick

For Beginners Only: Stocks

Stocks are classified as common stocks or preferred stocks. Common stocks are classified in four groups. Blue-chip stocks *are typically large, well-established companies and usually offer less risk because of their solid track records.* Small company stocks, *also called "small caps" for "small capitalization," are companies with a relatively small total market value. They often offer increased growth and higher returns, but they are more volatile—their stock price may increase or decrease dramatically—and therefore riskier.* Growth stocks *are companies with the potential for strong earnings—the up-and-comers of the market.* Value stocks *are companies whose assets are considered undervalued or have turn-around opportunities and low P/E ratios.*

Holders of preferred stock sometimes receive preferential treatment; for example, dividends must be paid on preferred stock, while dividend payment on common stock is optional. Preferred stocks sound like a good deal: They pay a fixed high dividend, and they have the potential for growth. But if it's growth you want, you're better off researching common stocks, and if it's income you want, check out bonds.

You also hear about penny stocks, *which sell for $5 or less and have a sort of slot-machine appeal. You don't have to put much*

on the table, and you think you really might hit it big. But penny stocks, to my mind, are a case of you-get-what-you-pay-for. You're seldom buying quality. Penny stocks typically have no revenue, no income, no capital, and if you ranked companies by quality, they'd be right down at the bottom. That's why they're penny stocks. If you're really drawn to a penny stock, take a wait-and-see attitude, and watch for a while. Let it prove itself by going over $10 a share before you jump in.

exactly the right stocks at exactly the right time, or they won't be successful investors. The fact is that because the overall long-term trend of the stock market has historically been upward, it's usually more important to just weed out the unproven or worn-out stocks than to pick the exceptionally good ones. Choosing the companies that you want to invest in isn't very different from making purchasing decisions in the rest of your life: Value and quality are what you're looking for.

There's no magic involved; you're just trying to find a good product—in this case, the product is a company—and you go about it just as you would go about buying a refrigerator or a new set of golf clubs. You don't rush into it; you don't try to intuit what to buy, or make a purchasing decision on a whim. Instead you do some research, you look at your choices, you think it over. You're looking for a company you believe in. And then, based on your experience and what you've learned, you make your choice, knowing that it was an informed decision.

Start by looking for a company that is healthy and thriving, sort of the way you'd look at plants at a nursery. Remember, a company is designed to grow, and I'm suspicious of one that isn't growing in terms of measurable things like products offered, revenue, and earnings. Beyond that, there are a lot of ways to choose specific companies.

There's a lot to be said for buying what you know—in other

words, investing in industries that you know something about. Paying attention to the world around you can help you spot what's selling. You can also watch for "product stocks"—companies that have a hot product. And many investors enjoy watching and investing in small-cap companies—meaning those with a market capitalization of less than $1 billion—because of their higher potential for growth. That said, if you venture down the small-cap path, be particular, and be sure that you're ready, willing, and able to tolerate some significant price fluctuations. (And remember that if you're really excited about the small-cap world, a small-cap mutual fund may be a better choice than lots of individual stocks.)

Finally, once again, I encourage you to look for growth stocks. Income investors (and retirees are often income investors) typically base their decisions on the dividends produced by the stock, and they look for dividends in the range of 4% or better. Companies that pay dividends of this rate generally have a pretty stable stock price. But growth investors don't want big dividends—they want the company to be reinvesting those dividends for growth, fueling that company's expansion, which should be reflected in a growing stock price. So, as appealing as income stocks are, think long-term—think growth—and look for those companies that are growing.

Once you've narrowed your search, you're wise to do a little research and keep an eye on the stocks of any companies you're interested in. To start, I look at the company's track record. Generally speaking, stocks of established corporations are usually more predictable than stocks of young, unproven firms. Smaller companies often have high growth potential but no track record, so consider the trade-offs between investing in well-established companies versus newer ones.

I also look for quality by tracking a company's earnings trend. Earnings are the company's net income or profit, and

Earnings Per Share (EPS)

$$EPS = \frac{\text{total earnings}}{\text{number of shares outstanding}}$$

Goal: You want a company's EPS to increase.

they are given in millions of dollars. The more helpful number is *earnings per share* (EPS), which is the company's total earnings for a period divided by the number of shares outstanding. For example, a company with earnings of $50 million and 20 million shares outstanding would have an EPS of $2.50. This number has meaning when you compare it to earlier EPS numbers for the same company, and to similar companies. Your hope is that the EPS is increasing, year after year. The easiest way to find a stock's current EPS is on the Internet. Just about any stock report should include it.

And I look for value, which means that I'm hoping to pay a price that's under historic levels for that stock. Strangely enough, the best measurement for a stock's value isn't its price. That just tells you what the public thinks of the company on any given day. A better measurement is the company's price/earnings ratio, or P/E, which represents the relationship between the price of the company's stock and its earnings for the past year. You get a company's P/E by dividing its current price by its EPS for that year. For example, a stock selling for $50 with an EPS of $2.00 has a P/E of 25 ($50/$2.00). Stock P/Es can vary tremendously, from as low as 0.5 to over 100. Many companies have a P/E reported as NMF, which stands for "not meaningful." This occurs when the company's earnings are zero or negative. While there are no hard-and-fast rules about what to watch for, in general a low P/E can be a good sign because it may indicate that the stock price hasn't risen to reflect the company's earnings ability, which means the stock may be undervalued—in other words, a bargain. A high P/E is not worrisome in and of itself, but it should prompt you to do some homework so that you understand the reasons for it. It can result from a runaway price or depressed earnings, both of which are reasons to be wary. But it can also mean that the market feels the company has high growth potential.

Remember that you're not just buying a name or a P/E ratio or a rating. You're buying into a company you believe in.

A great resource for researching stocks is the stock charts available through the stock chart publishing division of Babson-United, a company that supplies independent, unbiased investment research. The stock charts combine market prices and trading volumes with important statistics on the companies themselves, including earnings, dividends, and relative strength when compared to other companies. The *SRC Green Book of 5-Trend 35-Year Charts* is a publication that gives a thorough look at a large number of companies, industry groups, and market averages over a long period of time through various economic conditions and historical events. The charts help you follow a company's earnings, dividends, and price patterns, and you can see where its stock stands today relative to points in its past. Babson also publishes a wall chart that traces the economic history of the United States for more than 100 years. You can reach Babson at **www.babson.com**, or at 888-223-7412.

Demystifying the World of IPOs

It's easy for small investors to feel they're standing on the sidelines where IPOs (initial public offerings) are concerned. It seems as though there's a new one every day, and those debuts are often surrounded by a lot of hype. So what's the true story? Are IPOs as great a deal as they can seem to be?

You can get the idea from the media that just about any IPO out there is a sure thing. That's a long way from the truth, especially for individual investors. According to a Prudential Securities study of 1,700 IPOs between 1994 and 1996, investors who bought at the close of the first day of trading posted flat returns, on average, over the first three months.[2] For every star IPO, there are dozens more that don't do so well.

Second, the really hot IPOs are often unavailable to small investors, so if you're able to buy shares on that first day, that may not be a good sign. That's because the demand for hot IPOs is usually substantially greater than what's available. The firm underwriting the IPO typically allocates the shares among its top clients, and to the more active customers of brokers who regularly participate in underwriting syndicates. Not only that: Those handpicked clients often buy their shares at a discount, usually around 15% under the estimated market value. Even when online trading firms work with Wall Street underwriters to make some portion of new issues available to their clients, those clients are still often in that "top client" category. When all is said and done, there's often not much left over for the small investor—or what is left is not so hot. This situation is called "the winner's curse" because the IPO that individual investors "win" the opportunity to invest in are often the less desirable offerings.

There's another catch. While the way in which an IPO performs on its first day might be off-the-charts positive, the chances of smaller investors realizing those high average returns are small. Because of the way in which IPOs are allotted, the smaller investor's average IPO dollar can do poorly. And even if you do manage to buy on that first day, that's no guarantee. Here's why. Suppose you're watching two companies about to go public and you place orders for 1,000 shares of each of them. Both of them have an initial public offering price of $10. Company X turns out to be hot, and it goes up 100% on its first day, closing at $20. Company Y isn't so hot. It falls 20%, to $8 a share, and remains there.

2 "Letting in the Little Guy," *Investor University* at *Individual Investor Online.*

In the larger scheme of things, it looks as though you did fine (assuming you received your full allotment of shares of both stocks). Your 1,000 shares of Company X is worth $20,000, and although your 1,000 shares of Company Y have fallen to $8,000, your total for the two stocks is $28,000, a 40% gain on your $20,000 investment. Not bad.

Maybe. But unfortunately, just because you placed an order for 1,000 shares doesn't mean you got them. Suppose, for example, you did get your 1,000 shares of Company Y (because the demand for that stock was low), but you got only 100 shares of Company X because it was in much greater demand. In this case the picture changes: You're down $2,000 on Company Y, and you're up only $1,000 on Company X, which gives you a net loss of $1,000—about 9% of your $11,000 investment.

Believe it or not, this is not an unusual scenario. As I said, the hottest offerings are hard to get, usually reserved for a brokerage's best customers. If you're in that group, you may do great with IPOs in the long term. But if you're not—if you're a more typical small investor—you may receive more of the IPOs that are likely to underperform, and fewer of the star performers.

If you're truly interested in IPOs—and assuming you've heeded the warning above—there are some things you can do. Most important of those is to examine the prospectus, which is the best source of information on a company's stock before the company goes public. This preliminary prospectus is often called a "red herring" or S1. The goal of this document is to provide prospective investors with useful information, in compliance with SEC regulations. You may find some warning signs here. You can get a company's preliminary prospectus free of charge, through the SEC's EDGAR Web site. Because every domestic company is required to file its preliminary prospectus with EDGAR, you can learn about almost any company you're interested in at **www.sec.gov/index.htm.** (Other Web sites to check out for IPO information include

Hoover's IPO Central [**www.hoovers.com**], which gives a detailed listing of new registrations, and Bloomberg's IPO Center [**www.bloomberg.com**], which includes the Bloomberg IPO Index, an index that measures the performance of stocks during their first publicly traded year. Quote.com's IPO Edge [**www.quote.com**] also has current information on upcoming offerings.)

Here's what to look for in the prospectus:

- ***Who is underwriting the IPO?***

The cover of the red herring will list the underwriting firm or firms that are bringing the new issue to market. You do see second- and third-tier investment banks underwriting solid new issues, just as you sometimes see a new issue fail to pan out, even though it's underwritten by a top firm. But, statistically speaking, you're probably in a better position if you stay with name underwriters whose reputations attract the cream of the IPO crop.

- ***Who's selling, and how much?***

In a section of the red herring often called "The Offering," you will find a list of the stockholders who are selling. It's possible that early private investors such as venture capitalists are selling their stake in the IPO. If you see that pre-offering investors are selling large blocks of stock, you may have reason to be wary. That sell-off could mean a lack of confidence on their part. Conversely, if you see that company management is holding on to a substantial stake (look in a section usually called "Principal and Selling Stockholders"), that may be a good sign.

- ***How is the company doing financially?***

In the section called "Consolidated Financial Data," you'll find information about how the company is doing financially, including past and present revenues, earnings, and operating margins. If the company has seen a slowdown or decline in growth, be careful. You may find an explanation under "Management Discussion." If you do, make sure that that explanation is thorough and convincing.

• ***How is the company using its investors' money?*** You can also learn how the money you invest in the company will be used. You'll find this information under "Use of Proceeds." If the company is using investors' money to pay off debt (as opposed to funding future growth), that may be reason to believe that the company is facing financial difficulties. If the company is vague about where the proceeds are going, that too may be cause for concern.

Can a Stock Split Make You Money?

In today's market environment, the announcement of a stock split gets a lot of attention. Stock splits have become a hot item, with entire Web sites devoted to them. Many people view them as a way to make a quick dollar. But what does a stock split really do for stockholders?

First, here's how it works: When a stock splits, the company issuing the stock gives "investors of record" (shareholders who officially own stock on a specific date chosen by the company) additional shares, based on the number of shares they own. The most common split ratio is 2-for-1, but you also see ratios of 3-for-1, 3-for-2, and 5-for-4.

There are several dates to pay attention to when looking at a stock split:

1. The declared date is when the split is first publicly announced.

2. The record date is the date by which you (the stockholder) must officially own shares in order to receive split shares.

3. The split date is when the new shares are awarded.

For example, suppose you own 250 shares of XYZ stock. On January 1, XYZ declares a 2-for-1 split for investors of record as of February 1, with the split effective on February 5. If you are a shareholder of record on February 1, on February 5 you will receive one additional share of stock for every share you own, *and the stock's price will be adjusted accordingly. If you had 250 shares priced at $120 before the split—an investment worth $30,000—after the split you'd have 500 shares worth $60 each. You haven't lost or gained anything. Your investment is still worth $30,000.*

Splits can also work the other way, through what's called a reverse split. For example, a stock that reverse splits 1-for-10 exchanges one new share for each 10 existing shares, raising the stock's price by a factor of 10 in the process.

So what has the split changed? From a bookkeeping standpoint, almost nothing. You've basically exchanged 10 dimes for 20 nickels. Your investment is still worth the same amount, and neither the company's market capitalization nor its key measurements (things like its P/E ratio) have changed. The only thing that's changed is that there are more shares outstanding (or fewer, in the case of a reverse split) with the price adjusted accordingly.

If that's true, you may be wondering why a company goes to the trouble. Companies declare stock splits to reduce the price of their shares. Lower-priced shares, they believe, are more attractive and affordable to investors. The hope is that the stock split will push up the price of the stock. There are a lot of investors out there who believe this as well, and they often try to anticipate stock splits. With reverse splits, the idea is that a stock trading at $20 looks better than one trading at $2. A reverse split drives the price of the stock up by reducing the total number of shares.

There are a handful of Web sites that offer predictions about which companies might split in the near future. You can arrange to be alerted via e-mail when a stock splits, but is it worth it? It's true that some stocks do rise in value faster than the market as a whole when a split is announced, but there's no guarantee that a stock will perform well after a split is announced. Many split stocks perform poorly or just languish after a split. And while there may be some evidence that splits cause certain stock prices to rise, I question the idea that splits add value over the long term. People with split pagers clipped to their belts are usually short-term traders looking for a quick profit. For the long-term, buy-and-hold investor, a better strategy may be to stick with fundamentals like strong management, a solid balance sheet, firm earnings, and consistent growth. If you follow the long-term buy-and-hold approach, you're likely to end up owning one or more stocks that subsequently split, which is probably good news. After all, stocks most often split because their prices have risen to high levels—which is what most investors want.

A final note: When one of your stocks splits, be sure to keep good records because the split will affect your cost basis—the amount you've invested in each stock share. For example, if you paid $50 per share for a stock that subsequently splits 2-for-1, your new basis will be $25 instead of $50. This is important, because your cost basis will determine your capital gains and therefore the taxes you owe when you sell the stock.

For the More Sophisticated Investor: Measuring Stocks with Beta and Alpha

We'd all like to have a way of predicting how a certain stock will perform. And while there doesn't seem to be a sure-fire method to do that, there is a way that you can compare the risks of specific stocks to the overall market. It's an approach called the "modern portfolio theory" (MPT), and it's become a valuable tool for measuring and comparing the risks of individual stocks, and even entire portfolios. It can help you look for the best balance between risk and return in your entire portfolio—and two of its measurements, *beta* and *alpha,* can also help you look at the risk and performance of specific individual stocks.

We'll start with beta, which measures something called "systematic risk," the part of a stock's volatility that can be explained by the stock's sensitivity to changes in the overall market. (You can also get beta information for mutual funds.) Beta compares a stock's historical volatility with that of a benchmark. For stocks, the most commonly used benchmark is the S&P 500 Index. A stock with a beta of 1 is expected to exhibit the same volatility as the S&P 500. A stock with less than 1 is expected to exhibit less volatility than the S&P 500, and a stock with a beta greater than 1 is expected to exhibit more volatility than the S&P 500. For example, a beta of 0.5 means that that stock is expected to exhibit half the volatility of the S&P 500, meaning that it will move about 1% for every 2% move in the S&P 500. A beta of 2.0 means the stock is expected to move 2% for every 1% move in the S&P 500.

Alpha, the second tool, measures the percentage of total return unique to an individual company, that part of the return not dependent on the general market. Alpha measures the stock's specific risk (or residual risk). Some investors and professional money managers view a high alpha as a sign that a stock may offer returns above its historical average. A stock can also have a negative alpha. This occurs if it isn't performing as well as its beta suggests that it should.

Alpha and beta won't tell you everything you need to know, but they can provide a piece of the puzzle when you're evaluating a stock. Looking at stock betas can help you diversify your portfolio more effectively. For example, if most of your stocks have betas above 1.0 (the beta of the benchmark), you may want to balance those investments with some stocks with lower betas (below 1.0). If you want your portfolio to simply track the S&P 500, you might look for stocks with betas close to 1.0. For a more aggressive portfolio, you could look for stocks with higher betas (more than 1.0).

Here's an example. Let's say that the stock for the company XYZ Inc. has a beta of 1.5 relative to the S&P 500. If the return for the S&P 500 for the year is 28%, the stock's 1.5 beta suggests that XYZ Inc. stock would increase 1.5 times as much as the S&P 500, which would be 42%. But suppose XYZ Inc. went up not by 42%, but by 50% in the year. Of that 50%, beta attributes the first 42% to the general rise in the S&P 500, and to the stock's sensitivity to that market. That extra 8%, according to this theory, is due to positive developments in the company itself—its rate of growth, for example, or its earnings per share. That 8% represents the stock's positive alpha. There are different ways of arriving at an alpha number, but all of them are based on the outperformance of the return suggested by the stock's beta.

You can find stock betas in the Value Line Investment Survey weekly stock analysis service (800-577-4566—also available at many libraries) and on many Web sites.

Simplifying the World of Fixed-Income Investments: Treasury Notes and Tax-Exempt Munis

Fixed-income investments, particularly in the form of bonds, have several qualities that make them attractive: They may provide income in the form of interest, they may have only minimal risk in terms of keeping your principal intact, they may reduce the effect of market declines, and they may offer tax advantages. Institutions and individuals who invest in bonds generally do so for dependable income, safety of principal, and diversification. Institutional investors such as insurance companies, mutual funds, pension funds, banks, corporations, and state and local governments account for the majority of bond investors. If you're interested in bonds, you can follow interest rates by watching the yield on the ten-year Treasury note, a sort of bellwether of the bond market, similar to the Dow Jones Industrial Average or the NASDAQ for the stock market.

Bonds play an important role in most diversified asset allocation models by helping to manage risk and generate income. However, I have to say here that I find fixed income the least exciting part of investing and that, generally speaking, I'm not much of a bond enthusiast. Bonds don't protect you from inflation, and they don't provide any growth. But as I've aged, I know that I need to have a portion of my portfolio in fixed-income securities to protect my income in turbulent times—just as we witnessed in 2000 and 2001. I include bonds in my own portfolio to satisfy my need for diversification because research shows that including both stocks and bonds in your portfolio (rather than only stocks or only bonds) gives you the likelihood of better long-term results. So, even though bonds seem dull, they have their place in most portfolios.

Fixed-income securities are a necessary part of every balanced portfolio for the second half. But, as you can see by the figures in the sidebar below, the world of fixed income is huge. So how do you narrow it down? I do so by looking at risk, in terms of both the risk involved in different types of fixed-income investments and the risk involved in various lengths of time.

First, types of fixed-income investments. I see fixed-income investments in terms of three levels of risk: those

For Beginners Only: Fixed-Income Investments

Fixed-income investments are like IOUs for borrowed money, and most produce a steady stream of income in the form of interest payments. The borrower (or "issuer") can be a municipality, a state, or the federal government, or a corporation, or a bank or a savings and loan. In each case, they're borrowing money from investors as a way to raise funds, and they promise to repay the money at a set date, called the maturity date, plus interest, which they usually pay twice a year, but sometimes pay as a lump sum at maturity. The interest rate is usually fixed at the time the security is issued, and remains constant throughout the life of the loan. If you want to, you can usually sell fixed-income securities in a secondary market at their current market value, so your money isn't locked in until maturity.

The fixed-income market is huge, far larger than the stock market in the U.S. According to the Securities Industry Association, there are only a few thousand stocks traded, with a market value of about $5.3 trillion. But there are over 1.5 million fixed-income issues traded, with a market value of over $7.6 trillion.

investments that have minimal risk, those that entail a small risk, and those that carry unwelcome risk—that is, more risk than I want to take. U.S. Treasury notes, to my mind, have minimal risk. Investment-grade bonds entail a small risk. And everything else brings along more risk than I want to take. Then I look at the length of time that my money will be tied up in a specific investment. A maturity of two years or less is pretty risk-free; a maturity of two to five years has some risk, but one that I'm willing to assume. Any bond with a maturity greater than ten years brings with it, to my mind, an unacceptable level of risk.

I end up with two fixed-income investments that I prefer: five-year Treasury notes and, for investors in higher tax brackets, tax-exempt municipal bonds. What follows gives you some basics, but buyer beware: Fixed-income investments are a little trickier than others, so I strongly encourage you to take the time to discuss your personal needs with a fixed-income specialist.

Five-Year Treasury Notes

U.S. Treasury securities are debt obligations of the U.S. government that are issued through the Department of the Treasury. They're backed by the full faith and credit of the U.S. government, so they're considered virtually free of the risk of default. Treasuries also have tax advantages, as the income they produce is exempt from state and local taxes.

There are three kinds of Treasuries. Treasury bills, or T-bills, are short-term, highly liquid investments available in maturities from three months to one year, with a minimum investment of $1,000. Treasury notes and bonds are intermediate- and long-term investments that pay a fixed rate of interest semiannually and return their face value at maturity. The minimum investment is $1,000 for short-term notes and $1,000 for longer-term notes and bonds. Of these, my preference is for five-year Treasury notes, because they capture more than 80% of the yield curve of bonds without the risk of long-term bonds. Here's why: The yield curve is the yield of the three-month Treasury bill versus the yield on the 30-year long bond. Suppose the three-month T-bill yields 4.98%, and the 30-year long bond yields 6.09%. That means that the yield curve has a spread of 111 basis points (6.09 – 4.98 = 1.11). If the yield of the five-year Treasury note is 5.9%, you're getting 83% of the yield curve, without incurring the risk of the long-term bond.

There are several ways to buy Treasury notes. First, you can buy Treasury notes new at regularly scheduled auctions, or you can buy previously issued Treasury notes through what's called a secondary market. The advantage of buying through the secondary market is that you usually have a wider choice of maturities and interest rates, and you can buy at any time, instead of only on auction days. Secondary market availabilities are published daily in the financial press, which lists notes and bonds by maturity date, and gives the institutional price and yield information.

Either way, new or previously issued, the easiest way to buy Treasuries is through your broker. True, you can buy new Treasuries at the Treasury Department's regularly scheduled auctions throughout the year, but this is usually less convenient since you have to invest according to the Treasury Department's schedule. (For example, new five-year Treasury notes are usually auctioned during the third week of the month.) The only advantage of buying through an auction is that for smaller trades it's possible to get a better price than you would when purchasing issues in the secondary market at the same time. But because the average auction price and interest rate are set during bidding, you don't learn the actual price you receive until after you place your order.

A popular strategy that I like to use with Treasury notes is "laddering," which means buying notes with increasing maturities that are staggered so that they produce a steady income stream from the interest, and they moderate the effect of a change in interest rates. In Chapter 5 we'll talk more about laddering as part of creating a cash flow.

For Those in Higher Tax Brackets: Tax-Exempt Munis

Municipal bonds, or "munis," are debt securities issued by state and local governments and their agencies. Munis typically pay interest at a fixed rate twice a year, and the issuer promises to return your principal at maturity. The typical minimum investment is $10,000. Terms can range from one to 30 years or more.

The attraction of munis is tax-free income. The interest is free from federal tax, and if the bond is issued in your state of residence, the interest may be exempt from state and local taxes as well. As a result, munis are popular with investors in high tax brackets because they can provide better after-tax yields than other fixed-income investments. Be aware, however, that some munis can trigger Alternative Minimum Tax (AMT), a tax that applies to the interest on some state and local bonds. This is a somewhat complicated tax matter, so be sure to consult your tax professional before investing in munis. For information on tax-free yields, see Section 8 of the Appendix.

You can buy munis individually or through a mutual fund (and either way, you can purchase them through your brokerage firm). How do you decide between individual munis and muni bond funds? There are several factors to consider, but let's start with the fact that in the bond market in general, most individual investors are better off buying individual bonds than bond mutual funds. This may sound strange since the opposite is usually true with stocks—in that arena, most investors fare better with mutual funds, with perhaps a handful of individual stocks. But the world of bond funds is a complex one, in part because bond funds don't act like fixed-income investments. They don't do what individual bonds do, namely, give you a fixed yield and the guarantee of the safety of your principal, the reason being that there is no maturity, and the income fluctuates with interest rates. The risk in bond funds is tricky as well. With an individual bond, the longer you hold the bond, the less risk there is. But the risk level of a bond fund can go up or down, depending on the actions of the market as well as the fund manager.

That said, there are situations in which bond funds may be a better choice than individual bonds. In particular, if you're interested in corporate bonds, you're often better off with funds than with individual bonds. But let's get more specific and look at individual munis and muni funds.

There are several factors to consider when you choose between the two, mainly how much you have to invest, whether or not you'll need a specific amount by a certain date, and whether or not fixed returns are important to you.

• Individual bonds are probably a better choice than bond funds if you have $50,000 or more to allocate to fixed income and you won't need to liquidate the bond before maturity. Individual bonds are also a good choice if you need a specific amount at a specific date in the future; they give you regular income, usually semiannually, and their maturity values don't fluctuate as long as you hold the bonds to maturity. Bond funds, on the other hand, can't guarantee the return of a specific dollar amount. They typically provide monthly payments that fluctuate. If you do invest in individual bonds, remember that you'll want some diversification. That's one of the reasons for the $50,000-minimum recommendation. Most munis are sold in lots of $25,000, so to get any diversification at all you'd need $50,000, and $100,000 would be better.

• Bond mutual funds are probably a better choice if you have less than $50,000 to allocate to fixed income and you want tax-free income. Diversification, as mentioned above, is one reason. Another argument for bond funds is cost: You can invest in muni funds with as little as $2,500 to $5,000. Bond funds are also a good choice if you suspect you'll need the money before maturity, because they have greater liquidity than individual bonds. Remember also that bond mutual funds have the advantages of mutual funds in general: simplicity, diversification, and professional management. They are managed by professional investment advisors and operated by investment companies that pool money from many individual investors to purchase a variety of bonds. When you want to access your money, you sell shares in the fund at the current share price, which may be higher or lower than the price you paid for them.

Bond funds do, however, carry significant tax implications. In most cases, mutual fund earnings are taxed according to the kinds of securities in the fund's portfolio. For example, the earnings on corporate bond funds are subject to the same federal, state, and other taxes as the earnings from an individual corporate bond. When you sell your fund shares, your tax will depend on the share price at the time of the sale. If the share price is higher than your original purchase price, you'll usually be taxed on the capital gain (the difference between your original cost and the sale price). If the share price is lower, you may be able to deduct your loss from your taxable income.

For a comparison of specific features of individual bonds and bond funds, see Section 8 of the Appendix.

ZERO COUPON BONDS

Zero coupon bonds, also called "zeros," are bonds that don't pay interest until maturity. They are sold at a discount from their face value, and their value increases as they near maturity. Your return comes from the bond's appreciation. Zeros are suited to situations in which you have a specific goal in terms of how much you need and when you need it. The interest accumulates in the price, and your initial investment can increase dramatically. For example, if you invested $10,000 in a 20-year zero with a 6% yield, you'd receive over $30,000 at maturity—more than triple your original investment.

There are three types of zeros: corporate, municipal, and Treasuries. Of those, my preference is Treasury zeros called STRIPs, which is an acronym for the unlikely phrase "separate trading of registered interest and principal" securities. You purchase STRIPs from your brokerage firm—they're not available through the Federal Reserve—and they are the most popular and actively traded zeros. Here's why.

First, STRIPs are backed by the U.S. government, which means that you maximize the safety of your principal if you hold the bonds until maturity. Second, they offer tax advantages because the income you earn is exempt from state and local taxes. Third, they are often used by investors who want to lock in a rate of return for an extended period, often for a specific date—for example, for college tuition payments, or paying off a mortgage. One other way to save for these kinds of payments is simply through a money market mutual fund; you can often get a better return if you invest in STRIPs.

That said, you have to have the heart for zeros—they can be fairly volatile investments. Because the interest isn't paid until maturity, the value of a zero fluctuates more than the value of other fixed-income investments. If interest rates rise, the value of a zero will drop more than the value of other kinds of bonds with a similar interest rate. But if interest rates drop, the value of a zero will increase more than the value of other bonds, allowing you to take a capital gain. Remember also that even though the interest you earn on STRIPs isn't paid until maturity, a portion of the interest is subject to federal income tax each year you hold the bond. This means you may want to consider STRIPs for a tax-deferred account such as your IRA or 401(k).

Which Account: Regular or Retirement?

Once you've concluded that you want to include both stocks and bonds in your portfolio, how do you decide where each of them should be? Should you invest in stocks in your tax-advantaged account or regular brokerage account?

It's my feeling that you're better off including individual stocks and stock mutual funds in your retirement account (where taxes are deferred) and bonds in your regular account (which is currently taxable). There are a lot of people who will tell you just the opposite; their argument is that the income from bonds isn't taxed in a retirement account. But to my mind, stocks (and stock mutual funds) make more sense in retirement accounts because the tax advantages you get by just letting your stocks grow in a tax-deferred account are greater than the advantages from having bonds in a tax-deferred account. And the longer you have stocks in your retirement account—and the higher your tax bracket—the greater those advantages are. This is even more true if you're investing in value stocks (as opposed to growth stocks) because they typically produce larger dividends.

So, regardless of your time horizon, I believe you're better off with common stocks in retirement accounts, and bonds in your regular accounts. Income and capital gains in retirement accounts aren't taxed until you retire and begin to withdraw from that account (at which time you might be in a lower tax bracket, since your income may be lower). Investment income in your regular accounts is taxed when you earn it, and your capital gains are taxed when they're realized. This is also a big argument for a buy-and-hold approach in your regular accounts. By doing so, you minimize taxes and capital gains.

Cash-Equivalent Investments: Money When You Need It

The compelling reason for including cash-equivalent investments in your portfolio is liquidity. I recommend that you keep three to six months' living expenses in money market mutual funds. These are mutual funds that invest in short-term obligations from corporations and state or federal governments. Such funds are designed to maintain a stable $1 share value, but there is no assurance that they will be able to do that. It's usually easy to make deposits or withdrawals from money market funds, which makes them great parking places for cash between other, longer-term investments. Your money is available to you, but it's also earning more income than it would in a typical bank savings account. The key words for money market funds are *short-term investing, low risk,* and *lower return.* When you choose a money market fund, be sure you understand its objectives, and that those objectives match yours. For example, one fund may be geared toward generating tax-free income; another might go for higher returns. The minimum investment for a money market fund is usually between $1,000 and $5,000, and you can often write checks on the fund.

Choosing a money market mutual fund is, to a large extent, a matter of common sense. In the interest of convenience, probably the easiest thing to do is to use a fund from your brokerage or your mutual fund company so that you can easily transfer money. Eventually you'll be creating your own paycheck from your investments, so using a brokerage firm that is dedicated to customer service is important. You should also make sure that you can comfortably meet the fund's minimum balance requirement, and you should check the fund's expenses as described in the prospectus. As always, taxes can be a consideration. If you're investing in a regular, taxable account (versus a retirement account, where taxes are deferred), you may want to consider Treasury funds. The returns on those funds are lower, but their dividends are exempt from state and local taxes in most states. Such funds are usually good choices only for investors who fall into the higher federal tax brackets (28% or above), and who reside in a high-tax state. If that's you, you might also consider a state-specific, tax-free money fund that's exempt from federal, state, and local taxes.

Words to the Wise on Choosing Investments for the Second Half

• Asset allocation is dynamic. You'll be revisiting your decision every five years, at a minimum, so choose what you're comfortable with right now. This isn't a lifelong decision.

• As you develop your asset allocation plan, remember to consider all of your investing dollars—your investments in retirement accounts as well as those in your regular brokerage accounts.

• An asset allocation fund is a mutual fund that can mirror a specific asset allocation pie chart. It usually includes a mix of stocks, bonds, and cash equivalents to meet a specific growth objective. Over time, the fund automatically and professionally reallocates your money among investments, based on changing market conditions, so that your asset allocation doesn't fluctuate by an inordinate amount, despite the market's fluctuations. Aside from hiring a financial advisor to manage your investments, using an asset allocation fund is as simple as investing gets.

• The investments that I prefer are stock mutual funds for the core of your portfolio, five-year Treasury notes and tax-exempt municipal bonds for the fixed-income portion, and money market mutual funds for the cash-equivalent portion.

• Research shows that adding some fixed-income investments to your portfolio gives it a little more stability.

• Stock mutual funds are good for both building your nest egg and for generating income through dividends and capital gains.

• Investing in individual stocks is very appealing, but because choosing solid stocks can be tough, I suggest you allocate no more than 10% of your investing dollars to individual stocks.

• When choosing actively managed mutual funds, consider only no-load mutual funds.

• An index fund gives you simplicity and low fees. You're assured of closely tracking the market because the fund is engineered to track the performance of an index, or a group of securities considered yard-

sticks of market behavior. If the market goes up 10% in one year, so does the index fund.

• Choose funds with steady performance and a solid track record, not only for this year, but over the life of the fund. As you look at a fund's performance over time, make sure it's steady in up-and-down markets.

• In choosing individual stocks, look for quality by tracking a company's earnings trend. Earnings are the company's net income or profit. The more helpful number is earnings per share (EPS), which is the company's total earnings for a period divided by the number of shares outstanding.

• Also look at the company's price/earnings ratio, or P/E, which represents the relationship between the price of the company's stock and its earnings for the past year. You get a company's P/E by dividing its current price by its EPS for that year. For example, a stock selling for $20 with an EPS of $2.00 has a P/E of 10 ($20/$2.00).

• The compelling reason for including cash-equivalent investments in your portfolio is liquidity, and to that end, I recommend that you keep three to six months' living expenses in money market mutual funds.

• When you invest in bonds, you're generally better off doing so in your regular account (which is currently taxable) versus a retirement account (where taxes are deferred). Stocks (and stock mutual funds) are usually the better choice for retirement accounts.

5

Cash Flow in the Second Half: Creating a Paycheck for Yourself

In the past, a lot of people relied on bond interest and dividends for money to live on when they no longer had a paycheck. Most of us know that although that approach often worked in the past, it just won't cut it anymore. To have enough to live on from bond interest or dividends, you would have to be heavily weighted in bonds (more than any of the asset allocation models I recommend), and in stocks that pay high dividends. Companies that pay high dividends are not growth companies—and to my mind, they're not the best investment choice. As I see it, the best potential for long-term growth is to be invested in companies that have growth as their overriding goal—and one of the signs of that goal is a company's reinvesting their earnings for growth.

Many people don't have a clue about how they will get their money after their last paycheck. They imagine a Social Security check, but they haven't come to grips with withdrawing from their retirement funds. But remember—your original asset allocation is a balancing act between risk and return, and the way and rate at which you'll withdraw funds and create a second-half paycheck for yourself is also a balancing act. You don't want to take out so much that you're short in your later years; but you also don't want to skimp unnecessarily and deny yourself things that you've always wanted in the second half.

Simplifying Cash Flow by Consolidating Accounts

Generally speaking, figuring out cash flow will be easier if you consolidate financial accounts and deal with the fewest number of accounts and firms possible—you may even be able to deal with only one. This is one of the first issues you should look at. You may find that you want to move accounts between financial institutions or brokerage firms, and that can take time. It's often a good idea to consolidate your retirement accounts into one rollover IRA as well, the reason being that when you reach the age of 70½, the law requires that you take minimum withdrawals from each retirement account. If you haven't consolidated, that's going to get complicated. But if you do combine retirement accounts into one, those withdrawals will be pretty straightforward. In addition, one large account is just simpler than several smaller ones.

One more thing: Note that I started this sidebar by saying "Generally speaking." That's because there are some exceptions here, dealing with factors such as Roth IRAs, estate planning, and whether or not you return to work. When in doubt, check with a professional.

I need to add a word of caution here: Cash flow in the second half of life can be a complex issue, and you may want to consider getting some professional guidance, particularly if you're at one extreme or the other—if your situation is very complicated, or if your nest egg is on the small side. The less you have, the more important planning is. Chances are that if you're reading this and you're still in your fifties, you have plenty of time to learn how to do it. And if you do choose to figure out how to create that second-half paycheck yourself, start planning early, perhaps six months or so before your retirement.

Creating Your Second-Half Paycheck

No single withdrawal rate is appropriate for every individual. People have different circumstances and goals, so there really isn't any cookie-cutter withdrawal number. But as a result of research using historical data, various payout rates, and asset allocation models, I feel comfortable in suggesting a beginning withdrawal rate of 4% to 5% per year. That's based on asset allocation models of 60% stocks/40% fixed income and 80% stocks/20% fixed income.

You may read advice that suggests withdrawal rates from anywhere between 3% and 10%. But if you were someone close to me, I'd try to persuade you to start with 4% to 5%. That gives you the best chance of outliving your money. And while the difference between a 5% and a 10% withdrawal rate may not seem very significant, it is. If you want 30 to 40 years of income, an initial maximum 5% withdrawal rate is my recommendation because it's my belief that 6% or more is dangerous to start with. The idea is that you should choose a payout rate that is smaller than your after-tax rate of return, which takes taxes into account. (See the box on page 132 for more information.)

And that's your second-half paycheck. Once a year (or once a quarter or once a month—we'll talk about how often you do this below), you'll transfer 4% to 5% of the value of your portfolio to your money market account, and that's what you'll live on. As you age, you'll probably be able to increase that percentage, depending on your returns. You might go to 6% in your sixties, then to 7% in your seventies, but be wary of overspending in the first years of your second half, and don't be hasty about raising that withdrawal rate.

You'll want to review your withdrawal plan periodically to see how you're doing. Maybe your estimates will turn out to be on the conservative side, and you'll be able to increase the amount you're withdrawing. Or maybe you're spending too much, and you'll need to cut back. If so, it's better to know that now than later.

As you can see, basing your second-half paycheck on a percentage of your portfolio's value will give you a variable income. If your portfolio goes up, so will your paycheck. If the value goes down, so will your paycheck. Some people find that uncertainty unsettling, and it can take some getting used to. It also takes planning; it may mean putting off a major trip for a year or so, or holding off on a big purchase. But at least you know where you stand; if you stay with the 4% withdrawal rate, the odds are excellent that your money will outlive you. That peace of mind about the future is worth a little uncertainty in the present.

The 4% tells you how much you'll withdraw. You'll also need to decide how often you withdraw, and where you'll take the money from. How often is up to you. I'd suggest that at the end of the year you figure out what 4% of your portfolio is, then withdraw one fourth of that amount at the start of each quarter and put it in a money market account, where the money will continue to earn market-rate interest (higher than what you'd get in a savings account). If you think about it, this is something like reverse-order dollar cost averaging (see Chapter 3). You're taking money out on a regular basis instead of putting it in, but the benefits are similar. By withdrawing a fixed amount on a regular basis, you are smoothing out the variability in the market instead of trying to time it.

The quarterly plan is just my recommendation. You may be more comfortable with doing it annually. The disadvantage to that is that your money can work for you just a little longer if you don't withdraw the whole amount at once. Or you may prefer to withdraw one twelfth of that 4% on a monthly basis. To me, having to think about it every month is a bother. So that's why I suggest a quarterly plan—it's convenient, but it lets your money work for you.

To simplify things further, I suggest that you use a money market account with check-writing privileges so that you won't have to then transfer the money to your checking account. You can even set up regular automatic transfers from one account to another. For example, if you want to withdraw $1,000 a month from a mutual fund, you can have shares equal to that amount sold and the money transferred to your money market account. Most mutual funds have set up an "automatic withdrawal program" that lets you receive a check regularly in the amount you specify. You can also transfer or withdraw funds on an as-needed basis, instead of on a regular schedule.

That's the how-often part—now for the where. If you have a Roth IRA, I suggest you withdraw from it first since your withdrawals are not taxed. This postpones paying taxes on sales in other accounts. Generally speaking, though, you should plan to tap your *taxable accounts* (your regular brokerage account and any savings) first. If you've held those investments for over 12 months, that money will be taxed at the capital gains rate instead of at your income tax rate (which is usually higher). On the other hand, most money in *retirement accounts* (except the Roth IRA) is taxed at your ordinary income tax rate when you withdraw it.

Tapping your taxable accounts first is particularly wise until you reach what's been called the "magic age" of 59½—the age at which you can withdraw from retirement accounts without penalty. By delaying your withdrawals from your retirement accounts for as long as possible, you let that money continue to work for you, tax-deferred.

In general, consolidating retirement accounts is a good idea, but there are times when you're better off keeping them separate. First, if you have a Roth IRA and a traditional IRA, keep the Roth IRA separate. Second, if you have a traditional IRA to which you've been contributing, it's probably better to keep it and your workplace retirement accounts separate. And, third, there may be estate-planning reasons that argue for keeping things separate.

CALCULATING YOUR AFTER-TAX RATE OF RETURN

Your after-tax rate of return is a rate of return that takes taxes into account. Since taxes are the largest single drag on your investment return, a rate of return that ignores them isn't meaningful. Your *pre-tax* rate of return does represent how much money you're making on your investments, but it's not very meaningful for planning purposes because it doesn't take taxes into account. It's better to include taxes now and err on the conservative side than to think you've got more than you have, only to learn the truth in 15 years.

To start, you need to make sure that you know how all of your investments combined have performed—in other words, that you're looking at your total rate of return, instead of the return you're getting on a specific account (such as your IRA) or a particular investment (such as a mutual fund). A common mistake is reading that a mutual fund returned 12% in a given year and being lulled into the idea that that's the return for your entire portfolio. But if 50% of your money is only earning 4% in a money market fund, your total return is only 8%. That's why you'll want to look at the rate of return from the *total amount of money* you have in all your investment and savings accounts.

If you want to estimate your total return, you can do so based on the kinds of investments you have. If your entire portfolio is largely stocks, you'll use a higher rate of return than you would if your portfolio comprised mostly bonds or other fixed-income investments. The annual rate of return of the S&P 500 from 1970 to 2000 was 13% (including dividend reinvestment, but not taxes). Over the same period, bonds returned 9% and T-bills 7%. Rates of return for varying portfolios would be something like 8% for a fairly conservative portfolio, 10% for a moderate portfolio, and 12% for an aggressive portfolio. These rates are based on historical performance. I do, however, have to add a word of caution about estimating your rate of return, particularly when you're choosing a projected rate of return—the rate of return you anticipate in the future. Much of the time in financial planning, we build our strategies on average returns. But as I said in Chapter 3, "average" means 50% of the time you fall short of your goal and 50% of the time you exceed it. Choosing your projected rate of return is one time when I suggest you err on the conservative side. If you want to calculate your total rate of return, you can follow these steps:

1. Compare your last year's year-end statements to today's.
2. Subtract any new money you added during the year.
3. Add back any withdrawals you made during the year.
4. Total your ending balances and divide by your total beginning balance.
5. If the result is greater than 1, you're ahead. If, for example, your result is 1.12, you're up 12%.

Now for your after-tax rate of return. The total return you just came up with is a pre-tax figure, meaning that it doesn't take taxes into account. If you have a 10.4% before-tax return and you're in the 36% federal and state tax bracket, your after-tax return is really only 6.65%. (Note that 36% assumes all gains are taxed at your ordinary income rate, not at the capital gains rate. If any gains are from capital gains, your overall rate would be lower.) To calculate a conservative after-tax rate of return, do the following:

A. Estimate the rate of return that you believe your investments will maintain until you retire: ________

B. Enter your federal tax bracket: 10%, 15%, 27.5%, 30.5%, 35.5%, or 39.1% (for 2001) ________%
(Note: You may prefer to use the current maximum long-term capital gain rate, which is 20%.)

C. *Subtract your federal tax bracket from 1.00* ________

D. Multiply *A* (your original rate of return) by *C* (your after-tax rate): ________%
Your after-tax rate of return (rounded to the nearest 1.0): ________%

A computer spreadsheet is a great tool for calculating rates of return. Your brokerage firm's Web site or your financial advisor may also help.

Withdrawing from a Traditional IRA

First off, a couple of reminders about the government's rules regarding withdrawals from traditional (not Roth) IRAs. You may start withdrawing from your IRA after the age of 59½. You must start receiving the required minimum distribution from your retirement plan by April 1 of the year after you reach the age of 70½. When you begin to withdraw from your retirement account, you'll finally have to pay taxes on that hard-earned money. Withdrawals are taxed as ordinary income.

Those are the government's rules. I'll add to that my own suggestion: *Don't withdraw from your traditional retirement account until you have to.* The main reasons for waiting are the taxes you'll have to pay and the penalties for early withdrawals. The penalties are particularly painful if you're in a high tax bracket. If you withdraw money from your traditional retirement account before the age of 59½ and you don't meet any of the qualifications discussed below, you pay a 10% penalty tax, and you could pay as much as 50% in federal and state taxes. These staggering percentages can apply even to hardship withdrawals.

By not withdrawing, you avoid penalties and you delay taxes. But there's more to it than that. You also allow that money to continue working for you. So you're wise to hold off on withdrawing from retirement accounts for as long as you can.

Early Retirement—Taking Money Out of Your Traditional IRA Early

If you retire early and you want to start withdrawing from your traditional IRA before you're 59½, think twice. There are at least a couple of disadvantages. First, once you retire, you'll most likely stop contributing to your IRA. It will continue to grow thanks to growth and compounding, but it won't grow as it would if you were still contributing. Waiting until you're 60 or even 70 to retire makes a big difference. It may not be enough of a difference to affect your retirement age, but it's probably worth taking into account.

That said, early withdrawals from an IRA or a qualified retirement plan sometimes are the best alternatives. Here's how they work.

In response to so many people taking early retirements, the federal government passed legislation in 1986 that is known as SEPP, for Substantially Equal Periodic Payments (Internal Revenue Code section 72[t][2][A][iv]). To withdraw money before you reach the magic age of 59½ and avoid the 10% penalty on early distributions, you set up a schedule of regular equal payments that will last for your life expectancy (if you're single), or the joint life expectancy of you and your spouse (if you're married). The IRS calculates the amount of the payments using life expectancy tables and a presumed interest rate. If you want to use a SEPP to access your retirement early without a penalty, have a financial advisor familiar with this method help you set up a schedule. The payments must continue for five years or until you reach the age of 59½, whichever is longer. Once you've received the payments for that length of time, you can give up the payment plan and take withdrawals in any amount you want without penalty.

There is one other way to take early withdrawals from your IRA without penalty: The Taxpayer Relief Act of 1997 allows penalty-free distributions before 59½ for first-time home purchases (up to $10,000) and qualified higher-education expenses.

Withdrawing from Your Traditional IRA After the Age of 70½

When you turn 70½, you have to start withdrawing money from your retirement plans, regardless of whether or not you need the money, and even if you're still employed. The IRS calculates how much you must withdraw using your life expectancy at the time of distribution. These mandatory withdrawals are called Minimum Required Distributions and they are not to be taken lightly: There is a harsh 50% excise tax on the amount required to be taken that wasn't. The exception to the minimum required distributions rule is Roth IRAs, which have no requirement for minimum distributions.

You have to take your first traditional IRA withdrawal by April 1 of the year following the year you turn 70½, whether or not you're retired. (This date isn't as easy to calculate as it seems. Think it through carefully.) After the first year, you have to withdraw the required amount no later than the end of the calendar year. You can defer that first withdrawal if you want to (for tax reasons, for example), but doing so would mean you'd have to receive two payments the next year, the deferred one for 70½ as well as the one for 71, which you'd have to withdraw by the end of December. Be careful; taking both payments during the same year might bump you up to a higher tax bracket, so check it out before you defer that first withdrawal.

Note that if you have several traditional IRAs, you'll be required to take minimum withdrawals from each IRA when you reach 70½, which means that you're probably better off consolidating IRAs when you can. There are restrictions on this; you'll need to check with your tax advisor to find out if it's possible for you.

Withdrawing from a Roth IRA

One of the advantages of a Roth IRA is its flexibility, particularly where withdrawals are concerned. It's easier to withdraw from a Roth IRA without penalty (versus a traditional IRA, as described above), and you aren't required to begin withdrawing from a Roth IRA at any specified age. The rules governing withdrawals from a Roth IRA distinguish between withdrawing your *profits* and withdrawing your *contributions.*

First, withdrawing your *profits.* Once five years have passed since you opened your Roth IRA, you can withdraw your profits tax-free if any of the following is true:

- You're over 59½.
- You're a first-time homeowner, which, in this situation, means that you haven't owned a home during the past two years. If you're married, this applies to your spouse as well. You can withdraw the $10,000 as a lump sum or in smaller amounts. You can then buy or build a home for yourself, your spouse, your child, your grandchild, or your parents.
- You are disabled.
- After your death, your beneficiaries can withdraw money tax-free.

You can withdraw the amount you've *contributed* to your Roth IRA tax-free at any time, and for any reason. If you want to withdraw an amount greater than your contributions, the amount you withdraw will be subject to income taxes if that withdrawal doesn't meet one of the requirements above. Also, if you're under 59½, those withdrawals are also subject to a 10% penalty.

Beyond Your Second-Half Paycheck: Other Sources of Income

The second-half paycheck you create from your IRA is one source of income, but it's not the only one. You may also have employer retirement plans, and there are ways to use your investments to provide income as well.

Social Security

Since its inception in the early 1930s, Social Security has changed dramatically. At that time, the retirement age of 65 was chosen because the average American's life expectancy was only 67, which, in theory, meant that retirement would last all of two years. Although the days when retirees could count on Social Security to meet most of their needs are long gone, it can still be a help. Think of it as a windfall.

When Should You Start Receiving Social Security?

You have a choice about when you'll begin receiving your Social Security benefits. You can retire early and begin receiving your checks as early as age 62, or you can wait until "full retirement age." Traditionally, that's been 65, and for those born before 1938, that's still true. But as of the year 2000, that age is gradually being bumped up, based on your year of birth, as shown in the table below:

Your Year of Birth	Full Retirement Age (year/months)
Before 1938	65
1939	65/2
1940	65/6
1941	65/8
1942	65/10
1943–1954	66/0
1955	66/2
1956	66/4
1957	66/6
1958	66/8
1959	66/10
1960 and beyond	67/0

So, should you start receiving Social Security early and collect less, or wait until full retirement age and collect more? Or can you wait even longer and increase the amount of your benefit? These are good questions, and it's worth looking at them from both sides.

The advantage of starting early is that you receive checks earlier, money that you can use as needed. You can certainly put that money to work for you by investing it, and that's a strong argument. By waiting until full retirement age, you miss out on three years of investing. But you do pay a price: early retirement reduces the amount of your checks—for the rest of your life—by 20% if you were born before 1938. This reduction is five ninths of 1% for each month that benefits start before full retirement age, and it adds up. Here are a couple of examples of that reduction:

- Suppose you were born in 1937 and your benefit at full retirement age (65) was $10,000. If you decided to collect before the age of 65, you would receive only 80% of your benefit, or $8,000.
- Suppose you were born in 1960 or later, and your benefit at full retirement age (67) was $10,000. If you decided to collect at age 62, you would receive only 70% of that amount, or $7,000.

Just as your checks decrease if you collect early, they increase if you wait beyond full retirement age to age 70. You've probably guessed the advantage of waiting: For every year you delay retirement until the age of 70, your check increases by a set percentage, as set out in the table below. The percentage will gradually increase to 8% in 2009 for each year you work past normal retirement age. In other words, the older you are when you start receiving Social Security (until 70), the larger your checks will be:

If you turn 65 in this year:	Your benefits will increase by this percentage each year that you delay receiving Social Security:
1998–1999	5.5%
2000–2001	6.0%
2002–2003	6.5%
2004–2005	7.0%
2006–2007	7.5%
2008 and beyond	8.0%

As you can see, the decision about when to start receiving Social Security can be a tough call, in part because you don't know how long you'll live. According to a calculation by Deloitte & Touche, the break-even point is about 12 years. So if you expect to live beyond age 74 (and I hope you do), *and* you don't need the income, it's my feeling that you would be better off waiting until full retirement age to begin receiving your Social Security payments.

How a Paycheck Affects Your Social Security Benefits

You can work and still receive Social Security benefits. The laws that affect this were changed in April of 2000, and now the way in which a paycheck affects your Social Security payments depends on how old you are relative to "full retirement age." While you're working, your benefit amount will be reduced only until you reach your full retirement age. Starting with people born in 1938 or later, full retirement age will gradually increase until it reaches 67 for people born in 1960 or later.

- If you are under full retirement age when you start getting your Social Security payments, $1 in benefits will be deducted for each $2 you earn above the annual limit. For 2001, that limit is $10,680.

• In the year you reach full retirement age, $1 in benefits will be deducted for each $3 you earn above a different limit, but only counting earnings before the month you reach the full benefit retirement age. For 2001, this limit is $25,000.

• Starting with the month you reach full retirement age, you will receive your benefits with no limit on your earnings.

• Once you reach your full retirement age, your earnings no longer affect your Social Security payments. You can earn as much as you want and your payments will stay the same.

The Social Security Administration will know of your earnings from the IRS, so be accurate in reporting your earnings. If you're not, they can ask for refunds from any overpayments you received, as well as penalties on the overpayments. (For more information, see **www.ssa.gov.**)

Income from Your Pension: Lump Sum or Monthly Payments?

If you are fortunate enough to have a defined-benefit plan or a defined-contribution plan through your employer, your second-half income will be helped along (sometimes substantially so) by your payments from your retirement plan. The amount you receive, and how often you receive it (in a lump sum or in monthly payments), varies from plan to plan. Some plans give you a choice about how you receive the money; others decide for you. You'll need to check the details of your specific plan. But whatever the plan, and whatever distribution schedule you choose, remember that pension income is taxable. There's no way to escape that, but you can delay it if you take a lump sum and immediately roll it over into an IRA.

A defined-benefit plan is the most basic pension. You receive a monthly payment, which is taxable, for the rest of your life. The amount is usually fixed, which means that the payment looks great when you retire, and not so great ten years later, thanks to inflation. Some corporations add cost-of-living benefits, but those companies are rare. Government pensions usually do have a cost-of-living adjustment (although it may not match inflation).

Before you begin receiving payments, you may have a couple of decisions to make.

First, you may be asked whether you want the pension to cover you alone or you and your spouse. If the pension is covering only you, the amount of the monthly check will be larger, but payments will stop at your death. So, if your spouse will need those pension payments after your death, you'll probably want the two-life pension (joint and survivor) option. If you do this, you may also be asked whether, after your death, your spouse should receive the same amount you received as a couple, or a smaller amount. If your spouse will be very dependent on this check, you'll probably want the larger amount.

You may also be asked whether you want to receive it as one lump sum or as monthly payments. The amount of the payments is calculated based on life expectancy tables, each month for the rest of your life. In most circumstances, monthly payments are a given, but there are some employers who give you the choice of taking your pension as a lump sum.

If you do have the choice, don't be hasty. This is rarely an easy decision; there are pros and cons to both sides.

First, the pros and cons of taking a lump sum. If you have other sources of income (so that you won't be completely dependent upon pension monthly payments), you might consider a lump sum. You can roll the money into an IRA and put it to work for you—and defer paying taxes on the money. Another advantage is that with a lump sum you're in control. You can decide exactly what you want to do with it, and even if you just reinvest it, you can do so where and how you please. If you're a wise investor (or if you plan to work with a financial advisor), it's also possible that you'll come out ahead with a lump sum. If you invest it and do well, you may be able to get more than you would have from the payout plan, and you're more likely to beat inflation. A disadvantage that comes with a lump sum is simply the temptation to spend it. A survey conducted by the U.S. Department of Labor found that of workers aged 55 to 64 who had received lump-sum distributions, 20% of them spent the whole thing when they received it. Another 20% of them spent part of it. Only 60% of them saved it. Another disadvantage is the lack of certainty. With a payout, you know exactly how much you'll be getting each month. But if you invest the money, there are no guarantees. If that sort of uncertainty keeps you awake at night, you may be better off with payouts. Another, less common reason to consider a lump sum is if you are worried about the company's health (unless your pension is insured by the Pension Benefit Guaranty Corporation). And if you're fortunate enough not to need your pension money, take it as a lump sum, then roll it over into an IRA and leave it to your heirs or to a charity that is important to you.

Two technicalities about lump sums: A key point in deciding whether or not to take a lump sum is the "discount rate" that the company uses to calculate the amount of your lump sum. If you invest the money and get a return that matches that discount rate, you come out even. To come out ahead, you have to invest the money in such a way that your return beats that discount rate. If you're unsure that you can beat the discount rate, you're better off with monthly payments.

The biggest advantages of going with monthly payouts are simplicity and security. You don't have to make any more

Of Taxes and Lump Sums on Employer Stock

The IRS says that if you take a lump-sum distribution of employer stock, you owe taxes only on your cost basis of the stock (what you paid for it), instead of the stock's actual price. This means

you're paying taxes based on what you paid for the stock instead of what it's currently worth. If and when you sell the stock, you'll still have to pay capital gains on the amount that's appreciated, but it's still a good deal. There are very precise rules for this—naturally. For example, you must take all of it in one tax year. Be sure to consult a knowledgeable tax advisor.

decisions. Your planning, in terms of both finances and taxes, will be easier, too, because you'll know exactly how much money you'll be receiving. A monthly payout also has the advantage of being a sure thing—whether there's a drop in the market or in interest rates, you're getting a predictable check. But that certainty has a price—your money isn't growing. Not many pension plans do anything to account for inflation, so your payments' purchasing power will decrease over time.

Finally, if you die prematurely, your heirs will be left with less than they would have with a lump sum. Pension payments typically stop or decrease at death, so if you die early, you'll have received only a portion of your distribution. If you take a lump sum, you get the full amount regardless of your life span, and your heirs may be better off.

Defined-contribution plans such as profit-sharing plans, 401(k)s, stock-bonus plans, and Employee Stock Ownership Plans are a different bag, and there are several ways of taking

Annuities

An annuity is a tax-advantaged investment contract issued by an insurance company. You, the policyholder, make either a lump-sum payment or installment payments to the insurance company, and you can elect to receive income until you die. Your investment grows without the income being taxed until you withdraw your earnings. Fixed annuities pay a guaranteed rate set by the insurance companies. Variable annuities allow investors a wide selection of fund portfolios with the opportunity to earn greater returns based on the performance of the underlying investments. In both types, principal is guaranteed upon death. Regardless of the performance of the investment accounts you choose, your beneficiaries are guaranteed to receive the account value of the annuity or the original deposit, whichever is greater.

You should be aware that there are certain costs associated with annuities. These can include surrender charges and other expenses and fees that can vary greatly from one company to another.

I have to add that at my age I'm not a great fan of annuities for income. They are usually better for the elderly who want certainty and ease than they are for those in the early part of their second half. With fixed annuities, your money usually loses its purchasing power over time, and with variable annuities, your income depends on how the underlying assets perform, so your account value will fluctuate with changes in market conditions. As with all investments, be sure to read and understand the prospectus.

To my mind, purchasing an annuity is a way of buying peace of mind for folks who are very concerned that they'll outlive their money. So, if you or someone you love worries about this, an annuity is probably worth investigating closely. There are lots of decisions to make when you decide to buy an annuity. For more details, I recommend reading the chapter on annuities in Don't Die Broke *by Margaret A. Malaspina (Bloomberg Press, 1999).*

the money owed you by your employer. You might be offered a lifetime annuity, which comes in the form of monthly payments (for you or, better yet, for you and your spouse), and which your employer buys from the insurance company.

You might also choose periodic payments, which you would receive over a specified number of years. The payments in this method might be higher than they would be with an annuity, but at the end of the period they'd stop. You might be able to leave some or all of the money in the company plan until you're 65 (possibly longer if there is a systematic withdrawal option), which is the best deal, if you can afford it. You can still withdraw money (according to the plan's rules), but your money continues to work for you. You usually have to have a minimum of $5,000 in the plan to leave it with your employer. Or you might be able to take the money as a lump sum, in which case you should immediately roll it over into an IRA so that the money isn't taxed until you begin to withdraw it. The exception is for company stock held in any qualified plan, for example a 401(k) or an ESOP. Then the tax laws often benefit taking the distribution and paying the tax on the cost basis. Even if you have to pay a 10% early withdrawal penalty, it may make sense *not* to roll it over to an IRA. Then you can decide how you want to invest it.

MANAGING A LUMP SUM FROM A SOURCE OTHER THAN A RETIREMENT PLAN

Deciding what to do with a large amount of money from an inheritance, the sale of a house, or even a property settlement from a divorce is both an opportunity and a challenge. On one hand it's great news—you've got a good-sized chunk of money that might really make a difference to you—but on the other hand it's pressure. You want to do the right thing. If you find yourself in this situation, I'd suggest the following:

1. *Put the money to work while you decide how to invest it.* Don't let the check sit around in your checking or savings account. Put the money to work by depositing it in a money market fund (where it will earn a higher rate of income) as soon as you receive it.
2. *Take your time.* There's no hurry—it's fine to deal with a lump sum little by little. You can invest half of it now and think about the other half. You might even take a year or so to decide what you want to do—which is fine, as long as the money's work-

ing for you in the meantime (in a money market account, for example).

3. *Look carefully at how this sum changes your financial picture.* How does this sum affect your portfolio? Is it a significant enough amount that you'll want to change your asset allocation? You can use the money to do some rebalancing if you want to change your asset allocation (which we'll talk about in Chapter 6). Or you can spread the amount among several investments to keep your current asset allocation.

4. *Understand the tax implications.* Receiving a lump sum is definitely a time to talk to the pros—at least your tax advisor, and maybe a financial advisor as well. The tax implications are critical, and they vary from situation to situation. Money received in an inheritance is the net (or after-tax) amount, meaning that it's already been taxed, and you keep what you receive. Money received as a property settlement in the course of a divorce settlement is not taxable.

5. *Pay off high-interest debt.* If you're carrying debt with a high interest rate (such as credit cards, which can carry an interest rate of 14% or higher), using some of the lump sum to pay off that debt might be a wise move. It's a matter of simple logic: If the debt is costing you more than what you'd earn by investing it, you should probably pay off the debt. (Your mortgage can be an exception to this rule. See the box on page 72.)

6. *If you're tempted to spend, be careful.* One of the biggest worries about receiving a lump sum is simply the temptation to spend the money. If you just have to spend some of the money, do some planning. For example, allow yourself to spend no more than 5% of the total—or, if you've received a large amount, don't use the whole 5% at once. Put it in a separate discretionary spending account. Then invest the rest.

7. *Invest the money for growth.* Put the money to work for you in the same way you've invested the rest of your money so that it will take advantage of compound growth. And if you don't need the money, put it to work for someone else—for your children, or for the charitable cause of your choice. (See Chapter 10 for information on charitable giving.)

Creating Income from Your Investments

There are several ways to use your investments to produce income. For example, instead of reinvesting your dividends, you can request an electronic funds transfer to your checking account for the fund's regular distribution of interest or dividend income.

Laddering individual bonds is a popular way to produce steady income, and for good reason. For one thing, laddering keeps your investments fluid, and it protects you from having to invest all of your money at once if rates are low. You can also use laddered investments as a source of regular income. As bonds come due, you can put the money into more liquid accounts to use for living expenses. By planning those cash infusions, you can avoid having to sell off other investments that would continue to produce income, like stocks, longer-term bonds, or mutual funds.

Here's the strategy. The first year, you'd buy a series of Treasury notes or munis with different maturities. For example, you might buy five Treasury notes with maturities of one, two, three, four, and five years. As each note matures, you can use the money if you need it, but preferably you reinvest in another five-year note to keep the ladder going. The following sidebar illustrates what happens one year after your initial purchase.

I recommend that you not use maturities greater than five years. That way you're more likely to be able to hold the notes until maturity. Individual bonds fluctuate in price prior to maturity. If you hold to maturity, you'll get your principal back.

In addition to providing income, laddering bonds can help you weather a down market. Let's look at an example. Suppose you have five individual bonds worth a total of $100,000. And suppose those bonds pay annual interest of 5% to 6% with one bond maturing in each year for the next five years. This laddering scheme would give you a potential of

An Example of Laddering

Year 1

Amount	Yield	Maturity	Interest
$20,000	5.00%	1 year	$1,000
$20,000	5.25%	2 year	$1,050
$20,000	5.50%	3 year	$1,100
$20,000	5.75%	4 year	$1,150
$20,000	6.00%	5 year	$1,200
			$5,500

Year 2

Amount	Yield	Maturity	Interest
$20,000	5.25%	1 year	$1,050
$20,000	5.50%	2 year	$1,100
$20,000	5.75%	3 year	$1,150
$20,000	6.00%	4 year	$1,200
$20,000	6.00%	5 year	$1,200
			$5,700

One year later, the average yield of the portfolio is 20 basis points greater, with no change in the yield curve or average maturity.

$25,500 of income for one year ($20,000 from cashing in the mature bonds at face value and $5,500 in interest from the bonds during the year) without selling stocks—a particularly nice benefit during a down market. If the market stays down, your bonds would give you $24,500 the following year ($20,000 for cashing in the next maturing bond plus $4,500 in interest income). If you had $20,000 to $25,000 a year from laddering bonds, plus around that same amount from Social Security, you'd have an income of around $40,000 to $50,000 a year for five years without selling any stocks—and selling stocks is exactly what you don't want to do in a down market. During more normal market years, you could roll the maturing bonds over for another five years.

Once again, when you're dealing with fixed income, you're wise to sit down with a fixed-income expert before you go ahead.

Working in the Second Half of Life

The fact is that most people will continue to need a paycheck of some kind in at least their 50s and 60s. It's tough to stop working that early and rely on your investments for the rest of your life—say 30 or even 40 years—but a lot of people are finding that they also *want* to work. Almost half of today's retirees will tell you that leisure is a tough transition, and nearly a quarter of them say that they're unhappy no longer working.

So, as it turns out, needing a paycheck isn't necessarily bad news. Work can help to keep you active and involved, and it can add purpose to your life—*if* it's work that you value and enjoy. People are approaching employment in the second half with more creativity today. They're starting home businesses, and trying new things, and working at jobs they've always wanted to try—and some at jobs they'd never considered. Today many "retired" people are finding their most creative and fulfilling work in their second half.

Surprisingly enough, it's estimated that as many as 95% of Americans don't enjoy the work they do. I find that an alarming statistic, because work should be a fulfilling, creative endeavor, not drudgery. If you don't love what you do, it may be worth your while to consider whether or not a change is possible. Working at something you enjoy is obviously good for your spirits, but chances are it's good for your bank account as well. Studies have shown that when you enjoy your work, you do better at it, and when you excel at something, chances are you'll be better paid for it.

Whether or not you continue to work has implications beyond your paycheck. Your income affects other parts of your financial picture as well, and it's important to know what that ripple effect is. Two of the major areas that can be affected are your retirement plan and your tax bracket. Your Social Security payments can also be affected.

- If you continue to work, you can also continue to contribute to Keoghs, 401(k)s, and Roth IRAs after you've turned 70½. You cannot contribute to traditional IRAs or SEPs. Opening a Roth IRA is a great way to leave something for your heirs.
- Watch your tax bracket. Don't let yourself be unknowingly bumped up to a higher tax bracket, because of your earnings and your IRA withdrawals.

Borrowing from the Equity in Your Home: Reverse Mortgages

A reverse mortgage (also called a home-equity conversion) is a type of loan in which you tap the equity in your home. Think of it as getting the cash from your home without selling. Those suited for reverse mortgages are typically 75 and older, who need additional income.

A reverse mortgage can work in several ways. Basically, a lender loans you money against the value of your house. The amount you can borrow depends on your age, the age of your spouse, the amount of equity you have in your home, and the plan you're interested in. Unlike just about any other type of loan, the amount does not depend on your income.

You can usually withdraw the money in several ways as well—monthly checks, a specified number of checks, a lump sum, or a credit line. You don't pay interest on the money you borrow; instead, the interest compounds and you pay it when your loan becomes due—which is either when you sell the house or at the time of your death. The payments aren't income, they're a loan, so the money doesn't affect your income tax or your Social Security payments.

The advantage of a reverse mortgage is that the money it provides can allow you to stay in your home when you otherwise might not be able to. The checks might, for example, take care of live-in health care, if needed. Reverse mortgages are appealing to a lot of people, but beware: These loans can get complicated, so be sure you understand them thoroughly, and do some comparison shopping. Consumers can typically choose between a minimum of two programs, sometimes more, so if the agent you're dealing with offers only one, consider that a warning—it's entirely possible that you'd be better off with another company. As a start, the American Association of Retired Persons (AARP, **www.aarp.org**) has a good booklet available at no charge. E-mail **Rminfo@aarp.org** and ask for publication stock #D12894. Include your name, full postal address, the publication title (*Home-Made Money, a Consumer's Guide to Home Equity Conversion*), and stock number or order by phone: 800-424-3410.

Words to the Wise on Cash Flow in the Second Half

• For most people, to have enough to live on from bond interest or dividends means you would have to be heavily weighted in bonds (more than any of the asset allocation models I recommend) and in stocks that pay high dividends. Companies that pay high dividends are not growth companies.

• The minimum goal of any second-half investing strategy is to make your money outlive you. You can have the smartest and most solid asset allocation on the block, but if you withdraw too much, too fast, you can do some substantial damage to your second-half finances before you know it.

• Figuring out cash flow and managing your money in the second half is complicated, and the stakes are high enough that you may also want to consider getting some professional advice, particularly if you're at one extreme or the other—if your situation is very complicated, or if your nest egg is on the small side. The less you have, the more important planning is.

• Most everyone will continue to need a paycheck of some kind, thanks to our increased life expectancies, the cuts in Social Security, and the fact that, as a population, we're getting healthier, which means we're more active as we get older than we used to be.

• No single withdrawal rate is appropriate for every individual. People have different circumstances and goals, so there isn't any cookie-cutter withdrawal number. That said, I feel comfortable in suggesting a maximum withdrawal rate of 4% per year. That number is based on asset allocation models ranging from a minimum of 60% stocks (and 40% fixed-income) to 80% stocks (and 20% fixed-income). If you have a more conservative asset allocation, you shouldn't withdraw more than 3% annually.

• Don't withdraw from your retirement account until you have to. In general, you should plan to tap your taxable accounts (your regular brokerage account and any savings) first so that the money in your

retirement account will work for you as long as possible. This is especially true until you reach the age of 70½. By delaying your withdrawals from your retirement accounts for as long as possible, you let that money continue to work for you, tax-deferred.

• You may start withdrawing from a traditional IRA after the age of 59½. You must start receiving the required minimum distribution from your retirement plan by April 1 of the year after you reach the age of 70½, regardless of whether or not you need the money, and even if you're still employed. When you begin to withdraw from your retirement account, you'll finally have to pay taxes on that hard-earned money. Withdrawals are taxed as ordinary income.

• The IRS calculates how much you withdraw using your life expectancy at the time of distribution. These mandatory withdrawals are called Minimum Required Distributions and they are not to be taken lightly: There is a harsh 50% excise tax on the amount required to be taken that wasn't.

• The exception to the minimum required distributions rule is Roth IRAs, which have no requirement for minimum distributions.

• If you have other sources of income (so that you won't be completely dependent upon pension monthly payments), you might consider taking your defined-benefit plan as a lump sum. You can then roll the money into an IRA and defer paying taxes on the money.

• A key point in deciding whether or not to take a lump sum is the "discount rate" that the company uses to calculate the amount of your lump sum. If you invest the money and get a return that matches that discount rate, you come out even. To come out ahead, you have to invest the money in such a way that your return beats that discount rate. If you're unsure that you can beat the discount rate, you're better off with monthly payments.

• Laddering bonds is one of several ways to have your investments produce income for you. A good way to use this strategy is to buy a series of Treasury notes or munis with different maturities, ranging from one year to ten years. As each bond matures, you can then either reinvest the money or use it as needed.

6

Monitoring and Rebalancing Your Portfolio

It's human nature to want to know how you're doing in just about any endeavor that you pursue with any seriousness, and investing is no exception. Thanks to the Internet, it's getting easier all the time.

Chances are that, over time, your portfolio will stray from that asset allocation model you so carefully selected. And chances are even greater that you'll want to alter it as you move through your second half. When you want to change the way in which your investments are allocated among asset classes, it's called rebalancing your portfolio.

In general, you might rebalance for these reasons:

- ***Your portfolio no longer matches the asset allocation you chose.*** Over time, owing to the varying returns of different investments, your asset allocation can wander from its original percentages. For example, if stocks do particularly well one year and bonds fall, by the end of the year the percentage of your investing dollars in stocks will have risen, and your percentage in bonds will have fallen. If you started out with a portfolio based on an asset allocation of 80% stocks and 20% bonds, you could, over the next year or two, find that because stock prices have increased, you have 90% of your investing dollars in stock funds, and 10% in bond funds.

When you chose your original asset allocation, your decision was based on the risk you were willing to accept, and the potential rewards a specific allocation might offer. Given that, it follows that if your stock holdings rise above your original allocation, your exposure to risk increases, just as if your stock holdings fall below that original allocation, your future growth potential is probably lower. So the first question is whether or not you want to return to that 80/20 model. It's worth reexamining your asset allocation plan, but don't be swayed into changing your plan based on market performance alone. You're in this for the long term, and what the market did one year has little effect on what it will do the next year.

To return to your original percentages, you'll need to do some rebalancing. A nice side effect of rebalancing to bring your portfolio back in line with your asset allocation goals is that you get to realize the gains from your best-performing investments while at the same time adding to assets that have underperformed. This can help reduce your risk or loss during down markets. And it keeps your risk in line with your original strategy.

• ***You want to change your asset allocation goals.*** As I said in Chapter 4, you'll probably want to revise your asset allocation during your second half, or at least take a look at it. If you don't, you may act on opinions and attitudes that were formed years ago, and that may no longer be true. I think you can stay with an aggressive approach until five years or so after your last full-time paycheck. But sometime around there, you're probably wise to begin a very gradual shift toward a more balanced portfolio. "Gradual" is the key word. I suggest you look at your asset allocation percentages and consider changing them every five years or so, or whenever your life changes in a major way. Marriage, retirement, divorce, a significant change in health, a substantial inheritance—each of these life events can affect your investing strategy. (There are many asset allocation and rebalancing programs on the Web. You may want to look at them.)

• ***You want to modify a concentrated equity portfolio.*** "Concentrated equity" refers to holding a large amount of one company's stock in your portfolio. The most common reason for this is investing in company stock, usually through stock options, but a concentrated equity position can also be the result of inheriting stock. People use different definitions for concentrated equity; I see it as holding somewhere around 30% of your portfolio in one stock. If you have more than this, it's prudent to rebalance.

• ***You want to improve the performance of your portfolio.*** In addition to looking at your portfolio's asset allocation, you will also want to track the performance of your individual investments, so that you can see how you're doing relative to the appropriate market. If, after some analysis, you find that you're unhappy with an investment's performance, you may want to rebalance.

These are good reasons to considering rebalancing. I would also caution you that rebalancing should be a logical, well-thought-out decision and process. It's not an emotional decision, something you do because you're anxious about whatever the stock market's doing on a particular day; don't let your emotions run your investing strategy. Consider rebalancing once a year to improve the performance of your portfolio or to return to your original asset allocation, and, once you stop working full-time, every five years to tailor your asset allocation to fit your second-half needs.

Obviously, before you can know whether or not you want to change your asset allocation, you have to know what it is. (To see where you stand, follow the steps in the box on page 85 in Chapter 4.) Once you know what your current percentages are, compare them against the percentages in your original asset allocation. If you're doing this annually and you find that one asset class is off (plus or minus) by more than

5%, you may want to rebalance. But don't automatically assume that you want to return to your original asset allocation. Remember, things change. Take a moment to evaluate where you are, and look at whether or not your original plan still meets your needs.

Rebalancing to Change Your Second-Half Asset Allocation

During the second half of life, I recommend looking at your asset allocation every five years and gradually decreasing your stock percentage and increasing your fixed-income percentage, then rebalancing your portfolio to bring the proportions of investments in line with your new goal. Factors such as how you handle risk, how much money you have invested, and how much money you're withdrawing to live on will influence your asset allocation decisions.

The scenario below is, to my mind, ideal:

MY RECOMMENDATIONS FOR ASSET ALLOCATION IN THE SECOND HALF

Age 50: 95% stocks and stock mutual funds, 5% cash equivalents
Age 55: 90% stocks and stock mutual funds, 5% bonds, 5% cash equivalents
Age 60: 80% stocks and stock mutual funds, 15% bonds, 5% cash equivalents
Age 65: 70% stocks and stock mutual funds, 25% bonds, 5% cash equivalents
Age 70: 60% stocks and stock mutual funds, 30% bonds, 10% cash equivalents
Age 75: 50% stocks and stock mutual funds, 40% bonds, 10% cash equivalents

Retirees in particular have a tendency to keep too much of their money in cash, when it could be invested for growth. When you look at your cash, be sure to include money in your checking and savings accounts. It's my feeling that you should keep no more than six months' living expenses in cash-equivalent investments (money market mutual funds, Treasury bills, and CDs) until you begin withdrawing from your investments. Keep the rest of your money invested for growth.

You'll notice that in my scenario, you don't ever go lower than 40% stock mutual funds in your portfolio. My personal preference is to try to keep 40% of your portfolio in stock mutual funds for as long as you live, a strategy based on my confidence in the growth potential of stocks, as both investments and as legacies to pass on to our heirs.

So, if I'm such a growth enthusiast, and if I'm so sold on the long-term potential of stocks, why pull back ever? Even in the second half? We talked about the answer in Chapter 3: Averages lie, meaning that over time it becomes more dangerous to base your investing strategy on averages. So, as your time frame shortens, you need to pull back a little so that if there's a downturn in the market, you'll have time to recoup whatever losses you suffer. And you do that by adding some fixed income to your portfolio, giving it a little more stability for your second half.

Rebalancing to Change Your Current Asset Allocation

If you do decide that you need to rebalance either to return to your original allocation or to adopt a new one, go slowly. Rebalancing can be a tricky endeavor. The government rules on IRA withdrawals and transfers and the tax implications work together to make the task something of a tightrope walk, where a mistake can cause you to lose your footing—and some of the second-half money you've been so carefully investing. It is, at least, aptly named: Rebalancing is very definitely a balancing act. Fortunately, it isn't only a tricky endeavor; it's a creative one as well. There are often several ways to handle any rebalancing problem. What follows are some general guidelines to start:

- ***If possible, rebalance in your retirement account, rather than in your regular one.*** One of the things that can make rebalancing tricky is the fact that you're working with both regular accounts (currently taxable) and retirement accounts (which are tax-deferred). So your first decision is which account you'll do the rebalancing in. In general, you can simplify things by rebalancing in your retirement account—you have fewer tax considerations that way.
- ***If you do rebalance in a regular account, make sure you understand the tax consequences of any trade you consider.*** If you have substantial investments outside of a retirement account, you may need to trade in your regular account. In that case it's critical that you be aware of the tax consequences of any trades you consider. The biggest thing to avoid is holding an investment for less than 12 months—if you do, your profits are taxed as ordinary income. The next biggest concern is capital gains. If, for example, you sell an investment in a regular account, you have a taxable transaction. If you've held that investment for a long time, chances are that you bought it for a substantially lower price than you sold it for—which means that you've probably made significant profit, and that amount will be taxed at capital gains rates.
- ***If an asset class is high, consider buying more of what's low instead of selling what's high.*** When you compare your current asset allocation percentages against your original percentages and you find that an asset class (meaning stocks, fixed-income, or cash equivalents) is higher than the percentage you chose, selling something from that group can seem like the easiest way to rebalance. For example, if

you want your asset allocation to be 80% stocks and 20% fixed income, but, thanks to good returns on your stocks, your stock portion has inched up to 90%, selling off some stocks seems like the obvious answer.

Although selling is the most obvious solution, it's not necessarily the best one. In fact, it's potentially the most problematic and expensive in terms of taxes. If the investment you'd sell is in a regular account (as opposed to a retirement account), selling is really a last resort, thanks to capital gains taxes; if you sell, you may realize a capital gain, and that gain will be taxed. You've worked hard for this money, and you don't want it eaten away in taxes.

So, instead of selling off some of the investment that's high, consider buying some of the investment class that's low, to bring its percentage up. This approach can be a little harder to fine-tune, and you may sacrifice some accuracy, but you do avoid the taxes you'd have to pay if you sold.

- ***Redirect dividends or regular investing money to the investment class that's low.*** If you are investing regularly, you can also redirect what you're buying each month or quarter so that you're buying investments in the underweighted class.
- ***Use withdrawals to rebalance.*** Once you begin to withdraw from your accounts, you can use your annual withdrawals to rebalance by selling from the asset group you want to decrease. Or you can spread out your withdrawal amount among types of assets to bring them to the percentages you want. For example, if you're planning on withdrawing funds to live on for the next six months or year, and you want to reduce the stock portion of your portfolio, withdraw from that portion and don't replace those investing dollars.

Rebalancing a Concentrated Equity Portfolio

Banking on one company—*one company*—with a big chunk of your investing dollars is risky, plain and simple, and no matter how great the company, you have to be aware of the risks of concentrated equity. Underperformance is a concern, as is increased volatility. Concentrated equity may make it more difficult for you to reach your investing goals. The age-old rule that says you shouldn't have more than 10% of your investing dollars in any one stock makes more sense as you age, for the simple reason that you have less time to recoup your losses.

The most typical reason for concentrated equity is company stock and stock options, which are often a great deal—but it's also a place where too much of a good thing can be risky. Even if it's the greatest company ever, a concentrated equity portfolio can mean dangerous waters, especially as you age. You're truly putting all of your eggs in one basket. If your stock drops even 20%, you could be in real trouble. Don't be swayed by an emotional attachment to your employer, even if it has made you very wealthy on paper.

People use different definitions to define a concentrated equity; I see it as holding somewhere around 30% of your portfolio in one individual stock. Why 30%? Research tells us that when investors take positions (up to 20%) in a single stock and invest the rest of their portfolio in the market, the increase in risk is relatively slight. At a concentrated equity position of between 20% and 40%, there is a rise in the rate of risk. Beyond 40%, the rate of risk increases even more. About 30% seems to be a sort of midpoint in that progression.

Managing a concentrated equity portfolio is a special kind of balancing act. I'd recommend you do the following if you are a concentrated equity investor:

- ***See where you stand.*** If your portfolio is one in which concentrated equity plays a role—or if you even suspect it—the first thing to do is the numbers, to find out what percentage of your portfolio the stock actually occupies. As always, look at the big picture. You have to look at your entire portfolio, not just your regular account or your retirement account. Your 401(k) may consist of all or almost all of your company's stock, but you have to look at all of your investments to determine what percentage of your portfolio is invested in company stock.

• ***Consider cutting back on risk in other areas of your portfolio.*** Because a concentrated equity position can increase your risk exposure, you may want to cut back on other, higher-risk investments, such as emerging markets or Internet stocks, and move toward larger and more stable companies.

• ***Find out how liquid the stock is.*** In some company retirement plans, holding a lot of company stock is mandatory, but some allow you to start selling at 55. Do your homework (by talking with someone in the benefits office, for example) so that you'll know what your choices are.

• ***If and when you want to lessen your concentrated position, know what your choices are.*** If you find that you are in a concentrated equity situation and you want to lessen that concentration, selling is one answer, but it isn't the only one. There are several ways to do it. If you're still adding to your portfolio, you can invest the new money in fixed income rather than in stocks. This will cut back on the amount of rebalancing you'll have to do later. You'll have less to sell, because you will have done more to balance things out. You can also use the stock in a charitable giving plan.

• ***If you do want to sell, be thoughtful.*** Before you do anything, find out what the tax implications will be. Knowing your cost basis and holding period will help you to do this. If you do decide to sell all or most of the stock, you don't have to do it overnight. You can sell gradually, perhaps over six months to a year, to average out the variability in the market.

Rebalancing to Improve Your Portfolio's Performance

Once you're comfortable with the percentages of each investment class in your portfolio, look at your individual investments to see how they're performing. How are they tracking relative to the appropriate market? And how do they compare with their peers? Your statement from your brokerage firm—or their Web site—should give you the information you need. You just have to compare how each of your individual stocks and mutual funds is doing relative to its respective benchmark. When you do this, remember: *You don't have to beat the benchmark; you just want to be close to matching it.*

A good basis for comparison for large company stocks is the S&P 500 Index. There are those who like the Dow Jones Industrial Average as well, but I'm less enthusiastic about it. The Dow includes just 30 stocks, so it's narrower than other indexes.

Suppose a large-company mutual fund in your portfolio went up 10% in a given year, and the S&P 500 Index went up 10%. That's fine, because, as I've said, you don't have to outperform the market to do well. Matching the market is absolutely acceptable. If, on the other hand, your fund went down 2% and the S&P went up 8%, that's a sign that something's gone awry, and you better keep an eye out. Watch it for a while longer, and if the trend continues, it might be time to change. I think of a good fund as one that fluctuates in the top two-quartiles (50%) of performance rankings, but don't be overly concerned by an occasional dip lower; even good funds have bad years. I think of a bad fund as one that stays in the lowest quartile of performance rankings for its peer group (meaning 75% of mutual funds do better). Bad funds usually have high fees as well. You can easily find information on quartile ranking in Morningstar's reports or Schwab's Mutual Fund Report Card®.

In a down-market scenario, your growth fund might go down 15% when the S&P 500 is down only 12%. In my mind, this is an okay relative performance. I'd recommend holding on for the next up market. Your growth fund may be slightly more volatile than the benchmark, but if it's close, hold on.

Remember that it's important to use the right "peer group" when you're applying performance benchmarks. If your fund is an international equity fund, evaluate its performance against similar funds. A small-cap fund gets evaluated against other small-cap funds. And so on. What follows is a sort of bottom line of benchmarking. Here are my suggestions for the index to use for various types of investments:

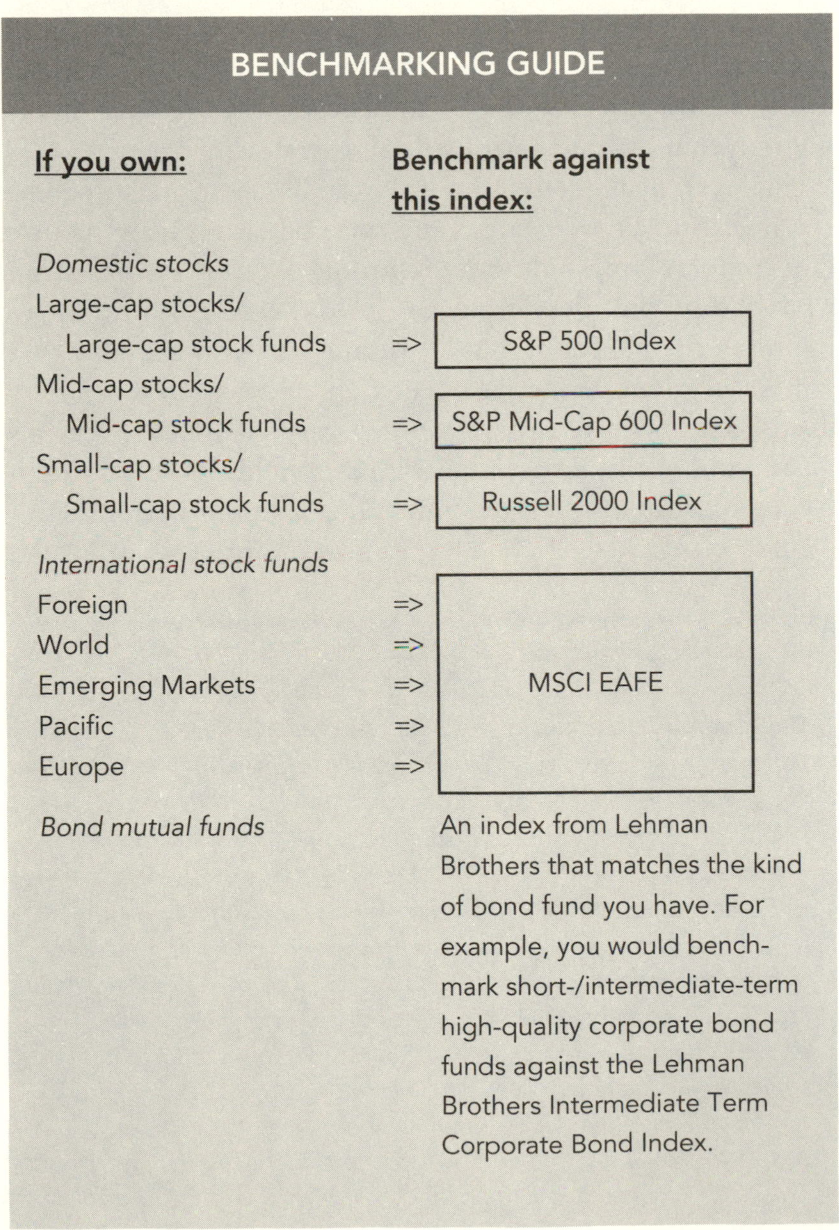

BENCHMARKING GUIDE

If you own:		Benchmark against this index:
Domestic stocks		
Large-cap stocks/ Large-cap stock funds	=>	S&P 500 Index
Mid-cap stocks/ Mid-cap stock funds	=>	S&P Mid-Cap 600 Index
Small-cap stocks/ Small-cap stock funds	=>	Russell 2000 Index
International stock funds		
Foreign	=>	MSCI EAFE
World	=>	MSCI EAFE
Emerging Markets	=>	MSCI EAFE
Pacific	=>	MSCI EAFE
Europe	=>	MSCI EAFE
Bond mutual funds		An index from Lehman Brothers that matches the kind of bond fund you have. For example, you would benchmark short-/intermediate-term high-quality corporate bond funds against the Lehman Brothers Intermediate Term Corporate Bond Index.

When Is Performance a Reason to Sell?

The fact is that our investment decisions don't always turn out to be good ones, and there are certainly occasions when it's time to cut your losses and sell a specific investment, which we'll discuss below. But you don't do this after a few weeks or a few months. Because of the market's emotional nature, day-to-day or even week-to-week fluctuations usually aren't significant buy-or-sell indicators; they're just movement in that organic entity we call the stock market.

The current publicity about day traders can make people see investing as a constant buy-sell endeavor. They picture day traders going online and trading like crazy, based on what the market does from day to day, even from hour to hour. It's the appeal of market timing at work: the idea that you get in when stocks are headed up, and get out when they head back down. But there are two very compelling reasons for staying in the market—buying and holding—rather than trying to get in at the right time: taxes and market timing.

First, taxes. Taxes have a huge effect on those rewards, and

On the Realities of Day Trading

Day trading has gotten a lot of press. The numbers of people actively pursuing this kind of short-term investing are having widespread effects. State regulators have taken notice, and begun to study the effects of day trading—and what they have found is compelling.

For example, one recent study by state regulators analyzed 30 randomly chosen short-term trading accounts from a retail day-trading firm over a period of ten months. The results are sobering. Of the accounts studied, 70% of them lost money. Only 30% of the accounts were profitable. The study concluded that if its analysis was representative of day trading, the majority of day traders will not only lose money in their short-term trades; 70% of the traders they followed will probably lose everything they invest. Only three accounts of those analyzed exhibited trading results and techniques that would bring profit to short-term speculation.

The study concludes with what I see as eminently wise advice: that the average public investor should refrain from short-term trading. Day trading isn't investing. It doesn't involve commitment. To my mind, it's gambling, not much more than guessing the outcome of the toss of a coin.

Source: "An Analysis of Public Day Trading at a Retail Day Trading Firm" by Ronald L. Johnson.

are a very strong argument for not selling. If you don't sell, you don't pay taxes. And if you don't pay taxes on the sale of an investment, the money that would otherwise go to the government stays in your portfolio and continues to work for you.

Second, market timing. As it turns out, the longer you're in the market, the more you're exposed to its rewards. And any losses you do incur are only "on paper" until you sell. During the 1990s, the S&P 500 compounded at an unusually high 18.3% annually. If you weren't invested during the ten top-performing days of that period, your rate of return would have been 14.0%. If you missed the market's 20 top-performing days, your growth rate would have been 10.9%. If you missed the market's 30 best days, you'd have earned 8.3%. And if you were on the sidelines during the 40 finest days—40 days out of ten years—your return would have been 6.0%. I know it's unlikely you'd sit out only the best days if you were timing the market. But the largest gains regularly are concentrated in short time periods and often come when conditions look darkest, and that's when you're least likely to be invested. So market timing can keep you out of the market at the wrong time. This is not to say that you can't improve success through studying market cycles and hands-on experience.

Instead of trying to predict the market's ups and downs and basing your buying and selling on those movements, a good alternative is to be in the market continually. Invest for the long term, and be very picky about when you even *consider* selling. Think about selling only when you want to rebalance your portfolio or change your allocation, or when, after a significant amount of time, an investment's performance isn't satisfactory in comparison to benchmark results.

What about when to buy? A lot of people seem to think there's a perfect time for buying stocks, and they become determined to spot it—so determined that they won't invest until that magic time. If the market's up, they won't invest because they say it's too high. But when the market goes down, they won't invest because they're waiting for it to go down even more. And on it goes.

But there really isn't any perfect time to buy or sell. Strangely enough, one time is almost as good as another. While someone who invests now might do better than someone six months ago or six months from now, in the long run the difference turns out to be negligible. Timing is a very minor player in the larger scheme of investing.

Evaluating the Performance of Individual Stocks

If you've done your homework and bought individual stocks only after a lot of thought, a drop in a stock's price is not, in itself, a good reason to sell. It may or may not mean that the stock is going downhill. Stock investments are long-term commitments, so a drop in price or a so-so performance over several years may not be reason for worry. If you've chosen a wide variety of stocks or invested in a broadly diversified stock mutual fund, it's likely your investment portfolio will appreciate steadily over time, overcoming most temporary setbacks.

That said, the time does come when selling is the wise thing to do. Maybe you just made a bad choice. Maybe you followed a hot tip or bought before you'd really researched the stock. Or maybe the stock has just run out of steam. That can happen for a lot of reasons. Whole industries can run out of steam. Or there may be more specific reasons for a stock's losing ground: legal troubles, for example, or tough competition, or misjudgment on the part of company management.

A change in a company's CEO is an example. A great stock can take a hit if the company leadership changes, for the simple reason that people are wary of change. But if it's still a great company, that downturn may not be a big deal, and the stock may bounce back. In that kind of situation, the company's competitive position isn't usually significantly affected. In the larger scheme of things, that leadership change often turns out to be just a blip on the screen.

A more serious indicator than stock price is market share. If you start reading about a company losing its market share, or if the stock prices of similar companies are going up and yours seems to be headed downward, it may be time to sell—your company may be losing its competitive position. Ask yourself this: "Knowing what I know now, would I still buy this stock? Does this stock look better than other stocks that I could buy?" You have to look at the bigger picture as well: Whole industries can erode, and if that seems to be the case, you have reason to be concerned.

Once you've done your research and the numbers show you that it's time to sell, don't hold on out of sheer hope. It's a mistake to hold on to a losing stock for too long just because you keep thinking that it's going to turn around any day now. Once you've done some research and you're sure that selling is the best decision, do it. Cut your losses and move on. The sooner you do, the smaller the loss, and the smaller the loss, the easier it will be to make up. It's the big losses you worry about—they're the ones to avoid.

We all make mistakes. It's very human to err by picking a bad stock. The important thing is to learn from your mistakes and to move on—and you can console yourself with your tax write-off, which can be significant. When you realize a capital loss, you're able to use it to offset any capital gains you realized in the same year. This decreases the taxes on your gains. That's not all: You can claim net capital losses of up to $3,000 in any given tax year, and you can use those against your ordinary income (which is taxed at marginal tax rates up to 39.6%). If you have capital net losses over $3,000, you can carry them forward into the next tax year. Realizing losses now and deferring gains until next year is a smart tax strategy.

There's plenty of information available to help you track stock performance, and once again the Internet is probably the best place to start. That's where you'll find the timeliest and most easily accessible information. Many magazines and newspapers publish analysts' reports on investments, economic trends, and developments in different industries. There are also many quality investment reference books and newsletters that provide professional and objective information.

Evaluating the Performance of Stock Mutual Funds

Mutual funds are core investments. As such, I don't see selling them very often. I tend to buy mutual funds and hold on to them for a minimum of three years, most of them a lot longer than that.

Evaluating mutual funds is really pretty simple: Over time, you simply watch and make note of the fund's performance. If the fund is performing as well as the benchmark (see page 165), you hang on to it, and possibly add to it. If and when you think, after a reasonable amount of time, that a fund isn't performing as well as it should be, you can switch to another. Morningstar's rankings of the relative performance of mutual funds are very useful in evaluating mutual fund performance. (These are available online at **www.schwab.com** or directly from Morningstar at **www.morningstar.com.** You can also phone Morningstar at 800-735-0700, or write to them at 225 West Wacker Drive, Chicago, IL 60606.)

I have to add that a drop in the performance of a fund is not, in itself, reason to worry. Sometimes a fund will underperform its peer group, simple as that. If you were careful and did your homework when choosing that fund—and its manager—don't worry. Managers, like the rest of us, have good years and bad. As long as the fund's objectives and the manager's philosophy haven't changed, be patient.

On average, recent research on fund performance provided these key findings:[1]

- Funds that have performed well in the past continue to do so.
- On average, funds with lower expenses perform better than those with higher expenses.
- Selling funds that underperform their peer groups can lead to slight improvements in portfolio returns (without considering tax and transaction cost implications).
- The best returns typically come from selling funds that have fallen into the bottom quartile for performance (i.e., the lowest 25%—funds that were outperformed by 75% of their relevant peer groups) on an annual basis.
- The difference in annualized returns, however, was slight—only 0.42%—suggesting that you consider the above strategy more a guideline than a mandate.
- Evaluating your fund's performance—along with your financial situation—every year is the critical first step in your decision-making process.
- Finally, when evaluating fund performance, make sure you compare your fund with the most appropriate peer group. Comparing apples with apples is the only accurate way to see how a fund is doing.

So when do you sell? I consider selling actively managed funds in the following situations:

[1]Schwab Center for Investment Research.

• ***When there's a change in the fund's manager or investment style.*** The departure of the manager from an actively managed fund can be a red flag. It's not necessarily doomsday, but it can be a warning. It's certainly possible that the new manager will do as well as his or her predecessor. What is more likely is that the new manager will substantially change the makeup of the fund. If your fund manager leaves, consider yourself warned.

A change in a fund's investment style is another red flag. If a fund changes direction in a major way—from large-cap stocks to small-caps, for example, or from domestic stocks to

Surviving a Down Market

There is a time when you don't want to sell, and that's during a down market, even though that's when you're most tempted to sell out of fear. The stock market's ups and downs are a given of investing, and you have to keep your emotions in check. This is particularly true when you face a formidable down market—and, like it or not, chances are you will during your lifetime. But remember that after each down market, stocks have rebounded and reached new highs. Investors who panic and sell during the downturn have a very tough time recovering. If you sell your stocks and move to cash equivalents and fixed-income investments out of fear, it can be almost impossible to catch up when the market does turn around. After a 30%, 40%, or 50% loss, you need a 60%, 80%, or 100% gain to break even.

Investing is an endeavor that requires commitment—and that means that you have to hold on in the tough times. During the past 100 years we've had 25 bear markets. Some were worse than others, but the typical bear market lasted about nine months and took the market down 25% to 30%. Every single one of them was followed by a bull market. Every one of those bull markets attained new highs. The sage investor remembers that record. I have ultimate confidence that the economy in America will be better this year than last.

international stocks—be on your guard. Once a year, check the Morningstar writeups for your funds, and look at the style box. If you see a change, keep a sharp eye on that fund's performance over the next year. If you see a downward turn, it may be time to shop around.

• ***When the fund performs below the average of its peer group of funds for more than two years.*** This is reason to pay attention, but before you sell, take a look at the shareholders' report to see if the manager has a satisfactory explanation. Maybe there was a reason for the drop. If you really think a lot of this manager, maybe you want to give it another year, or even more. But if the reasons for the lag don't justify it, it may be time to cut your losses.

There's a reason *not* to sell that's as important as the reasons to sell: Don't sell just because it's underperformed the S&P 500. It's not unusual for a perfectly good fund—especially growth and value funds—to fall behind the S&P 500 for a while, even for a couple of years. You'll get a more accurate reading of your fund's performance by comparing it with other funds in its peer group, not the whole S&P 500. (If you want a fund to perform just like the S&P 500, you're better off buying an index fund with that as its underlying index.)

Selling Stocks and Stock Mutual Funds

As you rebalance during the second half, chances are that you'll decrease the stock and stock mutual fund part of your portfolio, and increase the fixed-income part. Sounds easy enough, but selling stocks is not an easy task. It's easy enough to do the actual deed—to put the sell order in—but it can be tough if, like me, you're a real believer in growth. Whether you're talking about a stock that's done great for you or one that hasn't, selling is hard (which is one of the reasons for doing something besides selling to rebalance). Over time you can become pretty loyal to stocks you've invested in, and if that's the case, those may be stocks that you never sell. If the stock's done great and it's simply time to rebalance, it's hard to part with it, and even the profit doesn't entirely soften the blow. Selling a well-performing stock in a regular account is even tougher, thanks to capital gains taxes. When you sell, you finally have to pay the piper and realize a capital gain, and that 20% tax hit (if it's a long-term holding) hurts. In fact, taxes are the major reason that people resist selling, even when, in the case of a poor performer, they know that selling is the better choice. If the stock or mutual fund hasn't done well and you're selling for performance reasons as well as rebalancing, it's still hard, but it's pain of a different sort. You're finally admitting defeat and cutting your losses—which, while preferable to enduring more of them, hurts, too. So sell when reason tells you it's the right thing to do, but don't be hasty.

Selling Shares of Stock Mutual Funds

If you're considering selling shares of a stock mutual fund from a currently taxable account, keep the following in mind as well:

- ***If you're selling a fund that has gone down during the year, do so before it makes its year-end distribution.*** By doing so, you're not taxed on the dividend, in addition to a tax loss, if you bought the shares at a higher price. Many, if not most, funds make their capital gains payouts in December, and some funds issue an estimate of payouts in November—a nicety, since fund companies are not required to provide any advance warning of payouts.
- ***If you're selling only a portion of the shares you own in a particular fund or stock, it's possible to control the amount of gain or loss you report.*** Your profit or loss in the sale is the difference between what you paid for the shares plus any dividends that were reinvested (your cost basis) and the price you sold at (the sale price). If you bought shares

over a period of time, some shares cost more than others. If you sell 100 shares of a fund, the IRS assumes that you're selling the shares you bought first. The IRS calls this the "first in, first out" (FIFO) rule. Because the shares you bought first probably cost the least, the FIFO rule would give you the largest gain, and therefore work against you.

There is a way around this. Fortunately, you are allowed to specify which shares you want to sell, which means that you can, by doing a little homework, find the highest price you paid and sell those shares, thereby lessening the amount of your gain. You do this by referring to the date and price of the sale—for example, you might say that you want to sell the 100 shares you bought on August 2, 2000, at $50 a share, rather than shares you bought two years earlier for $30 a share. By selling the shares with the highest price, you minimize your taxes on that profit. You can also reverse this. If, for example, you wanted a large gain because you had losses to offset it, you could sell the $30 shares.

If you place the order by phone or online, follow the order with a letter and ask that you be sent written confirmation of the sale of the shares you specified. And as you can see, to sell specific shares, you have to know the price you paid for different shares, which means you need to keep thorough and accurate records of your mutual fund transactions.

Keeping Track of Your Mutual Fund Gains and Losses for Taxes

Figuring out the income tax on mutual funds in regular accounts is tedious at best—and that's if you keep accurate records. If you don't, it's a pain in the neck, and it's one of the main reasons for selling shares held in your retirement account rather than in your regular account, because the money isn't taxed until you withdraw it. With the exception of Roth IRAs, money you withdraw from a retirement account is taxed as ordinary income, period.

If you do sell shares in a regular account, the first thing to know is that you've got to have a system. Here are the basics:

• The money you make in the form of dividends and capital gains from the fund is easy. Each January, your brokerage firm or mutual fund sends you (and the IRS) IRS Form 1099-DIV, telling you the amount and character of distributions you received during the last year. This includes income that you never saw—dividends that were immediately reinvested in a fund, for example. You enter that amount on your tax return as either ordinary income or capital gains, and it will be taxed at the applicable tax rate.

• Selling is where things get interesting, to say the least. When you make a profit by selling shares of a mutual fund for more than they cost, you owe taxes on that profit. If you sell the shares for less than they cost, you have a deductible loss. Sounds simple enough until you think it through. The cost is, of course, what you paid for those shares—but what did you pay? Over time, you buy shares at differing prices. When you sell part of those shares, which ones are they? Which cost do you use to calculate your gain or loss?

There are two ways to calculate your cost. *Average cost basis* is the simpler way.

Cost basis is more complicated, but it can save you money on taxes. The best advice I can give you in terms of calculating your gains and losses from the sale of mutual funds is this: use a computer. There are software programs and Web sites that can make these calculations simple by keeping track of your portfolio and computing your tax basis. All you have to do is enter the information.

Deciding When to Sell a Losing Stock

When the time comes to sell shares of an individual stock, investors are often faced with a tough choice: *Do I sell the winner or the loser? Do I sell the stock that's made me money and take the profit, or do I sell the losing stock and cut my losses?*

Surprisingly, many investors decide to let go of their success stories rather than the stocks that have done nothing but decline. The reason is a sort of things-will-turn-around-soon mentality. People hope against hope that the losing stock will still recover. And as long as they don't sell, they don't have to deal with the other possibility: that the stock won't recover, and that it's been a loss.

But holding on to a losing stock may be costing you more than you think. For one thing, there's no guarantee that this is the end of your loss—it could get worse. And you're wise to take a close look at the company. If there are any basic problems with the company, its products, or its business prospects (things like a significant fall in earnings, weak management, or has-been technology), it's entirely possible that the stock will continue to fall. Second, even if the stock doesn't fall any more, it's tying up investing dollars that could be getting you a better return in another investment. Finally, that losing stock can cause you to lose something besides money—you can lose some tax benefits as well.

Stocks are a tax-deferred investment because you don't pay taxes on your gains until you sell your shares. When you don't want to realize a gain, it can make sense to hold off on selling appreciated stocks, as long as that's in line with your investment goals. But there can be a tax benefit to selling a losing stock and recognizing the capital loss. You can use that loss to offset any capital gains you may have realized. If you have losses left over after that, you can apply up to $3,000 of them against other income ($1,500 for married couples filing separately). If you still have losses after that, you can carry them forward to help reduce your taxes in future years, until you've used up the loss. In other words, selling appreciated stock usually increases your tax bill, while selling stock that has lost value usually reduces it. So, if you're looking for ways to bring down your tax bill, selling a poor performer may be one of those ways.

That doesn't mean you should sell a stock as soon as it starts to fade. Some ups and downs in stock price are usually part of the deal, and just as there are reasons to sell a losing stock, there are reasons to hold on as well, reasons that explain the decline in price. For example, maybe the company has taken a sizable balance sheet write-off that drove profits down for a quarter or two. Or maybe the arrival of new competition has driven the stock price down, but perhaps only temporarily. Or maybe the whole market has seen a decline. The point is to look beyond the stock price. The price in itself shouldn't be the only factor you consider in a sell-or-hold decision.

What follows are some suggestions about how to decide whether to sell or hold:

- ***Pretend you're a first-time buyer.*** Periodically research all the stocks in your portfolio with the objective mindset of a first-time buyer. Look at the things we talked about in Chapter 4: P/E ratios, company management, and the industry as a whole. Read the company's annual and quarterly reports and take a look at its balance sheet to see if anything there explains the price of the stock. And don't forget to look at the overall industry as well.
- ***Get help.*** A sell-or-hold quandary may be a good time to get some professional advice. Doing an investment-by-investment review of your portfolio with a pro can be a tremendous help. If you and the advisor decide that it's time to let go of any investments, he or she can help you in the process.
- ***Look at the tax side of the issue.*** If you're doing this evaluation toward the end of the year, and you've realized significant capital gains during the year, you might consider selling stocks in which you have unrealized losses (stocks that have decreased in value, but whose losses can't be used for tax benefits until you've sold the stock).

• ***Listen to the experts.*** If many analysts are saying that it's time to sell, and you're holding on out of stubbornness, it may be time to reconsider. There are certainly times when cutting your losses is the wise thing to do. But don't act on the advice of only one analyst. And be sure those you listen to have good reputations.

On Trading Stocks in Fast Markets

A fast market is typically the result of an imbalance of trade orders in one direction or the other—for example, there are all buys and no sells. This type of market is then spurred on by certain events or announcements in the news, things like the announcement of an analyst's strong recommendation for a certain stock or sector, or the debut of a popular IPO. In a fast-market stock, when the sudden demand to buy or sell shares outpaces the supply of shares offered, we can see dramatic price movements. It's not unusual to see a 10-, 20-, or even 30-point move over a short period.

Investors can encounter a variety of problems in fast markets. First, price quotes might not be accurate. In a fast market, prices move so quickly that there can be a big difference between the price you're quoted one moment and the price at which you buy or sell just moments later. Even what are supposed to be real-time quotes can lag behind what's really happening. If you place a simple market order (an order at the market price; see the sidebar for more information), you can end up buying or selling shares at a price that differs significantly from the market price displayed just moments earlier. For example, in a fast market you could place a trade at a projected price of $10 and end up paying $40. It can and does happen.

Not only that: The number of shares available at a certain price (called the size of a quote) can change quickly, which can have an effect on the price you're being quoted. And there's more of a chance that market orders, especially large ones, will be filled in segments. In a typical market, the number of shares available at a given quote gives you an indication of the price at which a market order might be filled. Even in the best of market circumstances there is no guarantee that you'll get the quoted price with a market order, but in a fast market, because of the backlog and quotes that may not be current, there's more of a chance that the shares will no longer be available at the quoted price. It's possible that by the time your order is filled, you'll get the quoted price on only a portion of your order, and a different price for the rest of it.

Finally, the rapid pace at which orders are submitted during a fast market can result in a significant backlog, which means there can be a substantial delay—as much as 30 minutes or more, for example—between the time you place your order and the time it's executed. In the short time between when you place your order and when it's executed, trade orders in line ahead of yours can change the price of your stock. So that quote you get can be much more of an indication of what already happened than of what's happening now.

As you probably know by now, I have always advocated a long-term investment philosophy. I urge you to be cautious in

For Beginners Only: Market Orders and Limit Orders

A market order *is an order to buy or sell a stock at the best price available at the time the order is executed in the market. Market orders are usually placed on a day-only basis, and are executed on a first-come, first-served basis. They are usually filled very quickly (which means they usually can't be changed or canceled). In a fast market, as a result of minute-by-minute changes in stock price, the price you pay or receive on a market order can differ substantially from your expectations.*

A limit order *is an order to buy or sell a stock with an upper limit (for buy orders) or a lower limit (for sell orders) on the price. A limit order can help you to set your price, but it doesn't guarantee that your order will be executed.*

fast markets, and to do what you can to protect yourself from the risks that come with volatile markets. If, knowing all of the above about fast markets, you're still interested in trading in a fast market, there is something you can do to help lessen your risk. For example, if you decide to place an order in a fast market, entering a limit order (instead of a market order) lets you establish the maximum amount (for a buy order) or the minimum amount (for a sell order) that you want to pay or receive. In other words, you have some control. A limit order can help reduce the risk of trading at a price that you haven't expected. With a limit order, your trade may or may not be executed, but at least you lessen your chances of trading at a price that you don't want.

Words to the Wise on Monitoring and Rebalancing Your Portfolio

• In general, there are four reasons to consider rebalancing: to return your portfolio to its original asset allocation percentages; to change your asset allocation goals; to change a concentrated equity portfolio; and to improve the performance of your portfolio.

• You should revisit your asset allocation goals once a year to see if they still meet your needs. Once you turn 60, consider changing your asset allocation every five years.

• You should also reexamine your asset allocation any time your life changes in a major way. Marriage, retirement, divorce, a significant change in health, a substantial inheritance—all of these life events can affect your investing strategy.

• Once a year, take an investment snapshot of your portfolio by comparing its current percentages against those of the asset allocation you chose. Then consider whether or not you need to rebalance.

• In general, if you do want to rebalance, you can simplify things by rebalancing in your retirement account—you have fewer tax considerations that way. If you rebalance in your regular account, be sure you're aware of the tax consequences of any trades.

• Selling isn't the only way to rebalance. You can also add to your low investment classes, redirect dividends, and, once you begin making withdrawals, make your withdrawals from the asset classes that are high.

• A concentrated equity portfolio is one in which 30% or more is invested in the stock of one company. You should be aware of the inherent risks of concentrated equity.

• When monitoring the performance of stocks and stock mutual funds, remember that you don't have to beat the index. You just want to track it.

• Taxes are a very strong argument for not selling. If you don't sell, you don't pay taxes. And if you don't pay taxes on the sale of an investment, the percentage of the profit that would otherwise go to the government stays in your portfolio and continues to work for you.

• Market share is a good indicator of when to sell a stock. When a stock price is headed downward because its competitive position is eroding, or because its industry is eroding in what looks like a permanent way, those are serious issues. If the stock prices of similar companies are going up and yours is going down, you may have reason for concern.

• As a long-term investor, consider selling only once a year. Don't even think about it the rest of the year. To minimize taxes, sell some losing investments to offset the gains from your success stories.

• If you're selling a fund that has gone down during the year, do so before it makes its year-end distribution. If you're selling only a portion of the shares you own in a particular fund or stock, it's possible to control the amount of gain or loss you realize.

II

Putting Your House in Order in the Second Half

7

Getting Help If and When You Need It

I'm a real believer in learning from the pros. If I had the time, I'd schedule a golf lesson at least every week or two, and I'd gladly head off for golf school once or twice a year and hit a couple hundred balls a day while I worked on my golf game. I've fly-fished with guides in Montana, Alaska, and New Zealand. These folks not only knew where the fish were hiding, but also helped me with the casting and fly selection that are crucial to success with catch-and-release fly-fishing. And I've taken classes in Chinese cooking in Hong Kong and learned about French cooking in San Francisco. Whether it's golf or fishing or cooking or tennis or skiing—I've found that help from a pro can make a big difference.

The reason for all that instruction is simple: I love to do well, and I love to get better at what I do. The things we love to do aren't just about the end result; much of the joy is in the process of improving. There's always room for growth.

Investing is very definitely a place where a professional can help, for all kinds of reasons. Some people feel they lack the time to make good investing decisions; others have complex financial situations that benefit from more intricate investment strategies. And still others simply want a lesson of sorts, some instruction to help them become better investors. At my firm we offer a lot of educational opportunities to our customers at all levels of expertise, because we want people to feel confident with investing. Some investors are confident and comfortable directing their own investments, while others may seek guidance and advice to validate their approach before they invest, and still others may wish to delegate the work to a financial advisor.

That said, I have two caveats regarding hiring a financial advisor. First, because of the simple economics involved, it probably doesn't make sense to hire someone to manage your money if you have less than $100,000 to invest or already invested. If you're in that category, you're better off doing it yourself. In addition, the world of investment professionals is a big one. This is not a time to just grab the Yellow Pages and pick up the phone. You'll be much more able to make a good decision when you understand your choices, and when you have a personal referral. And that just takes a little thought and time.

Second, even if you end up paying someone to validate your strategy or to manage your money, become educated first. It's still important to understand investing in general and your financial situation in particular. Deciding to get help doesn't mean you forget about your financial life and just hand the whole thing over to someone else any more than you'd let your lawyer or realtor or doctor make all the decisions for you. Remember, we're talking about your future, and once again, you're wise to do your homework. When you have, you'll be able to make good decisions in terms of the kind of help you need and where to get it. And you'll have not only a sound investment strategy but peace of mind—which is what this process is all about.

Generally speaking, you have two decisions to make: first, the degree to which you want professional help; and, second, who that person should be. They're important decisions—in a way, two of the most important decisions you can make.

When to Get Help

Some people take to investing like fish to water, and there's no stopping them once they've learned the basics. Investing becomes part of their lives, and keeping track of their portfolio is as much of a given as going to the market or getting the car washed. They invest regularly, they stay current on research and investing news, and they check their portfolios online, keeping a watchful eye on their investments. The task of investing is up close and personal to them, and the idea of getting help would never occur to them.

But that's not everyone, and maybe it's not you. While it's true that I am a great enthusiast about managing your own investments, I know that it takes some time and attention and patience—not a lot, but some—to manage your money well. It's a commitment and a continuing process that involves a variety of tasks: researching investments, deciding on the best asset allocation, monitoring performance, and rebalancing when necessary. Doing all that may take only a few hours every few months, but maybe that's too much. Or maybe it's not a question of time, but of interest or comfort level or expertise. Or maybe you're just hoping to simplify your life. The goal of financial planning is having enough for your second half, which in turn gives you peace of mind. If the planning itself makes you overly anxious, or if you truly don't enjoy the process, maybe it's time to get some help.

Another reason that people seek professional help is complexity. You can reach the point where your finances are too complicated to handle alone. That can result from a retirement distribution, or an inheritance, or a complex tax situation. Maybe you're changing jobs and you need help rolling over your 401(k) plan distribution. Or maybe you're getting close to company retirement and you need help investing your retirement distribution.

Concern over performance is also a reason that people go to a pro. It can be a very valid reason, but don't overreact.

Give it time. Just because you don't see good results immediately, it's not necessarily an indication that you've made a mistake. Harvey Penick, the great golf teacher, said, "If you play poorly one day, forget it. If you play poorly the next time out, review your fundamentals of grip, stance, aim, and ball position. Most mistakes are made before the club is swung. If you play poorly for a third time in a row, go see your professional." There's a similar axiom for investing: First make sure you've done your homework and learned the basics, then ask yourself whether you still feel overwhelmed or uninterested—or if you just don't have the time to devote to it. If that's the case, then get help.

Whatever your reason for considering professional help, you have a lot of choices in the type of help you get, and in your level of involvement. You can work with someone who helps you define your goals and develop an asset allocation strategy to meet them, puts that plan into action, and then manages your portfolio on an ongoing basis. Or you can go to the other extreme. Maybe you just want to meet with someone once or twice to get help with your strategy or to get some feedback on what you're already doing. At my firm we recognize that people's needs for help vary, which is why we provide a whole spectrum of choices in terms of help and advice. So, if you need help, get started in finding it.

To start, ask yourself the following questions:

- ***Do you want help with your investment plan alone, or do you want someone to manage your portfolio on an ongoing basis?*** In other words, do you want someone just to help you devise an investing strategy, or do you want someone to fully manage your money? Maybe you just want some guidance, a professional to help you develop an investment plan, which can include anything from a basic asset allocation plan to a complete financial evaluation, including estate planning, tax planning, and insurance needs. Then, once you have the plan, you want to put it into action and monitor it yourself.

• ***Is an individually tailored portfolio important to you?*** Some professionals offer to develop an investment plan that's specifically for you. An investment manager chooses specific investments that he or she believes are the best choices for your situation. You can then make changes to your portfolio as you and your manager see fit.

Other kinds of investment management offer you a selection of preset asset allocation plans that meet a variety of different investment goals. You fill out a questionnaire that deals with your goals and your attitude toward risk, and, based on those answers, you're matched up with one of several asset allocation plans. You then give the investment manager the authority to trade on your behalf through a limited power of attorney, and your plan is adjusted periodically to make sure that it stays in sync with your goals. This process works especially well for long-term investors.

• ***How much control do you want your manager to have? Do you want him or her to have authority to trade on your behalf?*** Professional investment management can be *discretionary* or *nondiscretionary.* With discretionary management, you retain control of your assets, but your manager handles the day-to-day investment decisions. Once you and your manager agree on an investment plan, you give him or her a limited power of attorney, which allows the manager to make trades for you without your having to give prior approval for each one. Your manager can buy and sell for you, but he or she cannot withdraw or transfer money from your account. In a nondiscretionary relationship, your manager advises you on your strategy and on specific trades, but you place the actual buy and sell orders.

• ***Do you favor certain types of investments? Are there others you'd like to avoid?*** Some investment managers specialize in specific types of investments. For example, one manager might prefer an all-mutual-fund approach, while another might include all types of investments in international as well as domestic markets. If you have preferences for or against certain investments, you'll need to be sure they're in sync with the manager you choose. If you're looking for ongoing management, is it important to you to deal with only one person, or is working with a firm acceptable?

Different types of management offer different levels of personal contact. In some instances you work directly with one individual, the same individual all the time, who manages your money. In other situations the investment management firm handles your portfolio, and you may or may not deal with the same person each time you have contact with the firm. If working directly with the person handling your money is important to you, that will affect your choice of managers.

More About Investment Management

Generally speaking, these are sources of help, each with its pros and cons:

Independent financial advisors and investment managers are individuals who work directly with you to advise you on investments and/or manage your portfolio. They are not employed by a brokerage firm; they may or may not be part of an *investment management* firm. The manager works closely with you to develop and plan, then puts your plan into action and monitors your portfolio. Once you begin working together, you will probably give your manager discretion over your account, meaning that he or she can buy or sell investments without your prior approval, though he or she cannot transfer or withdraw money from your account. Your manager will make investment decisions, handle the details, keep you informed, and meet with you regularly.

If you work with a manager whose compensation is fee-based (described below), you are charged a percentage of your assets being managed. To my mind, an independent, fee-based investment manager is the best choice for ongoing investment management. You get help and guidance that's unbiased and free of conflict of interest, personal service, an individualized portfolio, and ongoing management. You are charged a set fee, usually 1% to 2% of the assets managed. For this type of professional help, the minimum asset value for accounts generally starts at $100,000.

Mutual fund companies have as their main service the buying and selling of mutual funds, but some offer a type of managed account called a *wrap account.* In this kind of account (also called a "wrap program"), the mutual fund company typically offers you a preset asset allocation plan that's suited to your goals and attitudes toward risk (as indicated by a questionnaire that you fill out). Once you're matched up to an asset allocation plan, the company invests your assets in its funds, then manages those investments for one all-inclusive set annual fee, which is usually around 1% to 3% of the assets managed. Rather than hearing from the individual managing your portfolio, you're typically kept informed on the performance of your portfolio through an account representative, which makes a wrap program the least personalized of your choices. Mutual fund companies set a minimum level for the assets they'll manage; those minimums vary from around $25,000 to over $100,000.

For the Affluent Investor

If your net worth is $5 million or more, you may want to work with an investment management company that specializes in serving affluent individuals and families. Such firms offer investment advice and wealth-management services such as private banking, estate, tax, and retirement planning, and fiduciary services. Their specialized knowledge and personalized service can be a great benefit for the affluent investor. I recommend that you look for a firm with a long history in advising affluent individuals and families. Northern Trust, Bessemer Trust, and U.S. Trust (which is affiliated with Charles Schwab & Co.) are good places to start.

The Name Game

At first glance, it can seem that the world of investment management is populated with an amazing variety of professionals. There are financial consultants, financial planners, financial advisors. There are investment advisors and investment managers, portfolio managers and money managers, and the list goes on. There are a lot of people out there calling themselves professional financial advisors, and it's hard to know whom to trust or where to start.

The title doesn't tell you anything about the individual's qualifications to advise you—or about his or her method of compensation. So be wary. The fact that someone tells you that they are a financial advisor may or may not mean that they're qualified to give you professional investing advice. They may have had very little education or experience in investing; or they may be not much more than salespeople after a commission. To learn these crucial pieces of information, you have to ask questions.

Second, for the purposes of this chapter, I'm going to stick to the terms "financial advisor" and "investment manager"; in these pages the two terms are interchangeable. Both refer to a professional who is qualified to help you in the planning and ongoing management of your investments. More specifically, they refer to individuals or members of a firm who will work with you to develop an investment plan and then, if you want, manage your portfolio for you according to that plan. They monitor your investments and, as needed, can buy and sell investments on your behalf. Some advisors offer additional services as well, such as estate and tax planning. Some use a specific methodology for investing (value-based investing or sector rotation, for example), while others work only with mutual funds. You usually work directly with the person making the recommendations, which means you can ask questions and make sure he or she understands your needs. You and your advisor work together to put your investment plan into action. Funds are held at a financial institution or brokerage firm.

In addition to those generally used names, there are several types of certification available to financial investment professionals:

Certified Financial Planner (CFP).[1] A professional planner who has met the Certified Financial Planner Board of Standards' requirements in education, experience, and ethical conduct, which involves passing a ten-hour comprehensive examination in investment, tax, estate, retirement, and insurance planning. The individual must also agree to follow a code of ethics.

If you're looking for a comprehensive financial plan, a Certified Financial Planner is often a good choice. This type of manager can offer you tax planning, estate planning, and advice on insurance needs. Once you get an overall picture of how best to plan for your financial security, you can decide whether you want ongoing management as well. In most cases a Certified Financial Planner can offer you discretionary portfolio management to support the objectives of your overall plan.

Chartered Financial Analyst (CFA). A financial analyst who has met certain standards of experience, knowledge, and conduct as determined by the Institute of Chartered Financial Analysts. The successful candidate must pass three six-hour examinations, one each over a three-year period, covering economics, security analysis, portfolio management, financial accounting, and standards of conduct.

Certified Public Accountant (CPA) who is a Personal Financial Specialist (PFS). A CPA who specializes in financial planning and has earned the PFS designation from the American Institute of Certified Public Accountants. (Phone 888-999-9256 for a state-by-state list.)

[1]CFP and Certified Financial Planner are federal trademarks owned by the CFP board.

The Cost of Professional Help: Understanding Compensation

Once you've decided you want help, probably the most important thing to know is how investment managers are compensated. More specifically, you need to know the difference between fee-based and commission-based compensation.

Financial advisors are compensated in one of three ways: by the hour, by a set fee based on a percentage of the assets managed, or by commission:

- ***By the hour.*** If you primarily want help with planning versus ongoing management, you'll probably be charged on an hourly basis. This is often the case when you meet with someone on a short-term basis—to help you evaluate your needs or develop a plan, for example, or to assess your current one. Helping you develop a basic investing plan might take as few as two meetings, totaling three or four hours. A more complicated plan, including an estate plan and insurance, could take many meetings over several months. Hourly rates vary tremendously, but a ballpark figure is $150 to $250 or higher. A comprehensive financial plan might cost $3,000 to $6,000. The minimum charge is typically around $1,000 or $1,500.
- ***By a set fee.*** This is called *fee-based management,* and if you're interested in ongoing management, I think it is your best choice in terms of compensation. When you work with a fee-based manager, you're charged a percentage of the assets in the manager's control, usually around 1% or 2%, subject to a minimum. To my mind, fee-based management gives you the best combination of advice and ongoing management with the greatest assurance of unbiased, no-pressure service. There's no conflict of interest with fee-based compensation, and no pressure to buy and sell. You and your advisor share the same goal: to meet your financial goals. Not only that: It's in your advisor's best interest for your assets to increase in value. The greater the value of your portfolio, the greater

their earnings: 1% of $100,000 is $1,000; the same percentage of $150,000 is $1,500. This means your goals are aligned, and everybody wins.

- ***By commission.*** A commissioned advisor or manager gets paid on a per-transaction basis by the company whose investments he or she sells. In other words, that person is in many ways a salesperson, which means that you may be pressured to buy some investments over others simply because of the manager's potential commission. To me, that's conflict of interest, and I encourage you to stay clear of commission-based management.

Choosing an Independent, Fee-Based Financial Advisor

Just as no two investors are alike, neither are any two financial advisors. Background, experience, size of firm, and investment philosophy can all vary, which is why you should take your time in finding the advisor who's right for you. The process isn't hard. You just need to compile a list of potential advisors, interview all or some of them, and make your decision. And if you have a spouse or partner, he or she should be included in deciding who is the best financial advisor for the family.

Step 1. The List

The first step in finding a financial advisor is to compile a list of potential advisors. An easy way to get started is by taking advantage of the complimentary Schwab AdvisorSource™ referral program, which provides you with a list of local, independent, fee-based advisors. All of these advisors have been pre-screened by Schwab in terms of their background and qualifications. Schwab looks at the advisor's form ADV ("Application for Investment Advisor Registration"—see the box on page 204), his or her licenses and registrations, and Dun & Bradstreet reports, which give information about the advisor's credit history. To be listed with AdvisorSource, an advisor must have been a registered investment advisor for at least three years, have a minimum of $25 million in assets under his or her management, be compensated primarily by fees (as opposed to commissions), and have at least one of the following: a bachelor's degree from an accredited four-year institution, a CFA (Chartered Financial Analyst) designation, or ten years of experience managing money and investments as a primary occupation. They also pay a fee to participate. (To use Schwab's AdvisorSource service, visit a Schwab office or phone 800-979-9004.)

Word of mouth is also a good means of finding someone. Ask other professionals—your lawyer or accountant, for example. Or ask a friend who you know uses an advisor.

Remember that how the manager is compensated is an extremely important consideration. I strongly encourage you to consider only managers whose compensation is fee-based rather than commission-based. (That said, for some investments, such as annuities, investment managers receive commissions in addition to their advisory fees.)

Once you have a list, make some phone calls and ask potential advisors to send you information about their business or firm. Try to learn as much as possible about any certifications and state and federal registrations. You can also ask for and follow up on professional references. Finally, if you're something of a detective, you can look at Dun & Bradstreet reports to check the credit history of the firm and the advisor.

As a minimum, I would suggest that any potential advisors meet these requirements:

- be a Registered Investment Advisor (RIA) for at least three years;
- have at least $25 million in assets under his or her management;

• have one or more of the following: a bachelor's degree from an accredited four-year institution; a CFA (Chartered Financial Analyst) certification, or ten years of experience managing money and investments as a primary occupation; and

• meet all applicable state and federal registration and licensing requirements.

Step 2. The Interview

Once you have a list of potential advisors, it's crucial that you set up some interviews. There's no substitute for meeting someone face to face. Sometimes you can learn more about someone in five minutes in person than you could in an hour-long phone call. So, even though it can take some time, interviewing your potential advisors is crucial. Most advisors are more than happy to speak with you about your financial goals and investment needs with no obligation, so don't hesitate to call for an interview. Ask open-ended questions and encourage the advisor to talk. And by all means, interview more than one candidate, even if you're crazy about the first one. Don't be in a hurry. Take your time.

One of the main goals of the interview is just conversation. You want to know more about this person, and you do that by engaging him or her in a conversation. This is a lot easier if you've prepared beforehand by thinking of some questions. And it's a two-way street; your potential advisor will want to know about you so that he or she can begin to assess your needs and consider a course of action. You can also ask your advisor for any brochures or résumés the firm can provide on the firm itself and its employees.

In the interview, you're trying to accomplish a couple of things. First, you just want to get a feel for what this person is like, and whether or not the two of you will get along. The interview gives the two of you a chance to get to know each other, and to determine whether or not you have the personal chemistry and mutual understanding that are essential to a good working relationship in any field. It's important to work with someone you're comfortable with, someone who you feel understands your needs and will be responsive to them. Those kinds of intangibles—things we can't measure or research—are every bit as important as an individual's expertise and training.

You'll also want to learn about the manager's experience, background, and expertise—and you'll want to be able to tell him or her about your financial goals and needs. You should come with a list of questions to ask, and with financial statements and tax returns that reflect your financial situation. Discussing this with a stranger can feel odd, but remember that everything you tell him or her is confidential. And he or she will need some information about your financial situation in order to advise you wisely.

If he or she is with a firm, you might want some information about the firm. The decision to work with a small firm or a large one is a personal preference. A large firm may have more resources, while a small one may offer more personal attention. You might find it helpful to know the size of the firm, the number of people it employs, the total value of assets managed, the number of clients, and the size of the average portfolio. In addition, find out if you'll be working exclusively with the person who is managing your money, or with a representative of the firm. If working directly with your investment manager is important to you, you'll want to choose an advisor who encourages an ongoing personal relationship.

Finally, ask for references, but be specific. Ask for the names of clients whose financial objectives are similar to yours. And then call them, and ask how satisfied they are with the help they're getting.

If the whole idea of an interview makes you nervous, rest assured that you're not alone. A lot of people dread this kind of appointment. They put off working with a financial advisor until they have to, until events force them to—a divorce, a death in the family, an early retirement opportunity. But with financial planners, just as with other professionals in your life, the best time to find one is before you need one, especially if you know that you have an important financial decision down the road. Doing the legwork now will make that decision easier later on.

To be able to discuss your financial situation in detail, you may want to bring your brokerage statements and tax returns. In any case, you should be able to discuss the following:

- Your assets and liabilities (what you have and what you owe)
- Your monthly expenses
- Your income
- Your financial goals
- What retirement benefits you'll receive from your employer
- Your personal circumstances (married or single, children and their ages)
- Insurance
- Any lump sums you expect to receive
- Your attitude toward risk
- Future financial obligations (children's education or support of parents, for example)

You should also have a list of questions for the advisor. You may want to photocopy the worksheet on page 43 and use it for your questions and notes. What follows is a list of general questions:

What is your education and professional background? Ask how she got where she is today, including education, continuing education, special certifications, memberships, employment history, and areas of specialization. Professional designations (e.g., CFA or CFP) will give you information about her interests and specialties.

What is your management style and philosophy? What's

the best investing decision you've made in the last few years? The worst?

He should be able to briefly explain his philosophy of money management. Does he favor a long-term buy-and-hold approach, or does he trade frequently? How does he choose investments? Does he have a strategy for when to sell? Later on, you'll want to compare his answers with your feelings about these same issues, to make sure that the two of you are in sync.

How are fees set?

If the advisor is fee-based, ask how fees are calculated. Fees can be a percentage of the assets managed, an hourly rate, or a flat fee based on the size of your account and the services required. Asset-based fees generally fall in the range of 1% to 2% of assets. Ask the advisor if he or she sometimes receives commissions and, if so, under what circumstances. Knowing the fees in advance will help you decide whether the services are worth the price and also indicate whether any conflicts of interest exist.

Do you prefer one type of investment over another?

Investment managers sometimes specialize in specific types of investments. For example, one manager may prefer to invest completely in mutual funds, while another may choose from a wider range, including all investment types, both domestic and international. If you have a preference for certain types of investments, be sure to find out whether the advisor agrees—and whether he or she has experience in that realm.

Have you had success with clients similar to me? What has your past performance been for clients with financial objectives similar to mine?

Explain your investment objectives and your attitude toward risk, and ask the advisor to describe past performance for clients with goals similar to yours. Also ask him or her to explain how the portfolio was tailored to the client's objectives, and how client portfolios performed in both up and down markets. You might then compare the results with relevant benchmarks such as Standard & Poor's 500 during the same period.

When you look at performance, focus on the advisor's long-term record—not just the last quarter or even the last year. Every investment strategy has short-term ups and downs; performance over time is what you're interested in. Remember that a manager's performance can vary depending on the goals and risk tolerance of his or her clients. If you have a low tolerance for risk, your portfolio will be managed more conservatively than a portfolio for a more aggressive investor. If you have a long time horizon, investment returns should be measured over years, not months or quarters.

How will you help me define my investment objectives? Will you provide a customized investment plan? How often will you review my portfolio with me?

Ask how often you can expect updates on your investments. You should receive written reports at least quarterly, and formal reviews at least once a year. In addition, the advisor should accommodate your requests for telephone and face-to-face contact, and be available as needed.

Where will my assets be held?

Your assets should be held in your own account with a broker or other financial institution, not with the financial advisor. Because the account is in your name, you always have access to your funds. The advisor may handle the day-to-day investment decisions and place trades on your behalf, as authorized by a limited power of attorney, which you will sign at the beginning of the relationship. This legal document allows the manager to execute transactions on your behalf; it does not allow the manager to withdraw or transfer funds from your account.

Step 3. The Final Decision

Once you've interviewed a few potential advisors, take some time to choose the one who you feel will be best for you. Ask more questions if you need to; follow up on references. This is an important decision. Take some time to review your notes and other materials before you decide. As you choose the person you think will serve you best, look for someone industrious and encouraging, but not overbearing or defensive. You don't want someone who encourages you to become or stay dependent on them, or who tries to take more control than you want to give them.

CHECKING THE FINE PRINT: FORM ADV

As you can see, it's crucial to know whom you're dealing with as you begin to look for help. Fortunately there are ways to evaluate potential advisors and managers. You start by looking at things like their background, qualifications, and method of compensation. But your most detailed tool is Form ADV.

The Securities and Exchange Commission requires all investment advisors who manage more than $25 million in customer assets to register by filing Form ADV, Application for Investment Advisor Registration. The form is also used to disclose financial and disciplinary information about advisors to their clients. Once you've met with a potential advisor, you can check on his or her background by looking at the ADV. By law, investment advisors are required to give Part II of the ADV (which we'll discuss below) to prospective clients within 48 hours of their first meeting, or a brochure that contains the same material. If a potential advisor doesn't do that, that's a red flag, and you should consider whether or not you want to do business with someone who violates the law.

The form describes the advisor's education, business background, and current business practices. It's important because it gives you background information, services offered, and investment philosophies for investment management individuals and firms—all important information when making a decision.

Form ADV can be filed in a standard SEC format or in another form, as long as all the required information is included. In either case, it has two parts. The part of the form that you're interested in is Part II, pages 1–6, and, if applicable, Schedules E–G, which are specialized schedules.

Part II is an overview of the advisor's business, including basic operations, services offered, fees charged, types of clients advised, educational and business backgrounds of associates, and other business activities of the advisor.

Detailed information is provided in the schedules attached to the form. They explain responses to questions in Part II, and provide additional information about the advisor's background, fees, education, and disciplinary issues. Not all schedules are required for all advisors, so don't be alarmed if you find some missing. The schedules you'll want to examine are the following:

- Schedule E contains information on disciplinary issues. If any disciplinary issues (current or past) have been reported to the SEC, NASD (the National Association of Securities Dealers), or another regulatory body, those issues are described in Schedule E. If there have been no disciplinary issues, then this schedule is omitted.
- Schedule F contains detailed information about fees, types of services provided, types of clients, their investment philosophy and methodology, professional affiliations, and any conflicts of interest.
- Schedule G contains the investment advisor's balance sheet. It is completed when the advisor requires a client to prepay fees six or more months in advance, and when the advisor takes custody of the client's assets.

One last detail. The form contains something called an "OMB expiration date." This date pertains to the form itself, not to the information provided on the form, so an expired date does not indicate that the firm's information is outdated or invalid. If the advisor files with the SEC before the form's expiration date, he or she can keep using that form and just provide updates to specific pages.

Managing the Relationship

Once you've made your choice, your advisor will guide you on what happens next. He or she will handle the details associated with opening the account and establishing the relationship. And you'll be on your way.

The process you'll follow is similar to the one we've talked about in this book. You and your advisor define your financial objectives, based on your tolerance for risk, your time horizon, your income needs, your tax situation, and your personal preferences. Remember that you've hired this person to help you with your finances; it is his or her job to advise you and to manage your portfolio, but you're the boss. Pay attention to the relationship. Keep the following guidelines in mind as you work together:

- Once you've carefully chosen someone, plan to stay with him or her for a full market cycle—three to five years—so that you can truly evaluate performance.
- Communication is critical. Be open and candid when discussing financial matters with your advisor, not only when you're getting started, but throughout the process. Be sure to report any changes in your objectives or your personal circumstances (marriage, divorce, inheritance, or retirement, for example) so that he or she can see if your investment strategy needs updating.
- When you receive investment documents in the mail (a prospectus or annual report, for example), read them carefully and ask questions about anything you don't understand.
- When discussing performance with your advisor, remember to do so within the context of your objectives and time frame. For example, if you have a low tolerance for risk, your portfolio will be managed conservatively and therefore may not produce high returns. If you and your advisor have agreed upon a long-term investment strategy, try not to be concerned with daily market fluctuations. This is one of the reasons for staying with an advisor for a full market cycle before considering a change in managers.
- Remember, you're talking about your future, which means your dreams, plans, hopes, and aspirations for the second half of your life. Financial advisors are dealing with far more than your finances. They're dealing with your life.

Words to the Wise on Getting Help

• *Think about the level of help you want. Do you want guidance in developing an investment plan that you'll put into action and monitor, or do you want someone to manage your investments on an ongoing basis?*

• *Consider only fee-based independent managers, and interview at least three.*

• *Be prepared for the interview. Bring information on your financial situation as well as questions for the advisor, and take notes during the interview. They'll refresh your memory later. Ask for clarification of any statements you don't fully understand.*

• *Be yourself. This person will be helping you to plan for your future. The better an advisor knows you, the better he or she will be able to do that.*

• *After the interview, review the advisor's Form ADV and follow up on references.*

• *Once you've chosen an advisor, try to stay with that person for a full market cycle—three to five years.*

8

The Assurance Called Insurance

Deductibles. Premiums. Co-payments. Waiting period. Underwriting. Sound important? The language of insurance, like the language of investing, can lead you to believe that it's all about paperwork and statistics and what-ifs that will never occur. But believe me, that's a misconception. The paperwork is necessary, the statistics do apply, and despite our hopes and best efforts, those what-ifs we hope never to encounter do become real sometimes.

What insurance is about is peace of mind, plain and simple. It's about being able to sleep at night and not having your worries wake you up. It's about taking care of yourself and those you love. It's about care and concern for your life. If you're reading this book, you need to read this chapter, whether you're young or old, single or married, with children or without.[1]

Health insurance can guarantee that you'll be able to pay for medical care. Disability insurance can protect your income and can guarantee that you'll still receive income if you are

[1]The views expressed in this chapter are solely my own. This chapter does not purport to advise any specific individual on insurance matters, and does not constitute the offer or solicitation of any insurance services or business.

unable to work because of illness or injury. Long-term-care insurance can make certain that if you ever require nursing-home care, those substantial expenses will be covered. And life insurance guarantees that if you die prematurely, your family will receive enough money to maintain their standard of living. There are, of course, other types of insurance: auto insurance, homeowner's, renter's, umbrella policies. Their intent is to protect your possessions, and they are often appropriate (and, in the case of auto insurance, often mandatory) for adults of all ages. But in this chapter we'll consider the types of insurance that become even more important as you begin the second half. These policies protect not your possessions but your future, your life, and the lives of those you love.

The types of insurance we're talking about can seem irrelevant ("Those things will never happen to me") and boring and as dry as dust, and therefore unimportant. But being adequately insured is one of the most important things you can do, for both yourself and your family. It's not only important—it's generous. The planning you do now can turn out to be a huge gift, for if any of those sobering what-ifs do come true, adequate insurance can make what are fundamentally difficult situations that deal with illness and disability and death easier for everyone. And who doesn't want to make hard things easier for those you love?

That may include your parents. If they haven't dealt with some of the issues discussed in this chapter, one of the biggest favors you can do them is to gently and tactfully raise those issues and do what you can to help them negotiate the necessary tasks. Caring for your parents in this way isn't always easy, but it is the honorable and right thing to do. It's an opportunity to do something good, a way in which you can show them a small portion of the care and concern they've probably shown you for your entire life. I speak from experience here; I helped both of my parents in their later years, first my dad and later my mom, and I wouldn't trade the ways in which I was able to help for anything.

And if you've avoided this subject, take heart. Understanding what types of insurance you need, and even how much of each, isn't that hard. You'll know by the time you finish reading this chapter. But please read it, and if this is one of those areas that your partner handles, it's time to catch up. It can be critical to your well-being, and to the well-being of those you love.

That said, it may also be a time to steel yourself. It's not easy to think about some of the issues you have to consider. We're frequently asked to fill out forms where we list who should be contacted in case of emergency. We usually automatically scribble in the name of our nearest relative without thinking about the circumstances that would require calling that person. You can take a similar attitude here; it can help to approach this material soberly but matter-of-factly. Go through the process, do the necessary tasks, and then you'll rest easier. But don't delay. The younger and healthier you are, the better your chance for getting a reasonable policy, and if you wait until you need insurance, it's often too late. Today is the day to make this right.

Health Insurance: Guarding the First Wealth

Ralph Waldo Emerson tells us that "the first wealth is health," and it's a statement that I have taken to heart as I've grown older. The point of planning ahead for the second half of life is to do what we love and enjoy, perhaps even to fulfill some lifelong dreams. Our health is a key part of that plan, and by guarding your health, I mean two things: taking care of yourself physically, and addressing the financial issues that deal with health care. The most important of those issues is health insurance. *Good health insurance for you and your family is crucial.*

Don't worry, I'm not going to get long-winded about the benefits of taking care of yourself. I'll just say that while I've always known that good health is valuable, it's become even more apparent to me in the last 20 years.

Twenty-four years ago, when I was 40, I heard a lecture by Dr. Ken Cooper, a health specialist, on the benefits of aerobic exercise. As a result, I immediately gave up the social smoking habit I'd picked up, and I began to jog—not just now and then, but really making it a routine. Since then I've jogged approximately every other day, for 25 to 30 minutes, just fitting it in whenever I can, whether that happens to be at 6:00 A.M. or 6:00 P.M., on the treadmill in the winter, or on country roads or city streets when the weather's milder and the days are longer. If I travel, I take my workout gear with me. I prefer six o'clock in the evening, because it rejuvenates me. Afterwards I do a few sit-ups, some abdominal crunches, some work with low-level weights. It's pretty modest stuff, but it helps, and it's important. So, despite a pretty crazy schedule, I work it in.

Why? Simple: I really love to be active. Taking care of myself physically helps me to enjoy the things I love. It helps my golf: I have the energy to walk 18 or 36 holes. I don't tire during a day of fly-fishing. I ski better than I did when I was 35, and because my lungs are in good shape, the altitude doesn't bother me.

While the recognition of our mortality is startling, there is an upside to it. We're living at a wonderful time. There are more advances in medicine, more ways to keep us healthy most of the time, and our life span seems to be on a continuous rise. It's a time when you have a lot of help available in working toward the best health you can achieve. And to me, good health is an integral part of a satisfying second half.

As people look to their future and devise ways to free up more time so that they can do what they love, they often realize just how much they want to do, and how much there is to enjoy in life. In my case, spending time with my family is invaluable—along with the fly-fishing and golfing and skiing. Good health is key to all of those plans.

The second aspect of guarding the first wealth falls under the heading of taking care of business, and it involves making sure you have good health insurance. Hospital bills add up so fast that it's staggering, and if you don't have insurance, those bills are your responsibility. Good health insurance is simply a basic necessity. And the fact that medical problems become more prevalent after 50, and that people are changing jobs more and more frequently, makes staying on top of this issue more critical than ever.

Like most types of insurance, your best bet for good rates on health insurance is through a group plan offered by your employer. Group plans typically cost less than individual plans. If that's not an option (you're not employed, your company doesn't offer it, or you're self-employed), you'll need to find a plan yourself, but you don't have to rule out group coverage. Many professional organizations offer coverage to their members. If group coverage looks impossible, contact the insurance providers directly about independent coverage. When you look at your choices in terms of health plans available to you, I encourage you to get the most comprehensive health insurance you can afford. For general information on the types of plans available, see the Appendix.

Disability Insurance: Protecting Your Income

Once you're retired and no longer working, you no longer need disability insurance, but as long as you're still employed, it, like health insurance, is a key part of your financial plan. The reason is that disability insurance protects your earned income in the event of illness or injury. You purchase it and pay premiums, and if you become unable to work for a substantial length of time, the insurance company pays you a part of your salary, typically around 60% to 70% of your gross income, which usually turns out to be approximately equal to your take-home pay. With it, in the event of an injury or extended illness, you'll still receive at least a portion of your salary.

One of the first questions people usually ask about disability insurance is "What about worker's compensation?" Worker's compensation is similar in that it too replaces income that's lost due to injury, but it applies if and only if you are injured while performing your job. Disability insurance replaces your income no matter what the cause or circumstances of the injury or illness. Regardless of where you became ill or injured, disability insurance means that you'll still have a portion of your income. Sounds like a good idea, right? Yet, surprisingly, more people carry life insurance than disability insurance, even though the odds of not being able to work because of injury are far greater than those of dying young.

Many companies provide disability insurance for their employees. This group coverage through your employer is typically the most economical coverage, so it's the best place to start. Large companies typically offer disability insurance; small ones don't. Some states make it mandatory for employers to offer disability insurance as part of their overall benefits package.

That said, check with your benefits office and make sure you understand the policy. Even if you are covered through your employer, that coverage may be inadequate. For example, most employer plans pay for only five years after you become disabled. Many of them also specify that you'll receive benefits for the first two years if you can't work at *your current job,* but after that you'll receive benefits only if you can't work at *any job.* That's a big difference. In fact, many of the definitions that disability insurance providers use can differ among providers, so be sure to find out exactly what is meant by the terms used in the policy (e.g., "disability" and "occupation").

If your company does offer disability, it's wise to sign up for it, and if that coverage isn't adequate, you can purchase an individual policy, just as you can if your company doesn't offer it or you're self-employed. Be forewarned that an individual policy can be on the expensive side. But don't let that deter you. If your group coverage truly isn't adequate, or if you don't have it, at least consider it. (For information on choosing a disability insurance provider, see the Appendix.)

Finally, a word about taxes. If you collect disability insurance and you've paid the premiums (instead of your employer paying them), the money you receive from disability is not taxed. But if your disability insurance is through your employer, that company is paying your premiums, which means that you will owe taxes on the insurance money that you receive. If your employer's policy pays 60% of your gross income, the money you keep will be far less because you'll pay taxes on it, which may be reason to look for a supplemental policy.

Durable Power of Attorney for Health Care

As long as you are capable of giving informed consent to health-care decisions, choices in your medical treatment are yours. But if you are unconscious or comatose or mentally incompetent, you can't make those decisions. A durable power of attorney for health care, or DPOAHC, is a legal document that specifies what type of medical treatment and life support you want if you're unable to make the decisions yourself. It also makes it possible for the person of your choosing to make those decisions for you so that your wishes will be followed. Without a DPOAHC, it is virtually impossible to remove someone from life support, regardless of their wishes, even if those wishes are known. It is one of the most important documents you can have in that it affects your life, and the care you receive. It also has financial implications. Most health insurance companies specify a maximum amount that they will pay for an illness or injury. That amount varies, but it's typically around $1 million. That may sound like a lot of money, but it's not when you're talking about receiving long-term critical care. It doesn't take long to run through it, and *after that the financial responsibility is yours. If you have not filled out a DPOAHC to specify that you do not want to be kept on life support, your estate could be wiped out in a very short time through the costs of life support. In the document, you make two general decisions: what you would want to happen, and who would be able to make health-care decisions on your behalf. See the Appendix for details.*

Long-Term-Care Insurance: Guarding Your Estate

As anyone who's gone through it knows, moving someone you love to a nursing home is an emotionally wrenching experience. And it's becoming more and more common. As a society, we've changed a lot in the last few generations. Our elderly used to be cared for by their children, or by other members of the family. But that's no longer the general rule, and increasing numbers of our older generations are requiring long-term care. Statistics tell us that the chances of needing long-term care will only rise, in part because we're living longer. And because women's life spans are typically longer than men's—today a 75-year-old woman's life expectancy is another 14 years, while her male counterpart's is just over 11—the odds are even greater that women will require this type of care. Men, because of their shorter life spans, are more likely to be cared for at home by their wives. Unconvinced? Walk around in a long-term-care facility and note the ratio of women to men. If your facility is typical, you'll find that far more than half of the residents are women.

Nursing-home care isn't only hard on the heart—it can be devastating in terms of finances. If you're married and you have to be moved to a nursing home—which, in the case of an event like a stroke, can happen overnight—your spouse pays for your care, and the costs are high. Good care—and this is a situation in which good care is crucial, for a visit to even the best of the best nursing homes is sobering—can easily be $30,000 to $80,000 a year or more.[2] Those are today's costs; who knows what they'll be in 10 or 20 years. It's easy to see that long-term care can wipe out an estate pretty quickly. In addition, in some circumstances the government can come back to an estate and demand restitution for long-term care, then collect by placing a lien on property. This is not a legacy that anyone wants to leave.

The good news is that this financial drain can also be avoided, thanks to long-term-care insurance, which covers some or all of the expenses incurred as a result of required long-term care. Policies can cover care in several types of facilities, such as nursing homes, adult day-care facilities, residential care facilities, and even your home. This type of insurance is a relatively new development in the insurance world, but it also appears to be a welcome one. The number of long-term-care policies purchased has increased dramatically over the last few years, while the cost has been decreasing. In fact, if you buy long-term-care insurance and end up needing this kind of care, it's entirely possible that the total of all of your payments would be less than the cost of only a year or so in a nursing home. Despite its newness, it's used more than any other kind of insurance—approximately one third of those who carry it end up using it. And if you buy it and never have to use it? Then consider yourself lucky, count your blessings, and know that you did the right thing by being prepared. You did the near impossible: You purchased peace of mind.

Long-term-care insurance has received a lot of attention in the last few years, much of it positive, but before you jump in, I think you're wise to consider your individual circumstances. You're the best judge about whether or not the cost is worth it. So when might you consider it? First of all, it's my

[2]Jane Bryant Quinn, *Making the Most of Your Money* (Simon & Schuster, 1997).

opinion that, generally speaking, you don't need to consider long-term-care insurance until you're 50 (the exception being family medical history or personal circumstances that would convince you otherwise). At 50 you can find fairly reasonable rates, and once you reach that age, the question to ask yourself is this: If I needed nursing-home care, what would my alternatives be? If your assets are close to $1 million to $1.5 million, you may conclude that you'd be able to handle the costs of long-term care yourself—in other words, to self-insure. If you're at the other end of the spectrum (with assets closer to $200,000 or less), the premiums may very well be too high. Generally speaking, long-term-care insurance probably makes the most sense for people with assets in the middle six-figure range.

But this isn't solely a financial issue. There are other situations in which the peace of mind you get from having long-term-care insurance may be more than worth the premiums. Health histories play a role here. If your parents required long-term care or if debilitating diseases such as Alzheimer's or Lou Gehrig's disease (ALS) seem to run in your family, these factors may make you more inclined to consider it. And there's the personal side. For example, Heather is 57 years old. Her husband died of cancer a few years ago, and her only child, a daughter, is in college. Thanks to the careful planning of Heather's husband, she and her daughter are secure financially. But she finds long-term-care insurance a comfort, for several reasons. First, having watched her husband go through a serious illness, she is all too aware of what medical costs can be. Second, if she needed long-term care, she would far prefer for the cost to be handled by insurance, so that more of her estate would pass on to her daughter. And, third, and equally important, she doesn't want her daughter to worry about having to take care of her in her old age. She views long-term-care insurance as peace of mind, and for her it's the right thing to do.

There's a lot of confusion about the types of care that long-term-care insurance covers. People think their health insurance will cover these, or that Medicare will (not to be confused with Medicaid, for which you must be legally "financially destitute" to qualify). The truth is that only a small percentage of our annual nursing-home costs are covered by Medicare, and that while there are circumstances in which Medicare will cover nursing-home care, those circumstances are limited and far from long-term. Specifically, as of this writing, Medicare will pay the cost of the first 100 days in a skilled nursing home only if you've first spent a minimum of three consecutive days in the hospital, and even then you'll be responsible for at least part of that cost from the twenty-first day on. In addition, Medicare does not cover long-term care for people who need custodial care as the result of a disease like Alzheimer's, or for people who need help with simple tasks like getting dressed and eating meals—in other words, custodial care, which is exactly the type of care that most long-term-care residents need.[3] (For more information on Medicare and Medigap, see Section 12 of the Appendix.)

And what about the cost? Long-term-care insurance can be fairly reasonable. There are two things you can do to improve your chances of getting a reasonable policy. First, the premiums for long-term-care insurance are based on how old you are when you purchase your policy, so applying while you're relatively young (say, 50 or so) can help lower your premiums. At 50, if your health is good, you may pay premiums of $500 to $1,000 per year. In your mid-sixties, premiums can be closer to $2,000 to $3,000 per year. You'll also have a better chance of qualifying for a policy, since you're more likely to be in good health at a younger age. Long-term-care insurance isn't available to those with serious health problems.

Second, the costs of long-term-care insurance can vary

[3]Quinn, *Making the Most of Your Money.*

tremendously, so comparison shopping is even more important than usual. As you compare the costs of various policies, be sure that you're comparing policies with the same benefits. Because state standards govern long-term care, what's available differs among states, and the type of coverage you're getting will affect the cost of the policy. There are several variables that affect the cost of your policy as well—things like the amount of daily coverage; the amount of time that you pay before your coverage takes over; your age when you buy the policy; and how long you want the policy to cover you. The amount of your premiums should stay the same for the life of the policy; they should increase only as a result of an across-the-board increase applying to all policyholders in a particular state or region with the same plan. (For more information on long-term-care insurance, including the tax implications, see Section 15 of the Appendix.)

Life Insurance: Looking Out for Those You Love

Life insurance is a protection against the financial crisis that can follow the death of a family's primary wage-earner or child-care giver, and it's something that every conscientious parent and spouse should consider. Simply put, it means that if something happens to you, those you leave behind will be taken care of financially, and believe it or not, having it can give you a security you can't get elsewhere. It can give your family cash when they need it most, so that the survivors can replace income, pay off a home, fund children's education, or cover an unexpected financial obligation. It can also help preserve your estate and allow it to pass to your heirs intact, protecting it from estate taxes. This is especially important if your estate consists of illiquid assets such as real estate or a family business.

We'll talk below about who should and shouldn't consider

Buyer Beware: Cashing In on an Existing Policy to Buy a New One Without Getting a Second Opinion

If an insurance agent suggests that you cash in an existing policy and just start over by buying a new policy, be cautious. If the agent is on commission, selling a new policy involves a good-sized commission, and his or her motives may not be in sync with your best interests. Get at least a second opinion before agreeing to this.

life insurance, but in general, if you are unmarried and you don't have children, you probably don't need life insurance. If you have dependents, you do need it, particularly if you are a single parent. This is true regardless of whether you work outside the home. When considering life insurance, you need to look at three issues: whether or not you need it; what kind to get, if you do need it; and how much to get.

Do You Need Life Insurance?

The general questions you need to ask yourself when deciding whether or not you need life insurance are these: Does anyone depend on you financially? If you were gone, would your family be able to make it financially? What kind of effect would the absence of your paycheck have?

More specifically:

1. ***If you are married and you don't have children*** (or if your children are grown and no longer dependent on you financially), you may not need life insurance. You might consider it if there is a discrepancy in your incomes, in which case you would insure the spouse with the larger income, so that the spouse with the lower income would be provided for.

2. ***If you are married and you have dependent children,*** you are wise to buy life insurance for both you and your

spouse. If something happens to the nonworking spouse, the parent who's left will have to hire someone to help with child care—and that takes money.

3. ***If you are unmarried and you don't have children,*** you probably don't need life insurance—unless you are financially responsible for someone (an elderly parent, for example, or some other relative). In that situation you may want to purchase life insurance and name the person you're responsible for as the beneficiary.

4. ***If you are widowed or divorced or unmarried and you have dependent children,*** you need to give some thought to who would be responsible for your children if something happened to you—life insurance is critical for single parents, working or nonworking—and then do what you can to make sure your children's needs will be met, including their college education.

What Kind of Life Insurance Should You Buy?

Believe it or not, there are hundreds of different kinds of life insurance policies. But two kinds are used by far the most often: *term insurance* and *permanent life insurance.*

Term insurance, which I like, is in effect for a specified period of time (usually a 5-, 10-, 15-, 20-, or 30-year term), after which you can renew it at a higher premium. It offers the maximum amount of coverage for the lowest cost. It doesn't pay interest; it doesn't have a cash value. It simply pays the beneficiary you name a certain amount in the event of your death—which is, to my mind, exactly what you want life insurance to do. If you have young children, you probably want a life insurance policy that will cover their needs until they're out of college—you want it to cover the period between now and the time when the youngest graduates.

Permanent insurance is in effect until the death of the policyholder, as long as the premiums have been paid. It includes a savings element. While term insurance is the preferred type of insurance far more often than permanent insurance, permanent life insurance can be effective in certain situations, such as estate planning, charitable giving, and caring for a special-needs child. It is a tool often used by attorneys and estate and financial planners.

How Much Coverage Do You Need?

Determining the amount of life insurance you need isn't easy. Everyone's situation is unique, and the amount you need depends on factors such as age, the number of dependents, and your financial situation. Here are three ways to calculate how much life insurance you need, ranging from the simplest to the most thorough:

1. ***A ballpark figure: calculating the amount as a multiple of your income.*** This is the simplest—and probably the least accurate—way to arrive at a figure. The general rule of thumb is that your life insurance coverage should be approximately six times your annual income. Using this example, if your annual income is $50,000, you may want to buy $300,000 coverage, taking into account any special needs and existing coverage.
2. ***Income replacement: calculating the amount that would cover your income.*** With this method, you buy enough coverage so that the death benefit, if invested at a high enough yield, would replace the income of the person who dies. For example, if you need to replace a $76,000 annual income, and you feel that 8% is a realistic return on investments, then you would purchase $950,000 of coverage ($950,000 × 8% = $76,000). If the assumption bears out, this amount would generate $76,000 annual income (before taxes) and allow you to retain the principal ($950,000) intact. If you believe you will receive a higher investment return, you can reduce the amount of coverage; if you believe you will receive a lower return, increase the amount.

3. ***A customized approach: calculating the amount based on your goals and current assets.*** This method weighs your specific needs and goals against your assets and liabilities, to arrive at a more customized figure. You do this by first estimating immediate cash needs at death (for example, administration expenses, debts, and loans) and future cash needs (including family income, education fund, and spousal retirement fund), then subtracting the value of your total assets (cash, savings, employee benefits) from that amount. That total is the coverage you would need.

See the Appendix for a worksheet that can help you to calculate the amount based on your goals and assets, and for important information on shopping for and choosing a life insurance provider and policy.

Words to the Wise on Being Adequately Insured

• Do not delay in examining your insurance needs and working toward adequate insurance coverage. This could be a crucial piece of your financial puzzle.

• When considering a provider for any type of insurance, make sure that it has a solid track record and good ratings, a maximum of two rate increases for current policyholders, and that it is active in every state.

• When choosing a policy, check group rates first and do some comparison shopping by getting quotes from at least four companies (through a free price-quoting service, for example). Make sure that the policies you compare offer the same coverage. Compare deductibles, premiums, co-payments, and the waiting period.

• Health insurance is not a place to cut corners; get the best and most comprehensive health insurance you can afford. Your best bet for good rates is probably through a group plan offered by your employer. Generally speaking, managed care offers lower cost and fewer choices; fee-for-service costs more, but offers far more choice.

• For disability insurance, group coverage through an employer is typically the most economical and the easiest to get. Large companies typically do offer disability insurance; small ones don't.

• A durable power of attorney for health care, or DPOAHC, specifies what type of medical treatment and life support you want if you are incapacitated and unable to make the decisions yourself. You can obtain the necessary forms at any hospital. Place one copy in your doctor's medical file and give another copy to the person named.

• Make sure you have a DPOAHC for all family members.

• Long-term-care insurance covers some or all of the expenses incurred as a result of required long-term care. It is used more than any other kind of insurance—one third of those who carry it end up using it.

• The cost of long-term-care insurance can vary tremendously. It

can be fairly reasonable, but rates can differ by as much as $1,500 a year or more, and there are a lot of variables to consider. Comparison shopping is crucial.

• Once you get some quotes on long-term-care insurance, make sure you can afford it, now and through your retirement. If you are unsure about your ability to afford it in the future, look for a "return of premium" option.

• Generally speaking, if you are unmarried and you don't have children, you probably don't need life insurance. If you have dependents, you do, particularly if you are a single parent. This is true whether or not you work outside the home.

• Term insurance, which is what I recommend, is in effect for a specified period of time (usually a 5-, 10-, 15-, 20-, or 30-year term), after which you can renew it at a higher premium. It offers the maximum amount of coverage for the lowest cost.

9

The Fine Art of Estate Planning

Contrary to what many people think, estate planning is not something that concerns only the rich or the elderly. Anyone reading this book—rich or poor, young or old—should have an estate plan. *If you are 50, and you don't have one, please follow the steps in this chapter and take care of this as soon as possible. You owe it to yourself and to your family.* The earlier you do it the better, even if you think you have very little to pass on. In fact, in a way, the smaller your estate the more important estate planning is, because if a big chunk of it goes to legal expenses or taxes, your heirs have lost a great deal. The time to do it is now. And once you've done it, you'll rest easier.

Taking care of the financial aspect of your life is like putting a puzzle together, and an estate plan is a big piece of that puzzle. It fits right in with financial peace of mind and security, and it's about the best thing in the world you can do for those you love. And though it sounds like a bunch of paperwork, about rules and regulations that most of us could do without, it's not.

As it turns out, estate planning is about choice. It's about taking a few steps now so that, after your death, your property and possessions will be passed on to the people or organizations that you want to have them. It's about protecting what you've worked for from taxes and needless legal expenses, so that more of it goes to the people or groups you intended it to, and less of it to legal expenses and the IRS.

A caution before we continue: Creating an estate plan is very definitely a place to get help from the pros—an experienced attorney, and possibly your financial planner or tax advisor as well. The basics aren't difficult to understand, but once you get beyond those, you encounter something of a labyrinth. The intricacies of estate planning are complicated, primarily because estate planning deals with the worlds of law and taxes, two of the most complex worlds I know of. The legal documents, such as wills and trusts, have to be done exactly right to be valid, and the laws concerning estate settlement are state laws that vary greatly from state to state and change frequently. And the fine print regarding estate tax goes on and on—and on. So get help. But do your homework first. The whole process will be simpler if you do.

The Best Reason for Having an Estate Plan: What Happens If You Don't

Estate planning at its simplest means figuring out what you want done with your assets after your death. Don't you *want* to have that choice? Don't you want your wishes followed? An estate plan can provide peace of mind that they will be.

But still people put it off; astonishingly, only 50% of those who die have an estate plan. People give lots of reasons for putting it off. They haven't had time, they don't understand the jargon, they find the process intimidating, they'll get to it next month, and—certainly not the least of these—they don't want to think about what happens after they die. Those first reasons are easier to do away with; this is just another thing you have to do, and it just takes a little time and a little discipline. As for the last reason, not thinking about what happens after your death, you owe it to those you love. The last things anyone needs when they're in the midst of grief are legal and financial nightmares. Doing the right thing now means that those surviving you will have fewer headaches later on.

Still not convinced? Read on, because what happens to your property in the *absence* of an estate plan is the most compelling reason I can give for developing one.

In short, if you don't decide and specify what you want done with your estate, someone else will. And you'll be leaving your heirs not the house or investments you'd hoped, but taxes and legal hassles and less control and definitely less money. And what happens with your estate may or may not be what you would have wished. For example:

The court will appoint a guardian for your children who are minors. If you're a parent with minor children, this is the one that sends chills down your spine. The fact is that if you haven't made legal provisions for your children, a judge will name a guardian for them—someone you might not have chosen.

Your beneficiaries will be designated by state law. There's an old joke that says that if you don't have an estate plan, the government will have one for you. True enough—state laws will distribute your property according to certain laws that specify what happens in the absence of a will. These laws are called *intestate* (meaning without a will) *succession statutes,* and they provide for the distribution of your property to your spouse and relatives in an established order. But while they aim at being fair, the results may go against your wishes. The ultimate nightmare would cause your assets to go to the state if you have no known relatives. (This is called *escheating.*)

Your estate may be subject to needless—and extremely high—taxation. Just as in life, taxes are a big consideration in estate planning. The federal government can take a surprisingly large tax bite from what you leave to your heirs. Any amount over the applicable exempted amount (an amount set by tax law, which says how high your estate can go without incurring estate taxes—you'll find more information later in this chapter) is subject to federal estate tax at rates that, believe it or not, can be even higher than income tax rates. They range from 37% to a staggering 60%. Unless you plan carefully, your children or other beneficiaries will be responsible for the taxes on your estate, and you won't be leaving them nearly as much as you'd hoped.

The good news is that with some careful planning, you can probably reduce, defer, or even eliminate the tax that they pay. A well-prepared estate plan can make a huge difference, which means that paying attention to the tax implications of your decisions—and, even better, having a tax advisor who pays even more attention to them for you—can mean that your heirs receive far more of what you leave.

Your estate will go into probate. Probate is a legal process that is used to value your estate, settle any debts, pay estate and other taxes, and make an orderly distribution (or transfer of title) of your assets to your heirs. At a minimum it can be an inconvenience for your heirs, but it can also be a time-consuming and extremely costly ordeal for them, thanks to legal, administrative, and probate fees. Skeptical? In some states, fees on an estate with a gross value of $500,000 can exceed $22,000; on an estate valued at $1 million, they can exceed $42,000.

If you use a will for your estate planning, your estate will still be probated. You can avoid probate by establishing a trust, instead of a will, as discussed later in this chapter. Many people seek to avoid the probate process by putting assets in joint tenancy. Often it works, but it can, in certain situations, have unanticipated results.

Planning Ahead with Your IRA

At the time of your death, the money (or assets) in your IRA passes to the beneficiary you named when you set up the account. It then becomes the property of that beneficiary—and part of his or her taxable income, with potentially substantial tax consequences. You can't avoid these taxes completely, but you can lower them by planning ahead. Make sure that you include your IRA (and any other retirement plans) when you set up your estate plan. Your tax professional and attorney may be able to protect your beneficiaries from unnecessary taxation.

One of the most important estate-planning steps concerning your IRA is also the simplest: Be sure to name a beneficiary. If you don't, your IRA assets might simply pass to your estate. Also, make sure that the beneficiary you name in your IRA is the person you want it to be. After a divorce or a death, for example, you will probably want to change it. Name a second beneficiary as well, in case your first beneficiary predeceases you. Keep a copy of the beneficiary information with your records.

The distribution of your assets to your heirs may be delayed. This depends on several things, but probate can take from a year to two years, or even longer. During the process, your assets cannot be fully distributed to your heirs.

Your estate can incur substantial legal and administrative fees. In the event of probate, your estate must pay for the probate attorney and the court-appointed administrator or executor who manages your estate during probate, which means that much less goes to your heirs.

What Do You Want to Leave Behind?

At the heart of doing an estate plan are some important questions about what you want to have happen to the things you've accumulated. We are body and soul, and certainly more than the sum of our possessions, but it's foolish to ignore the fact that some possessions and property are important to us—for what they represent, or for the good they can do, for example. And at least some of the allure and satisfaction of saving and investing is the prospect of passing something on. But whether you lean toward a "die broke" approach or hope to pass on a sizable estate to your family or charity, the decision about what happens to your money and possessions should be yours. And that takes planning.

If you're married and you have children, the answer to the question of what you want to happen to what you leave behind may seem obvious—you probably want to leave everything to your family. And there's nothing wrong with that. But think of the bigger picture: Beyond taking care of your family, are there things you'd like to do with what you've earned? Maybe you'd like some of it to go to your alma mater someday. Maybe there's a charity whose work you truly value. Maybe there's a friend or distant family member you'd like to help out. There's education, and financing a business, and putting money toward a first home. There's a world of possibility. An inheritance can truly make a difference in someone's life, or in the good works of a nonprofit organization.

Don't feel as though whatever you decide is set in stone. We can't anticipate the future, or even how we'll feel in a few years. Most types of estate plans can be revised and amended, for the simple reason that we change. But you're better off doing something now and amending it later than doing nothing at all.

What About the Kids?

The issue of whether or not to leave large estates to our children is a big one, and you'll find people's opinions run the gamut, from wanting to leave their kids everything, to wanting to leave them almost nothing. Warren Buffett, one of America's most successful investors, says that the right amount to leave children is "enough money so that they would feel they could do anything but not so much they could do nothing." He advocates leaving not more than a few thousand dollars to a college graduate.

A large inheritance can be a lot to put on a kid. Money can damper a person's incentive to work, and make individual accomplishments seem less important. If you want to leave a sizable estate to your kids, it's worth thinking about whether or not they're capable of managing large amounts of money. If the idea of leaving a large inheritance causes you more worry than enjoyment, it may not be the right decision. If you do want to leave something to your children, you'll need to think about the degree of control you want, and how long before you want your heirs to have total control of their inheritance.

If you have children who are minors, your estate plan addresses a far more crucial question in terms of your kids: It can name a guardian for them, in the event that your spouse dies or becomes unable to care for them. It may be another tough call, and it may be the last thing in the world you want to think about. But it's also potentially one of the most important decisions you can make. You can also use an estate plan to record your wishes about how your children should be raised and how old they will have to be to get their inheritance outright and free of trust.

I have five children, all of them grown, and I still struggle with the question of how to help them along the way. There just aren't any hard-and-fast rules, and it's even harder if you have more than one child, because you want to be fair to them all. And while balancing these things is never easy, there are two things I'm sure of: first, that the last thing a parent ever wants to do is take away the incentives for a child to create the world of his or her own independence; and second, that there is a great amount of joy in helping your kids while you're alive, when you're there to cheer them on, and to join them in celebrating their success.

Helping Those Who Help Others

Leaving something to a nonprofit or charitable organization is a wonderful act of giving. The choices are incredible and inspiring: cancer research, meals for the homeless, the art world, literacy programs, religious organizations. You can also leave a gift in memory of someone, or for a specific purpose, such as a gift toward the construction of a new medical building, or a field of research.

Surprisingly, leaving part of an estate to charity is uncommon. Less than 6% of American households include nonprofits in their estate plans. But this is a place where you can truly make a difference. There are lots of ways of doing it. You can leave a specific dollar amount to a good cause, or you can specify that a percentage of your assets be given. You can even leave them a specific asset such as your car or a piece of real estate. You can name a nonprofit organization as the beneficiary of your pension plan, or you can name a nonprofit as the beneficiary of an existing or new life insurance policy. Or you can designate a charity as the beneficiary of your retirement plan, which, because charities and nonprofit organizations are tax-exempt organizations, can give you significant tax savings.

If leaving something to charity appeals to you, talk with someone at the group of your choice and learn how your gift will help. Let your estate planner know of your intentions, and you're on your way.

The Tools of the Trade: Wills and Trusts

Say you're at an Italian restaurant. You look at the menu and you see *bucatini all'Amatriciana, bagna caôda, bollito misto, suppli al telefono, salsa di noce gratinata.* It's going to be hard to choose if you don't know what those are, and even if you recognize one, you'll have a better chance of getting what you want if you know what the others are, too. An informed choice makes a world of difference.

You could say the same thing about estate planning, the world of which is certainly more complicated and intricate than the world of Italian cuisine. To make a good choice, even though you'll probably be dealing with an estate attorney, you're better off knowing a little bit about your choices. You'll be more comfortable with the process if you're reasonably conversant.

The two most basic estate-planning tools are wills and trusts. There is a third—title registration, the simplest form of estate planning, which refers to the way in which you record ownership for a piece of property. But while title registration is a simple way to transfer property, it's limited in terms of estate planning and can have unintended results in certain situations.

A *will* is a legally binding document that states how all property in your name is to be distributed at your death. It can also name an executor for your estate—the person who will be responsible for making sure that your wishes are carried out after your death. Traditionally, preparing a will has been a very basic step in estate planning, sometimes the only one. In a properly drafted will, you can arrange for your assets to be distributed in any way you wish, and you can make certain that the settlement of your estate is supervised impartially by a local court.

A *trust* is a legal agreement in which you place specific assets (which can be anything you own, including bank accounts, real estate, investments, and personal property) in trust for the benefit of one or more people, whom you name in the trust. Trusts are, for many, the tool of choice, and for good reason. With a properly and carefully drawn trust, your estate can avoid probate. Trusts also allow flexibility, control, and tax efficiency. A trust can be established as part of a will, or it can be set up under a separate trust agreement. In most jurisdictions you can be your own trustee without going to a trust company or bank, and you can set up the trust so that it can be amended or revoked during your life.

What You Need to Know About Wills

To many people, a will is the traditional way of specifying where you want your property to go after your death. "Property" can include whatever you own, including pets. A will can also designate a guardian for minor children, and it can specify how debts, taxes, probate fees, and other costs are to be paid. It is not effective until your death; until then you change it in any way you want, as long as you're considered mentally competent. If you consider a will, you should be aware that a will does not provide for your incapacity. It is effective only at death, so if you become incapacitated, the court might appoint a guardian or conservator for you. There are very specific requirements concerning the legal validity of a will, so the only way to be certain that it will be effective is to have an attorney prepare it.

A will is not valid until it has been executed, and for that to happen, there are certain requirements that must be met. They vary from state to state, but in general you must be of sound mind and legal age, you must declare the document to be your "last will and testament," you must sign the will or you must have an authorized person sign for you, and you must have your will witnessed and signed by two or more disinterested individuals. (Special provisions are made for those who are physically unable to sign.)

At your death, your will must be probated in most cases, if

there are any assets in your name, unless they are held in joint tenancy. Probate is a legal procedure for settling your estate that is supervised by the court. During this process, your executor notifies your beneficiaries of your death and your will becomes a matter of public record. A notice of death is published in a local newspaper and mailed to any ascertainable creditors, which gives them the chance to present unpaid bills and allows any interested party the chance to contest your will. Your executor then works with the court to inventory and value your assets, pay any outstanding debts, pay estate and other taxes, collect benefits, and file your final income tax returns. After these things have been done, the executor obtains an order of distribution from the court, makes distributions to your beneficiaries according to your will, and your estate is officially closed.

If you anticipate that there may be disputes about your estate, having a will (as opposed to a trust) will cause any disputes to be settled impartially through probate court. That's the biggest advantage of having a will—and there are some serious drawbacks. The cost of probate can be surprisingly high, and it can take an astonishingly long time. All fees are paid out of your estate, so your estate grows smaller, and distributions can be inordinately delayed by probate. Not only does this mean that your heirs and any charitable beneficiaries get less—it also takes longer for them to get it. If you own real property in states outside the one of your primary residence, a separate probate is required in the state in which it's located, and believe me, the idea of multiple probates is not good news. There's also a lack of privacy, since the will and all documents filed with the probate court are a matter of public record.

What You Need to Know About Trusts

For many people, trusts are, in the world of estate planning, a godsend. Properly drawn, they can save your heirs a lot of money in taxes and probate fees, and they allow your assets to be distributed in a far more timely fashion. And they allow a level of flexibility and choice that makes the whole process of estate planning easier and more attractive.

At the most general level, there are two kinds of trusts: irrevocable and revocable. The two types of trusts meet very different objectives; an estate plan can include both types, if that's what you need. Simply put, trusts function in the way their names suggest:

An *irrevocable trust* is permanent; it can never be revoked or changed. You relinquish ownership of whatever assets you place in the trust—which means they are no longer part of your estate. Properly and carefully drawn, such a trust should not be subject to estate tax. (The transfer of the property to the trust is treated as a gift at the time of transfer.) You establish an irrevocable trust when you are absolutely certain that conditions won't change, or that you won't want to change your decision. An irrevocable trust might be used to establish support for an incapacitated family member, to set up an education fund for children or grandchildren, or to fund a charity or an insurance trust. The establishment of an irrevocable trust is a weighty decision since it cannot be changed. You should bear in mind that even an irrevocable trust can be subject to estate taxes when you die if you retain rights or income with respect to it.

A *revocable trust* can be revoked or changed as long as you're alive. (It becomes irrevocable when you die.) The assets in a revocable trust remain in your control and ownership until your death, which makes them far more widely used than irrevocable trusts. Like all trusts, a revocable trust can be used to specify the age at which a child is to receive his or her inheritance, or even when it can be used for special needs such as education or the purchase of a home.

The two most common types of trusts used in estate planning are *living trusts* and *testamentary trusts.* Assets can be placed in the trusts (by retitling them) as soon as the trust agreement is signed and notarized. A living trust, which can be revocable or irrevocable, becomes effective after the legal documents are signed and notarized. Of course, the assets need to be retitled for a trust to become effective at directing assets in the event of death or incapacity. If you don't change the title in your assets, having any trust won't accomplish any of your estate planning goals.

A testamentary trust, which an attorney may include as part of your will, will become effective at your death through the probate of your will, which means that that's when the assets are transferred to the trust. This type of trust suffers the disadvantage of being required to go through the probate process. When probate is complete, assets are distributed to the trust, and your trustee takes over. An estate attorney includes the terms of the trust as part of your will.

Here's the bottom line: For many people, a revocable living trust is a good choice for estate planning. It gives you flexibility—you can change the terms or even cancel the trust at any time. It gives you control of your assets during your lifetime. If you wish, you can act as trustee, and you can, during your life, continue to manage the assets in the trust just as before, or you can appoint someone else as trustee. You can specify a succession of trustees to take control in the event you are unable or unwilling to continue as trustee, and you can even specify the timing, amount, and circumstances under which distributions are to be made (a certain amount solely for education, and at a given time, for example). And it can be designed to minimize estate taxes. In short, if you want to avoid probate, a trust can do exactly what a will does for you, and may have more advantages.

To establish a living trust, you meet with an estate attorney, who writes a trust agreement, which sets out the terms of the trust. The trust becomes irrevocable at your death, and it dictates what happens at that time. You can specify that you want your assets distributed to your beneficiaries at your death, or you can specify that assets remain in the trust for a certain period following your death, in which case your trustee would oversee their management.

One of the biggest advantages of a revocable living trust is that it avoids probate. Your assets are distributed to your heirs at your death, or at the time you've specified in the trust. Settling a trust can be far less expensive than probating a will. In certain situations a trust can also eliminate or reduce estate taxes. It also remains effective if you are incapacitated, and it allows you to avoid probate for real property held out of state.

If you want to leave all or part of your estate to a charity or other nonprofit organization, a *charitable trust* can help you do that. This trust, set up for a qualified charity, can be a living trust or a testamentary trust. The advantage of charitable trusts is that they can allow you to retain some interest in the assets in the form of either the income stream or the principal. And you receive a tax benefit for the portion of the donated gift.

The Taxing Side of Estate Planning

Tax laws change just about as fast as the weather in Denver, so you always, always, *always* have to check decisions that involve taxes with a specialist. In addition, it's wise to have a tax specialist look over your estate plan periodically to see if changes should be made in light of new legislation. And if you move to another state, you should certainly have a tax specialist examine your estate plan, since tax laws vary from state to state.

I'm going to assume you'll be working with a pro here. But once again it's helpful to be conversant. So what follows are some of the more common and useful tax strategies and considerations in the world of estate planning:

• ***Estate tax exemptions: the unified credit amount.*** Current federal law allows each individual to avoid estate tax on estates that do not exceed a specified amount that increases annually. That tax-free amount is $675,000 during 2001, and it will gradually increase to $1 million in 2006. Amounts over the tax-free amount are subject to estate tax, which can range from 37% to 60% as the estate increases. The part of your estate that exceeds the exemption is the part you have to worry about in terms of taxes.

• ***The unlimited marital deduction.*** This means that you can transfer any amount directly to your spouse (or to a certain type of trust for his or her benefit), free of estate tax. This can reduce or eliminate estate tax on the death of the first spouse. So, if your estate is valued at over the exemption, you can structure an estate plan that will take advantage of both the marital-deduction allowance and the exemption to eliminate estate tax completely when the first spouse dies. The only disadvantage is that when the second spouse dies, the beneficiaries must then pay estate taxes on anything passed on to them (over the exemption), so the tax is really deferred rather than eliminated.

• ***A bypass trust.*** This type of trust allows you to use the exemption for the first to die and the exemption for the second to die, to protect your assets from estate taxes. This is one of the most popular ways to provide a tax shelter for your children. A bypass trust can be set up as part of either a will or a living trust. If this device is not used, the death of the surviving spouse could trigger death taxes on the entire assets of the couple, with only one exemption then available.

Creating an Estate Plan

It's not hard, and it won't take all month. You just need to heed the following three steps. And you'll feel better once it's done because you will have accomplished something crucial for those you love.

1. Determine the Size of Your Estate by Looking at What You Have and What You Owe

You need to know what you have, and how much it's worth now. It's time once again to do your homework. The worksheet in Chapter 2 will guide you.

You may be surprised at the size of your estate, and if your estate is larger than you thought it would be, your taxes will be as well, unless you plan carefully. This is especially true if you bought real estate prior to a real-estate boom. What and how much you own will determine the estate-planning and tax strategies you use.

What You Have: A List of Your Assets and Their Values

Finding out what you have is easy: You just need to list your assets, which means everything you own—what you might want to pass on to your beneficiaries, and what you'll want to address in your will or trust. It's also crucial in figuring the value of your estate, so for each asset, you'll need its current market value (not what you bought it for, but what it would sell for). The worksheet lists possible assets in detail; generally speaking, your assets might include real estate, investments, a business, cash, personal possessions (cars, jewelry, furniture, collectibles), even intellectual property such as patents and copyrights. You should also watch for "hidden assets" such as retirement benefits and the anticipated proceeds from an insurance policy, which may be a part of your taxable estate.

You'll also need to know how the titles to your assets are held (in joint tenancy or as community property, for example) and the beneficiaries you've specified (on life insurance policies and retirement plans, for example).

What You Owe: Your Liabilities

You'll also need a list of your liabilities. Again, the worksheet will guide you, but in general, your liabilities include any type of debt: the mortgage on your home, investment-related debt, the total balance on all credit cards, other loans, and personal obligations.

The Value of Your Estate: Your Net Worth

Once you know the value of your assets and liabilities, you can figure out the value of your estate. You'll need to know this because it will influence how you set up your plan and your tax strategy. To do this, you subtract what you owe (your liabilities) from what you have (your assets) and that gives you your net worth, which is your estate's taxable value. (But remember, your gross estate may be subject to probate.)

What you have – what you owe =
the value of your estate

Or:

Assets – liabilities = net worth

2. Decide What You Want

The next step is to become specific about what you want to happen to those assets after your death. These are extremely personal decisions, and underneath them all lies that big question: What do you want to leave behind? If you're married, you'll probably want to provide for your spouse. Chances are you'll want your estate to pass on to your spouse and children in the order and proportion that you specify. If you have children who are minors, you'll want to arrange for their support and defer their outright ownership to a certain mature age. You should specify who will be responsible for your financial affairs, if you become disabled. If you're the owner or part-owner of a small business, you'll need to think about who will inherit your share.

You may want to set aside money for special family needs, such as education for your children or grandchildren, and for medical expenses and emergencies. You may want to supplement your children's income, or finance a home or business for them. You may want to leave something for a university, or to a charity whose work you value. The possibilities and opportunities are truly endless.

And because this is such a personal area, advice isn't always appropriate. It's truly up to you, and the one constant guideline is to be true to yourself. Make decisions you can live with; you have every right to do what you think is best. Careful discussions with your spouse are a must here.

3. Get It Done

Once you know your net worth and what you want done with your assets, you'll need an attorney to advise you on which type of estate plan will best meet your needs, and to draft the appropriate documents. You may also want a tax advisor to make sure that the plan takes the maximum advantage of state and federal tax laws.

Estate planning is, as I've said, a complicated and even technical endeavor, one that not every attorney is suited for. I encourage you to meet with an attorney who specializes in estate planning. If you don't know of one, there are several ways to go about finding one. You can contact your local bar association for a list of attorneys who specialize in estate planning. There are also legal assistance groups that provide referrals, or you can simply ask for a recommendation from another professional. Whatever your method, the attorney you choose should have an in-depth knowledge of trust and probate law and income and estate tax regulations.

When to Revise Your Estate Plan

One of the few things in life that don't change is that things change, and many of those changes can affect your estate plan. As your circumstances change, what you want your estate plan to do might change as well, so it's important to review it periodically. You should read through it once a year to make sure that it still reflects your values and wishes. In addition, the following events might cause you to make changes to your plan. Basically, any of life's big events can affect your estate plan:

Personal changes:

- Marriage
- A move to another state (probate and tax laws can vary greatly)
- The birth or adoption of children or grandchildren
- Divorce
- A change in family relationships
- Educational needs
- Maturity of family members
- The death of a spouse or another heir
- Serious illness or accident

Financial changes:

- A significant change in financial status (for example, from an inheritance)
- A change in employment, whether positive (a promotion) or negative (a layoff)

- The receipt of a substantial gift or inheritance
- The sale of property for a substantial amount of cash
- Change in property values

In addition, in the event of changes in state property or probate laws, or of changes to federal or state tax laws, you should consult your financial advisor and ask that your estate plan be reviewed to determine whether or not those changes can benefit you.

To change a will, you can have your attorney rewrite it completely or add a codicil. Most minor changes are made through codicils. To change a revocable living trust, your attorney rewrites it or prepares an amendment.

If you acquire additional property, you can add it to your trust. You should then change the title on that property so that it is held in the name of the trust. If you neglect to transfer all of your assets to the trust during your life, the asset(s) not transferred could be distributed to the trust by what is called a "pour-over will." When you create the trust, you will probably also execute a will, which states that anything that you may have neglected to place in your trust during your lifetime should be distributed to the trust at your death. Thus it "pours over" the asset to the trust.

A Final Note

If all of this begins to seem like paperwork and nothing more, be assured that it's not. Estate planning is one of the most important things you can do for those who survive you. Ask a recent widow whose husband was generous and careful enough to have things in order before she was left on her own. Ask a young adult whose parents died prematurely, leaving her with the responsibility of their estate. This may feel like a chore, but it is most definitely exactly the opposite: a gift of your time, plain and simple, and one of the most valuable you can give. I can assure you that you'll feel relieved once it's done—because you've done the right thing for those you love.

Words to the Wise on Estate Planning

• Remember the two basic estate planning goals: to shelter the maximum amount of your assets from taxes, and to make certain your instructions are carried out just as you intended.

• This is a place for the experts. If your estate and needs are complex, estate planning may be a team effort, including an attorney who is well versed in estate planning, an accountant, a trust officer, possibly even a certified financial planner and a life insurance underwriter. If you need help, get it. This is not a place for do-it-yourselfers.

• Do your homework. Yes, this is a place for the experts, but, that said, the more legwork you do ahead of time, the less time you'll need from the experts (and the lower your fees will be).

• Before an estate plan is effective, certain legal documents must be executed, and it is imperative that they be legally accurate. Because not just any attorney can draft sophisticated estate documents, one specializing in estate planning should be used.

• The consequences of neglecting to minimize taxes on your estate are huge, but there are also some efficient tax-planning vehicles to help you out.

• Plan for liquidity, which means make sure that there is some cash readily available in your estate to pay for expenses that follow your death and probate expenses. Depending on the size of your estate, your heirs may need some of it to pay for estate and inheritance taxes.

• Your heirs may also need cash for administrative and other expenses that follow death, such as funeral expenses, executors' fees, legal fees, accounting fees, appraisal fees, and medical expenses incurred during a final illness.

• Sources of cash include Social Security benefits payable to your survivors, separate income-producing property, cash in the bank, CDs, life insurance proceeds, marketable securities, and payouts from an employee benefit plan.

• Once you've created an estate plan, review it periodically, perhaps once a year, to make certain that it still reflects your wishes. You

should also review it if circumstances in your personal or financial life have changed.

• If there have been changes to state or federal estate tax laws, you should have your attorney or accountant review your estate plan to see whether or not the changes affect you.

• Stay flexible. Developing an initial plan is only a start; you can always revise your estate plan. Don't get too caught up in the details. Though we can't see into the future, we can plan for it, and you don't have to anticipate every possible what-if to do that. Create an estate plan that's good enough for today, one that is based on your current circumstances, knowing that you can revise your plan as needed in the future.

• Make sure your assets are titled properly, especially if you have a trust.

10

Giving Something Back: Some Thoughts on Charitable Giving

Look around you. Start in your own backyard, the neighborhood you live in, the community you work in. Think of the museums and symphony you love, the community centers that enrich the lives of your neighbors, the libraries that provide you with books. Look at the hospitals that care for you and those you love, and the university that gave you your education. Or look farther afield, at the statewide organizations that improve education or that work at keeping your state beautiful. Go up another level and look at national organizations that respond to disaster, conduct medical research, or create opportunities for youth nationwide.

What do you see? I'll tell you what I see: opportunity. All of these places are potential recipients of your time, your talent, and your financial support. They're places you might consider giving to, places where you might be able to fill a void—and, in the process, places that can give to you in return.

And what do you get when you give? A lot. You get a certain focus and perspective that come only when you manage to step outside yourself and see your role in the larger scheme of things. And you get the chance to be with people who share your values and your interests. Giving reminds us that we are part of a larger community, and while it's true that the institutions or causes that you hold dear may do fine without your help, it's you who are the poorer by not giving. In fact, there even seems to be a connection between well-balanced individuals and the practice of giving. Giving seems to set good things in motion.

A Note of Caution

In this chapter, I've tried to provide a very general understanding of charitable giving. But the tax issues involved can be difficult and complex, so please see a lawyer who specializes in charitable giving before you take action.

There may be a communal and very real benefit to giving, as well. It's possible that by giving, we can minimize confiscatory taxation, which is really the way our local, state, and federal governments try to fix the problems they face. If things continue as they are, governments have few other choices besides taxation. But if the wealthier members of our society give voluntarily and choose where they want the money to go, they can potentially relieve governments of the task of taxation.

Perhaps the most important considerations in planned charitable giving are the way you structure your giving, and the tax implications of your plan, both of which we'll discuss later in this chapter. Before we get to that nuts-and-bolts level of giving, I have a few suggestions about giving in general:

- ***Give something, no matter how small.*** Something is most definitely better than nothing. If you're unwilling or unable to give money (or appreciated assets), give your time, or something you no longer need, to an organization that can use it. Everyone has something to give.

• ***Make giving a habit, not an occasion.*** One-time gifts certainly help, but you can make a much greater difference with regular contributions, and you can make life a little easier for the cause you're giving to. It's very helpful for charities to be able to count on a certain amount of money each month or year. You might start by deciding on an amount that you can give every month, either as a percentage of your net income or as a dollar amount. It's important to make this gift meaningful, both in terms of the amount and the recipient. Give with intention, as a regular part of your life.

At my company, we encourage our employees to give back to their communities—to be "community investors." Like many companies, we offer to double-match monetary gifts that our employees make to the charities of their choice. I urge you to take full advantage of any matching gifts programs offered by your employer.

• ***Consider giving now, during your lifetime, not just after your death.*** A lot of people relegate the majority of their charitable giving to the distribution of their assets after their death, through a will or a trust. That's certainly worthwhile, and charitable organizations most definitely deserve that consideration. But you can also contribute during your lifetime through what's called "planned giving," a structured approach that enables you to leverage the charitable assets you have, and that will fit in with your financial plan. While the decisions involved in planned giving are highly personal ones that depend on complicated issues such as your financial situation, the financial needs of your heirs, and your tax situation, I encourage you to at least consider giving during your lifetime. I've found it extremely rewarding to witness firsthand the improvements brought about by sustained, planned giving.

• ***Look carefully at how much you can give.*** The most common way to give is to decide on a specified amount, either as a dollar amount or as a percentage of your income. Money manager and author Claude Rosenberg Jr. has done a substantial amount of work on what he calls "affordability potentials"—how much people can give. After a great deal of research, he came to the startling conclusion that, on average, people give far less than they could. "The charitable donations of the IRS's top income group averaged less than 10 percent of what they could safely afford," he writes. "And a similar pattern existed for other income categories, particularly the higher earners."[1] To put that into real terms, if people think they can safely afford to give $10,000 a year, in his view (and based on his research), it's likely they can actually afford to give up to $100,000 a year. The reason is that people tend to base the amount they give on a percentage of their current income rather than on their net worth. Furthermore, he suggests that what he calls "enlightened philanthropy" can produce greater happiness than, for example, personal spending.

The significant tax advantages are another reason that you may be able to give more than you think. Because of the tax deduction you receive for charitable contributions, the after-tax cost of your donation is significantly lower than your original donation. And the higher your tax bracket, the lower the after-tax cost of your contribution. The table below illustrates this. It's an important point to remember when you decide how much to give; you may be able to afford more than you think.

Federal tax rate	Contribution (cash or equivalent)	Simple tax savings	After-tax cost of donation
39.6%	$10,000	$3,960	$6,040
36.0%	$10,000	$3,600	$6,400
31.0%	$10,000	$3,100	$6,900

Source: Schwab Fund for Charitable Giving.

[1]Claude Rosenberg Jr., *Wealthy and Wise—How You and America Can Get the Most Out of Your Giving* (Little, Brown and Company, 1994).

• ***Be creative.*** Remember, giving doesn't refer solely to financial gifts. Gifts of money are certainly valuable and worthwhile, but there are many more ways to give. Almost any asset is a potential gift—securities, real estate, artwork, cars, jewelry, antiques, fine wine, even life insurance and frequent-flyer mileage. There are many charitable organizations that can make excellent use of a home or a piece of property. Organizations can sell appreciated stocks, and they can include in fund-raising auctions tangible gifts such as artwork, jewelry, and antiques. You can also be creative with your financial assets. Annual bonus payments, stock options, and inherited assets can all be viewed as potential donations.

You can also earmark money or holdings that you don't yet have for giving; setting aside your annual bonus or stock options is a great way to give. You can also set aside inherited assets, which can be transferred directly to the charity of your choosing through an estate plan, providing significant tax advantages. (See the Appendix for more specifics on different types of donations.)

You can even name a charity as the beneficiary of your retirement plan assets, although I have to add a note of caution: It can be difficult to exclude family members and leave assets to charity, even if you're certain that a substantial amount would go to taxes. But if you do leave a retirement plan to charity, you can avoid substantial taxes. You won't pay federal income tax, which can be as high as 39.6%, and your estate can avoid as much as 60% in estate taxes. A disadvantage of doing this is that the IRS does not view charities as designated beneficiaries, which means you can use only a single life expectancy factor to calculate your required minimum distributions. And that means higher withdrawals.

Fortunately, there are other ways to do this. One way is to leave the assets in the retirement plan to the charity at your death. By doing so, you avoid income tax, and you can lower your estate taxes because the full value of those assets will be deducted from your estate. Finally, if the assets in your retirement plan exceed $1 million, you can leave the plan to your spouse, then have him or her specify that the assets will fund a private foundation.

Finally, don't limit your thinking to money and tangible gifts. Consider volunteering your time and talent, and the expertise you've developed in your professional life. It's possible that those intangible gifts are some of the most valuable assets you have, and that your personal involvement with a charity—through your participation on its board, for example—can make a significant difference. Organizations are always in need of people with financial marketing, management, and other business experience. Others need photographers, designers, cooks, gardeners, tutors, artists, writers, event volunteers, and more.

CLAUDE ROSENBERG JR. ON INVOLVING YOUR FAMILY IN PHILANTHROPY

Money can be a curse. It has destroyed many family relationships, and it requires delicate handling. Since philanthropy involves the use of money, it has to be handled delicately, too. How children are treated, how involved or uninvolved they should be in their parents' finances (including their philanthropy) is a book unto itself. Properly handled, however, philanthropy can be a great teacher of sound values. It can be a cohesive element—a fine common interest—forming a ladder of generations within a family, and potentially a bond between all family members. It can also be a practical tool that helps young people learn about business. In sum, philanthropy can represent a psychological boost for people of all ages and of all income levels, including those of inherited wealth, who often suffer from low self-esteem and even guilt stemming from their receipt of money they haven't "earned."

If you think you need guidance, there are consultants who help donors isolate the most effective charities to meet specific areas of need, and there are others who specialize in individual and family involvement in philanthropy, or simply in the broad subject of "dealing with wealth." H. Peter Karoff's Boston-based "Philanthropic Initiative, Inc." offers a fine questionnaire that can be of real help. Karoff has combined his views with those of Bob Graham's Namaste Foundation to produce the following list of positive effects of philanthropy on a family's well-being: a reduction in the sense of alienation from the larger world that people of wealth often experience; a view of money as a blessing that can benefit many people beyond the possessor's narrow family unit; a greater sense of emotional wealth and self-esteem; the establishment of a family purpose and team spirit; a forum for meaningful intergenerational communication; training in "letting go" for the older generations; and a forum for practicing family democracy and power sharing.

In fact, the relationship between friends or between spouses, as well as between parents and children, can benefit from joint involvement in charitable giving. As with parental involvement, the right kind of philanthropy can provide a way to nurture others and cultivate a sense of pride that can foster closeness and provide greater fulfillment and happiness for generations to come.

Adapted from Claude Rosenberg Jr., *Wealthy and Wise—How You and America Can Get the Most Out of Your Giving,* with permission of Claude Rosenberg Jr. (Little, Brown and Company, 1994).

Deciding Where to Give

These days there are charities for almost any worthy cause that you can name, groups that cover an amazing spectrum of needs. Most of us receive requests for donations almost daily, and the idea of choosing the most worthy requests can be daunting. It's certainly a decision you shouldn't take lightly.

So how do you choose? Start by thinking about what's important to you, maybe even something that's affected your life directly. Giving to a cause that's important to you may sound obvious, but it's not uncommon for people to give sim-

What Keeps People from Giving

Oddly, selfishness usually isn't the reason for not giving. It's not that people don't want to give—more often it's that they're afraid that they won't have enough money to last their lifetime. Giving interferes with their sense of personal security. They think they can't afford it. Or they mean to give, but they just never get around to it, thanks to the kinds of daily distractions that keep us from a lot of important things we mean to do. Finally, some people put off giving simply because they find the task of figuring out just where to give overwhelming. Others worry that their money just won't have an effect.

Whatever your reason for not giving, whatever hurdle is in the way, I urge you to take a good look at it and overcome any resistance you feel. Take some steps to change your attitude, and to look for opportunities that will suit your values and your priorities. I feel certain that you will be richly rewarded.

ply because one organization or another calls at the right time, or sends a particularly effective mailing. But giving is far more meaningful when you give with intention—when you consciously and purposefully choose the recipient of your gift.

Our reasons for choosing a particular cause can be complicated, maybe even very private. Your values and the concerns of your heart will narrow the field down substantially, as will your preference for giving to several organizations or limiting your choices to one or two charities. Personally, I've found a tremendous amount of satisfaction in giving to causes where I know that I can make a difference. A case in point: One of the most worthwhile charitable endeavors I've pursued has been the creation of the Schwab Foundation for Learning. I cofounded it in 1989 as a clearinghouse of information for parents and teachers trying to understand kids' learning disorders.

The reason for my interest is that I'm dyslexic, a fact that became apparent only when I was 47. Even then, I only learned of my own dyslexia because my youngest son was diagnosed with the learning disorder. He was having a tough time in school, and tests gave the diagnosis. His struggles were familiar to me, and once he was diagnosed, I was certain that he had inherited it from me.

I began to learn about the disorder, and others like it, and I found that a lot of kids who are very bright and deserving fall through the cracks because they have difficulty learning. I learned that what was needed was information, because if these learning disorders are identified, the kids can get help, and do just fine.

The help provided by the Schwab Foundation for Learning is important to me, and it's been a commitment that has given me a tremendous amount of satisfaction, in part because of its connection to my life.

But maybe you'll be more fulfilled by helping more causes in smaller ways. Either way, I encourage you to choose causes that you deeply care about. Once you've narrowed your choices to a handful of possibilities, you'll need to research those organizations. "A healthy skepticism," as Claude Rosenberg Jr. says, is necessary here; the fact is there are fraudulent organizations, and there are certainly organizations that are less than efficient, where your dollars won't do as much good as they might elsewhere. So don't hurry, and never say yes to an organization simply because it has pressured you.

But while this is a time to be cautious, the fact is that most requests for help come from good people who are truly trying to make a difference. These people deserve our respect, and even our gratitude. Don't let your caution keep you from acting; there are plenty of deserving causes and organizations that need your help. In a way, choosing causes is similar to choosing investments. You do your research, you create a "portfolio of causes," and you monitor the results of your community investments from time to time.

One good way to do that is on the Internet. You might start by visiting the Schwab Fund for Charitable Giving Web site (**www.schwabcharitable.org**). The Schwab Fund for Charitable Giving is an independent public charity established to increase charitable giving. The Fund can provide you with objective information and guidance on ways to give to charity. At the Web site you can research charities that meet your interests and goals, and, if you establish a Charitable Gift Account, you can make donations and track your contributions and the balance in your account. In the Appendix you'll find a list of other organizations that support planned giving.

Deciding How to Give

There are a variety of ways to give and tools you can use to maximize your tax benefits. The trick is devising a plan that will maximize the effect of your donation.

For a lot of people, donating means contributing to a charity, organization, or institution directly, by writing a check. And that's great—it's certainly better than doing nothing. But there are so many other ways to contribute, and many of them will give you more tax benefits, and will do more financial good for the charity or organization you've chosen.

To my mind, giving is most meaningful when it's a process and a lifelong endeavor, rather than a one-time event. To that end, I encourage you to develop a plan for your giving, a strategy that you'll periodically reevaluate and fine-tune as time goes by. A planned approach to giving can mean that you make more of a difference, and it can provide your cause with more benefits. This type of giving works best when it's part of your overall financial plan. It involves the following general steps:

1. Choose the cause or causes to which you want to give.

2. Select the specific organizations or charities that you want to help. Visit potential recipients and ask questions. Do some research online or at the library, if necessary, or talk to staff, current donors, or board members. You can also contact the independent organizations whose purpose it is to promote giving. Finally, you can also get information from investment managers, estate-planning attorneys, and the development offices of organizations you're considering. If you're giving a sizable amount, don't take shortcuts where research is concerned. The desire to give may begin in the heart, but choosing the recipient of your gift is an important decision.

3. Decide how much to give in terms of financial resources, as well as intangible ones such as your time and talents.

4. Set both short- and long-term goals that define specific results within specific time frames.

5. Monitor your progress. Stay in touch with the organizations you support. Give your community investments the same kind of attention that you give to your financial investments. True, the returns are harder to measure, but it's still possible.

6. Be open to change. Over time you may see new opportunities for giving, some kind of cause that's a better fit for your interest, goals, and values. Don't feel obligated to support an organization in the future simply because you've supported it in the past. Try to view community investing not as an obligation but as an opportunity.

The Tools of Charitable Giving

There are many ways to give. Some of the tools are complicated, and you may need the services of an attorney who specializes in charitable planning. What follows are some general descriptions of some commonly used tools.

Direct giving simply refers to outright gifts of cash, personal property, or securities. You can donate during your lifetime, or at the time of your death through your will. Direct giving provides immediate support to the charity and helps them with funding their daily operations.

Charitable trusts allow you to maximize the tax advantages of your giving. I think of them as win-win situations: The causes of your choice benefit from your generosity, while you in turn are able to write some of your donations off on your tax return. A *charitable remainder trust* enables you to donate your assets to one or more charities and to then provide yourself (or your beneficiary) with income. You contribute your assets to the nonrevocable trust, and you receive a tax deduction for the current year, based on the value of the asset less the present value of the future income. With a *charitable lead trust,* the reverse is true: By transferring your assets to the trust, you generate immediate income for the charity, but the assets themselves are eventually transferred back to you, your family, or another noncharitable beneficiary of your choice.

Donor-advised funds are offered by a number of public charities. Your contributions to a donor-advised fund are fully deductible (subject to adjusted gross income or AGI restrictions). In addition, when you give through a donor-advised fund, you aren't liable for capital gains tax when the fund sells any assets that have appreciated. Once you donate assets to a donor-advised fund, those assets are the property of the fund, and are no longer part of your taxable estate. Your contribution is invested and grows tax-free. You can recommend grants from the fund to any qualifying charity.

Pooled income funds are funds in which you pool your charitable contributions with those of other donors in an investment vehicle that gives income to the donor or any other noncharitable beneficiary. You contribute assets to a pooled income fund, and you may receive a tax deduction for the current year, based on the value of your donation less the present value of the future income.

Private foundations are a way in which, if your contribution is substantial, you can leave a lasting legacy and maximize your control over the distribution of charitable assets. Tax laws specify a minimum percentage of assets that private foundations must distribute each year through grants. The legal and administrative costs are significant, and this method is best suited—and offers the most benefits—for the affluent. To establish and maintain one of these trusts, you will very definitely require the services of an attorney who is experienced in charitable planning.

The Tax Advantages of Charitable Giving

A sort of windfall of charitable giving is the tax benefits that come your way when you donate, and while planning involved in charitable giving can be complex, the potential tax advantages are significant. Charitable giving can reduce your tax liability in very real and sometimes substantial ways. You can avoid capital gains on appreciated property or securities, you can receive a tax deduction from the donation, and you can lower your estate taxes, since donating assets lowers the value of your estate. And while these advantages aren't what motivate people to give, they certainly shouldn't be ignored. Using the various charitable tools offers you year-round peace of mind instead of year-end scrambling for charitable tax deductions. Being familiar with these advantages is simply another part of taking responsibility for your financial life. The more you save in taxes, the more you have to give.

There are three general factors that influence the tax advantages of a charitable contribution: what you're giving, how you structure your gift, and who's receiving it. The amount you can deduct in any one year can be limited by several factors as well: your adjusted gross income (AGI), the recipient, the gift, and how long you owned it. In addition, there are three different tax statutes that can affect charitable giving: income tax, gift tax, and estate tax.

Finally, you also have to be certain that the organization you want to give to qualifies for charitable deductions. The phrase "charitable organization" is fine for general use most of the time, but when you start talking about the tax implications of charitable giving, you have to get a little more specific. Gifts to some organizations may not qualify for charitable deductions. The IRS classification of the organization you're considering determines whether or not you're allowed an income tax deduction for the full value of your gift. To make matters more complicated, the way in which organizations qualify for income, estate, and gift tax deductions are similar but not identical.

For income tax deductions, you can consult an annual list published by the IRS. This index-style list, Publication 78 (also known as the Cumulative List or the Blue Book), lists all organizations qualified to receive gifts for income tax charitable deductions. This list is updated each year as of October 31. You can also use the list to check on gift and estate tax deductions. However, the book can be confusing and is often incomplete.

If the organization you're looking for isn't on the list, don't give up. It's possible that the organization is included in a parent organization, as is often the case with church organizations or national organizations with many local chapters. Many Web sites (Guidestar, for example) now carry the IRS list of organizations. If in doubt, contact the organization and ask for a copy of what's called their IRS determination letter, as well as written assurance that the letter is still in effect.

For more information on the tax advantages of charitable giving, see Section 18 of the Appendix.

Words to the Wise on Charitable Giving

• I encourage you to give something, no matter how small. If you're unwilling or unable to give money (or appreciated assets), consider giving your time, or something you no longer need, to an organization that can use it.

• Perhaps the most important considerations in planned charitable giving are the way you structure your giving, and the tax implications of your plan.

• Make giving a habit, not an occasion. You can make a much greater difference with regular contributions, and you can make life a little easier for the cause you're giving to.

• Start giving by deciding on an amount that you can give every month, either as a percentage of your net income or as a dollar amount. It's important to make this gift meaningful, both in terms of the amount and the recipient.

• Consider giving now, during your lifetime, not just after your death. Witnessing firsthand the improvements brought about by sustained, planned giving can be extremely rewarding.

• Look carefully at how much you can give. On average, people give far less than they could. The significant tax advantages of giving may mean that you can give more than you think. The higher your tax bracket, the lower the after-tax cost of your contribution.

• Almost any asset is a potential gift. There are many charitable organizations that can make excellent use of a home or piece of property. Annual bonus payments, stock options, and inherited assets can all be viewed as potential donations.

• You can also set aside inherited assets, which can be transferred directly to the charity of your choosing through an estate plan, giving you significant tax advantages.

• Develop a plan for your giving. With a planned approach, you can make more of a difference, and your cause can benefit more.

• Charitable giving can reduce your tax liability in very real and substantial ways. You can avoid capital gains on appreciated property or

securities, you can receive a tax deduction from the donation, and you can lower your estate taxes, since donating assets lowers the value of your estate. The more you save in taxes, the more you have to give.

• There are three general factors that influence the tax advantages of a charitable contribution: what you're giving, how you structure your gift, and who's receiving it.

• The amount you can deduct in any one year can be limited by several factors as well: your adjusted gross income (AGI), the recipient, the gift, and how long you owned it. In addition, there are three different tax statutes that can affect charitable giving: income tax, gift tax, and estate tax.

• Be certain that the organization you want to give to qualifies for charitable deductions.

EPILOGUE

Dear Reader,

I'd like to end with some final thoughts about investing in the second half—three pieces of advice that I hope will serve you well.

First: Remember what investing is all about. It can seem as though investing is all about profit and loss, about risk and reward and rate of return, but, as you know, it's about far more than that. At its core, investing is about *having enough.* Never lose sight of that fact. It's something you do in the here and now so that you and your loved ones can relax and know there will be enough for a good life. Investing is about growth. It's about taking action now to improve your future. It's about taking care of those you love. And it's about taking responsibility for your life. Those things can't be measured on a profit-and-loss statement—nor can most of the other things we truly value.

Second: Always invest in the things you believe in. I don't mean only the companies you admire. I'm using "invest" in the larger sense of the word. Don't limit your investing to the financial world. Invest in the causes that move you, the charities that pull at you, the things in life that have value for you.

Invest something of yourself, whether that's your time or money or talent, and you will be richly rewarded.

Third: Honor your second half. In these early years of the new millennium we are forging a new definition of that part of our lives that I'm calling the second half. It's a new time because unlike most of our parents and grandparents, we have so much choice. At 50, you truly are facing the second half of your life; you'll have the time, energy, and means to accomplish amazing feats. John Houseman received his first Academy Award at 71, and Katharine Hepburn her fourth. At 71, Georgia O'Keeffe flew around the world for the first time—she would live for another 28 years. Vladimir Horowitz performed in concert at 75. Eleanor Roosevelt was appointed the U.S. delegate to the United Nations at 77, Frank Lloyd Wright completed the Guggenheim Museum at 89, and Picasso painted until he was 90. The moral of the story? Don't waste this time. Anything is possible.

So go forward with hope. Invest in yourself, in others, in your beliefs and in your dreams. I wish you good fortune in all of those endeavors, financial and otherwise.

The first half of your life is known. What will you find in that great second half? *The answer is up to you.*

Charles R. Schwab

APPENDIX

The appendix contains the following sections, with the chapter where you'll find more information in parentheses:

1. Financial Inventory Contact List (Chapter 1)
2. 2000 Federal Income Tax Rates (Chapter 3)
3. Estimating Your Social Security Payments (Chapter 3)
4. The Guideline of 230K (Chapter 3)
5. The Investor Profile Questionnaire (Chapter 4)
6. Reading the Fine Print: What to Look for in a Mutual Fund Prospectus and an Annual Report (Chapter 4)
7. Comparing Mutual Fund Costs (Chapter 4)
8. Comparing Individual Bonds and Bond Mutual Funds (Chapter 4)
9. Tax Equivalent Yield Table (Chapter 4)
10. Learning More About Financial Advisors (Chapter 7)
11. The Ins and Outs of Health Insurance (Chapter 8)
12. Medicare and Medigap: What They Will and Won't Cover (Chapter 8)
13. Disability Insurance (Chapter 8)
14. Durable Power of Attorney for Health Care (Chapter 8)
15. Long-Term-Care Insurance (Chapter 8)
16. Life Insurance (Chapter 8)
17. Insurance Rating Systems (Chapter 8)
18. Some Tax Implications of Charitable Giving (Chapter 10)
19. Learning More About Charitable Giving (Chapter 10)

1. Financial Inventory Contact List

This list can help you keep track of your important financial records. You may also want to share it with your family.

	Company & Location	Account Number	Contact	Phone
BANKING Checking				
Savings				
Other				
INVESTMENTS Brokerage Accounts				
Mutual Funds				
Employer Plans (e.g., 401[k])				
Stock Options				
IRAs/Keoghs/SEP-IRAs				
Other				
INSURANCE Life				
Health				
Disability				
Homeowner's/Renter's				
Auto				
LOANS Mortgage/Home Equity				
Auto				
Other				
CREDIT CARD CHARGE ACCOUNTS				
OTHER Lawyer				
Accountant/Tax Advisor				
Investment Advisor				
Safety Deposit Box				

2. 2000 Federal Income Tax Rates[1]

SINGLE
IF YOUR ANNUAL INCOME IS:

More than	And less than or equal to	Estimated Tax Rate
$ 0	$ 26,250	.15
$ 26,250	$ 63,550	.28
$ 63,550	$132,600	.31
$132,600	$288,350	.36
$288,350		.396

MARRIED FILING JOINTLY
IF YOUR ANNUAL INCOME IS:

More than	And less than or equal to	Estimated Tax Rate
$ 0	$ 43,850	.15
$ 43,850	$105,950	.28
$105,950	$161,450	.31
$161,450	$288,350	.36
$288,350		.396

3. Estimating Your Social Security Payments

The Social Security Administration calculates the amount of your check using the contributions you will have made by retirement age. If you retire early, between 62 and the starting age, the amount will be reduced, and that reduction is permanent. The traditional age at which you begin receiving benefits is 65, but that age will be gradually increased to 67 by 2027:

Year of birth	Starting age for Social Security
1942 or earlier	65
1943–1959	66
1960 or later	67

[1]These tax rates are as of this writing. For the most current tax tables, consult the IRS.

You can find out approximately how much you'll be receiving from Social Security by looking at your Social Security statement. This is an annual statement that Social Security sends to everyone 25 or older who has worked under Social Security and does not yet receive benefits. You can also fill out a "Request for Earnings and Benefit Estimate Statement" (Form SSA-7004-SM) online at **http://www.ssa.gov.** Or you can call the Social Security Administration at 800-772-1213 and ask that a form be sent to you, or you can pick one up at a Social Security office. Once you turn 58, the Social Security Administration automatically sends an annual benefits statement to you. The chart below gives estimates of Social Security as of this writing. These numbers assume that you retire at age 65, and that you begin receiving your benefits at that time.

AVERAGE 2001 MONTHLY SOCIAL SECURITY BENEFITS

• **Retired worker: $845**
• **Retired couple: $1,410**
• **Disabled worker: $786**
• **Disabled worker with a spouse and child: $1,310**
• **Widow(er): $811**
• **Young widow(er) with two children: $1,696**

Source: "Understanding the Benefits," a publication (05-10024) of the Social Security Administration.

4. The Guideline of 230K

The tables that follow show you how I arrived at the guideline of 230K. Briefly, I asked the experts at the Schwab Center for Investment Research to test every 20-, 30-, and 40-year period since 1926 to find out how much money an individual would need to start with for every dollar he or she wanted to withdraw per month. (And this is adjusted for inflation, so that buying power stays the same.) These amounts represent the minimum starting value that would allow someone to make it through every time period since 1926 with something left after 20, 30, or 40 years. On the table a ratio of 230:1 means that for every $1,000 you want to withdraw monthly, you would need to start with a nest egg of $230,000.

After seeing the results for that first time period—1926 to 2000—and reflecting on them, I felt that that time period was not a good basis for the test, the reason being that the Depression skews those numbers. Our economy then differed significantly from what it is now, so I asked them to test a second time period, from 1950 to 2000, allowing for recovery from World War II. I feel that that second time period, 1950 to 2000, is a better representation.

The first two tables show the results of those two time periods; the third table compares those results.[2]

RATIO OF RETIREMENT DOLLARS-TO-MONTHLY WITHDRAWALS BASED ON HISTORICAL RESULTS ROLLING PERIODS 1926–2000

Asset Allocation

TIME IN RETIREMENT	Conservative	Moderately Conservative	Moderate	Moderately Aggressive	Aggressive
20 Years	280 : 1	240 : 1	240 : 1	250 : 1	260 : 1
30 Years	380 : 1	290 : 1	280 : 1	280 : 1	300 : 1
40 Years	470 : 1	340 : 1	290 : 1	280 : 1	320 : 1

The table above represents the ratio of dollars needed for every one dollar withdrawn per month over the periods noted. In this analysis, the ratios represent beginning dollar amounts to one dollar of withdrawal where at the end of the period a residual amount remained. This analysis looked at all possible outcomes over the rolling periods listed above from 1926 to 2000.

Assumptions: Based on annual withdrawals adjusted for inflation each year on a compounded basis, except during the first year of retirement. Withdrawals occur at the beginning of each year. This illustration does not include taxes or transaction fees. Asset allocations are as follows:

Conservative:

Pre-1970: Large-cap=20%, Bonds=55%, Cash=25%
Post-1970: Large-cap=15%, International=5%, Bonds=55%, Cash=25%

[2]Source for all tables is the Schwab Center for Investment Research.

Moderately Conservative:

Pre-1970: Large-cap=30%, Small-cap=10%, Bonds=45%, Cash=15%
Post-1970: Large-cap=20%, Small-cap=10%, International=10%, Bonds=45%, Cash=15%

Moderate:

Pre-1970: Large-cap=45%, Small-cap=15%, Bonds=30%, Cash=10%
Post-1970: Large-cap=30%, Small-cap=15%, International=15%, Bonds=30%, Cash=10%

Moderately Aggressive:

Pre-1970: Large-cap=60%, Small-cap=20%, Bonds=15%, Cash=5%
Post-1970: Large-cap=35%, Small-cap=20%, International=25%, Bonds=15%, Cash=5%

Aggressive:

Pre-1970: Large-cap=70%, Small-cap=25%, Cash=5%
Post-1970: Large-cap=40%, Small-cap=25%, International=30%, Cash=5%

RATIO OF RETIREMENT DOLLARS-TO-MONTHLY WITHDRAWALS BASED ON HISTORICAL RESULTS ROLLING PERIODS 1950–2000

Asset Allocation

Time in Retirement	Conservative	Moderately Conservative	Moderate	Moderately Aggressive	Aggressive
20 Years	250 : 1	240 : 1	240 : 1	250 : 1	260 : 1
30 Years	320 : 1	280 : 1	280 : 1	280 : 1	290 : 1
40 Years	340 : 1	280 : 1	250 : 1	230 : 1	220 : 1

The table above represents the ratio of dollars needed for every one dollar withdrawn per month over the periods noted. In this analysis, the ratios represent beginning dollar amounts to one dollar of withdrawal where at the end of the period a residual amount remained. This analysis looked at all possible outcomes over the rolling periods listed above from 1950 to 2000.

Assumptions: Based on annual withdrawals adjusted for inflation each year on a compound, except during the first year of retirement. Withdrawals occur at the beginning of each year. This illustration does not include taxes or transaction fees. Asset allocations are as follows:

Conservative:

Pre-1970: Large-cap=20%, Bonds=55%, Cash=25%
Post-1970: Large-cap=15%, International=5%, Bonds=55%, Cash=25%

Moderately Conservative:

Pre-1970: Large-cap=30%, Small-cap=10%, Bonds=45%, Cash=15%
Post-1970: Large-cap=20%, Small-cap=10%, International=10%, Bonds=45%, Cash=15%

Moderate:

Pre-1970: Large-cap=45%, Small-cap=15%, Bonds=30%, Cash=10%
Post-1970: Large-cap=30%, Small-cap=15%, International=15%, Bonds=30%, Cash=10%

Moderately Aggressive:

Pre-1970: Large-cap=60%, Small-cap=20%, Bonds=15%, Cash=5%
Post-1970: Large-cap=35%, Small-cap=20%, International=25%, Bonds=15%, Cash=5%

Aggressive:

Pre-1970: Large-cap=70%, Small-cap=25%, Cash=5%
Post-1970: Large-cap=40%, Small-cap=25%, International=30%, Cash=5%

5. The Investor Profile Questionnaire

The Investor Profile Questionnaire can help you learn what kind of investor you are, and what kind of investment strategy may best suit your needs. The questions address several important factors, but the most important of these involve your life stage and your attitude toward risk. The questionnaire assumes that the money you plan to invest will be used for your second half. Take a moment to read and answer the questions, then check the answers that apply to you and enter the corresponding points in the space provided. Then follow the instructions carefully. You'll probably want to make a copy of these pages before you begin, in case you want to retake the questionnaire in the future.

1. I plan to begin withdrawing money from my investments within:

A. Less than 3 years	*1 point*
B. 3–5 years	*3 points*
C. 6–10 years	*7 points*
D. 11 years or more	*10 points*
	Points: ________

2. Once I begin withdrawing funds from my investments, I plan to spend all of the funds within:

A. Less than 2 years	*0 points*
B. 2–5 years	*1 point*
C. 6–10 years	*4 points*
D. 11 years or more	*8 points*
	*Points:*________

Subtotal A. Add your points for questions 1 and 2: ________

If your score is less than 3, STOP HERE.

A score of less than 3 indicates a very short investment horizon. For such a short time horizon, a relatively low-risk portfolio of 40% short-term (average maturity of 5 years or less) bonds (or bond funds) and 60% cash is recommended, as stock investments may be significantly more volatile in the short term.

If your score is greater than 3, please continue.

3. I would describe my knowledge of investments as:

A. None	*0 points*
B. Limited	*2 points*
C. Good	*4 points*
D. Extensive	*6 points*
	*Points:*________

4. When I decide how to invest my money, I am:

A. Most concerned about the possibility of my investment losing value	*0 points*
B. Equally concerned about the possibility of my investment losing or gaining value	*4 points*
C. Most concerned about the possibility of my investment gaining value	*8 points*
	Points: ________

5. Review the following list and select the investments you currently own or have owned in the past. Then choose the one with the highest number of points and enter that number.

A. Money market funds or cash equivalents	*0 points*
B. Bonds and/or bond funds	*3 points*
C. Stocks and/or stock funds	*6 points*
D. International securities and/or international funds	*8 points*

Points:________

6. Consider this scenario: Imagine that over the past 3 months the overall stock market lost 25% of its value. An individual stock investment you own also lost 25% of its value. What would you do?

A. Sell all of your shares	*0 points*
B. Sell some of your shares	*2 points*
C. Do nothing	*5 points*
D. Buy more shares	*8 points*

Points: ________

7. Review the chart below. It outlines the average, best-, and worst-case annual returns of five hypothetical investment plans. Which range of possible outcomes is most acceptable to you, or best suits your investment philosophy? (The figures are hypothetical and do not represent the performance of any particular investment.)

Investment plans	*Average annualized return (1 year)*	*Best-case scenario (1 year)*	*Worst-case scenario (1 year)*	*Points*
Investment Plan A	*7.2%*	*16.3%*	*–5.6%*	*0 points*
Investment Plan B	*9.0%*	*25.0%*	*–12.1%*	*3 points*
Investment Plan C	*10.4%*	*33.6%*	*–18.2%*	*6 points*
Investment Plan D	*11.7%*	*42.8%*	*–24.0%*	*8 points*
Investment Plan E	*12.5%*	*50.0%*	*–28.2%*	*10 points*

Points: ________

Subtotal B. Add your points for questions 3 through 7: ________

Subtotal A represents your time horizon score.
Enter Subtotal A here: ________

Subtotal B represents your risk tolerance score.
Enter Subtotal B here: ________

Now plot your time horizon score and your risk tolerance score on the chart below and locate their intersection point. This tells you your investor profile, ranging from very aggressive to conservative. Once you know that, turn to pages 85–86 to find the pie chart that represents that type of asset allocation.

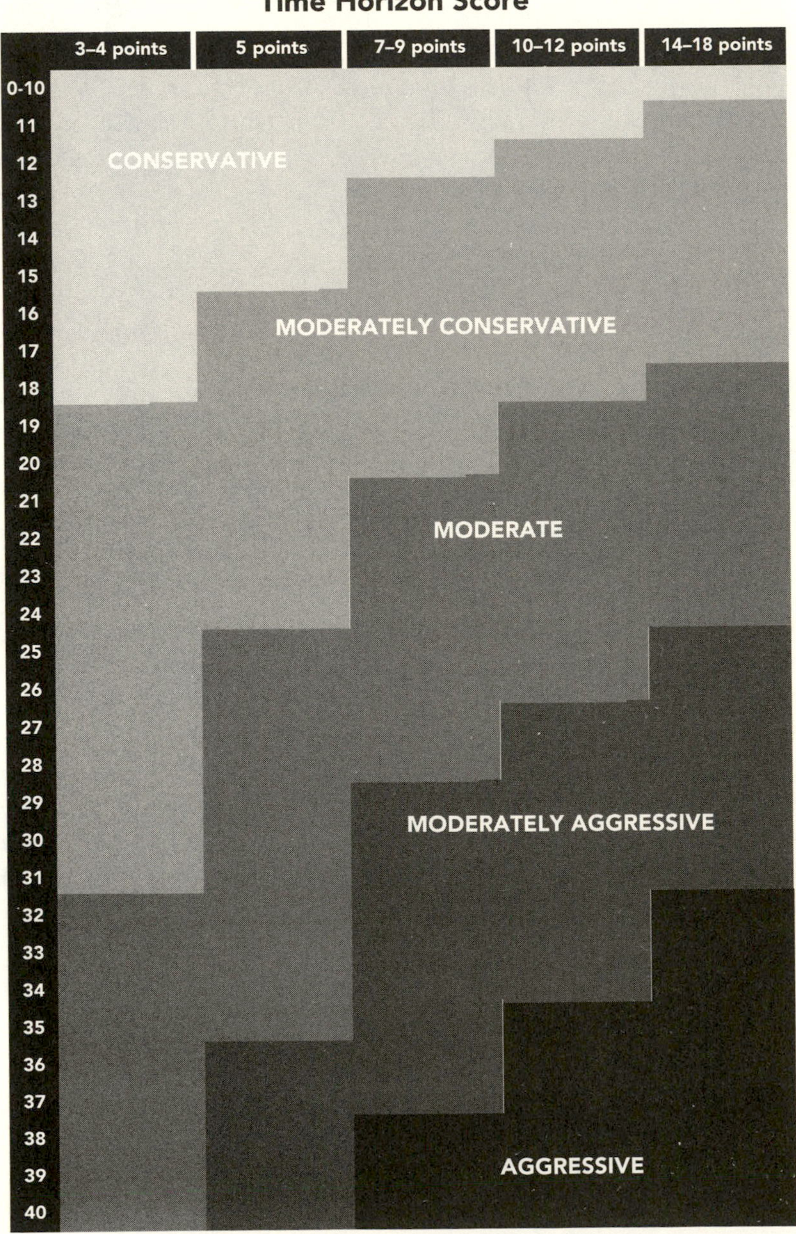

6. Reading the Fine Print: What to Look for in a Mutual Fund Prospectus and an Annual Report

Once you spot a fund that you think might suit your needs, call the mutual fund or your broker and ask for a prospectus and the latest annual report. The prospectus lists the fund's goals, restrictions, advisors, and fees. The annual report shows you what investments the fund is holding, and it reviews the fund's performance.

The Prospectus

The prospectus is a legal statement that describes the objectives of a specific investment. Every mutual fund is required to publish a prospectus, and to give investors a copy, free of charge. To get one, just call the fund itself.

Examine the prospectus carefully before investing. The most important pieces of information to look for are the detailed statements of the fund's investment policies (under "Key Features of the Fund"), the types of transactions the fund can execute, the types of securities that the fund can buy and sell (also under "Key Features of the Fund"), and the costs associated with buying the fund's shares and maintaining the investment (under "Summary of Expenses"). These costs are broken down by fee type.

More specifically, the prospectus includes the following:

- ***The fund's investment objectives.*** Make sure at the start that the fund's investment goals are in keeping with your own investment goals, and with your tolerance for risk. With mutual funds, as with other investments, the higher the risk, the greater the potential reward.
- ***The kind of securities the fund holds.*** Portfolios may include money market securities, bonds, stocks, precious metals and gold, options, warrants, and hedge transactions. This should be one of the first things you know about the fund, but it's wise to double-check and make sure the fund is investing in what you think it is.
- ***Investment minimums.*** Stock funds usually require an initial investment of $1,000 to $5,000. Subsequent purchases are less, often $50 to $500.
- ***Sales charges and fees.*** Mutual funds charge investors two main types of costs: sales loads and operating expenses. A *load* is a one-time sales commission the broker receives for selling the fund.

A *front-end load* means you pay a sales charge when you buy the fund. The charge can be as high as 8.5% of the purchase amount ($85 on a $1,000 investment), but it's more typically 4% to 6%. When you buy shares of a front-end-load fund, some of your investing dollars are used for the sales charge. So, if you invest $10,000 in a load fund with a 4% load, only $9,600 of your money is actually invested. You have to earn back $400 before you even begin to make a profit.

A *back-end load* is charged when you sell your shares. A specific type of back-end load, called a contingent deferred sales charge, decreases during the time you own your shares. It may reach zero if you hold your shares long enough.

Not all funds carry loads. Those that don't are called *no-load funds,* and a true no-load fund imposes no front- or back-end sales charges, which means that all of your investing dollars are going into the fund, not into commissions. I strongly urge you to invest only in no-load funds.

Operating expenses are just what the name implies: costs incurred by the fund in its day-to-day operations. Every fund is subject to some degree of operating expenses, which usually include the following:

Management fees, also called annual fees, are charged each year by all funds as the compensation for the fund manager. These fees are quoted as a percentage of the fund's average annual assets, and are often called the fund's operating expense ratio.

12(b)-1 fees (named after the regulation authorizing them) are annual fees assessed by some funds to cover the costs of marketing and distribution, as a percentage of the fund's total assets. For a fund to be considered no-load, its 12(b)-1 fee must be .25% or lower. These fees have no regulatory cap, and some funds charge another 1% or more. Fees are not paid directly by shareholders, but are taken out of the fund's current income before distribution to shareholders. So, the lower the fund's fees, the more the shareholder benefits.

Other expenses may cover administrative costs, maintenance fees, and costs resulting from customer reporting and servicing. (For more specific information on mutual fund costs, see Section 7 of this Appendix.)

- ***How often earnings are distributed.*** Funds distribute dividends and realized capital gains monthly, quarterly, semiannually, or even yearly. It may not be a good idea to invest in a stock fund late in the year; you could receive a large distribution of capital gains on which you'd owe taxes very soon. Ask the fund when distributions will be made, and postpone investing if it will affect your tax situation adversely.

• ***Recent change of the portfolio manager.*** There are turnovers in mutual fund management fairly often, and when the manager changes, you really don't know whether the new manager will match the previous manager's performance record. It's wise to find out whether or not the fund has recently changed managers.

The Annual Report

It's important to look at a fund's annual report both to evaluate a fund and to track its performance once you've invested in it. In the report you'll find information on how the fund did during the past year. There should be a somewhat detailed explanation, but if there isn't, you may have reason to do a little more research. The annual report also lists the trading costs that a fund incurs as it buys and sells securities. These are important to examine, as they can significantly affect your return, especially in a fund with a high turnover rate.

The annual report also includes a chart that shows how well the fund has performed compared to a standard market index during the last ten years (or for the life of the fund, if it hasn't been around that long). With this chart, it's easy to tell whether the fund is performing as well as other similar funds. And while the chart doesn't tell you everything—it doesn't give year-by-year performance, so if the fund has begun to go downhill, you won't be able to see that—the information that it does give is critical to your ability to evaluate a specific fund. Remember, though, that the manager responsible for that performance record may or may not be with the fund anymore. (For information on the fund's performance on a year-by-year basis, you can call the fund's 800 number and ask a fund representative, or you can go to *The Value Line Mutual Fund Survey* or *Morningstar No-Load Funds,* publications that are found in many public libraries.)

Once you begin investing in a specific fund, it's a good idea to follow not only the annual report, but other company reports as well. These might be distributed semiannually or even quarterly. Such reports will tell you what sectors the fund is investing in, and you'll be better able to understand and evaluate the fund's performance. For instance, suppose your fund is not performing as well as you'd hoped. If you look at what its holdings are, and find that 30% of the portfolio is in technology stocks, you can then compare it against the performance of technology stocks in general. If they are in a downturn as a group, then you'll know that the problem isn't just with your specific fund. And if you understand this, you'll be less likely to panic and sell prematurely.

7. Comparing Mutual Fund Costs

Although mutual fund operating expenses are usually lower than sales loads (typically between .5% and 1.75% of a fund's total assets), they are assessed annually. Those dollar amounts add up, and can become significant over time as your assets grow, so pay attention to operating expenses. It's helpful to think of investing as a business when looking at operating expenses; like any business, your hope is to keep expenses down.

Some comparisons can be beneficial, as operating expenses vary widely. But if you do compare expenses, be sure to compare the expenses of funds in the same category. The chart below shows average expenses of certain types of funds:

AVERAGE OPERATING EXPENSE RATIO

Fund Category	Actively Managed Funds	Index Funds
Domestic stocks		
Large-cap blend	1.34	0.61
Large-cap value	1.40	0.66
Large-cap growth	1.45	0.88
Medium-cap blend	1.47	0.33
Medium-cap value	1.45	n/a
Medium-cap growth	1.58	n/a
Small-cap blend	1.52	0.69
Small-cap value	1.55	0.25
Small-cap growth	1.68	0.25
International stock funds		
Foreign	1.74	0.93
World	1.86	n/a

Fund Category	Actively Managed Funds	Index Funds
Balanced asset allocation funds		
Domestic hybrid	1.30	0.20
Bond mutual funds		
Ultrashort bond	0.79	n/a
Short-term bond	0.83	0.45
Intermediate-term bond	0.98	0.39
Short government	1.03	n/a
Intermediate government	1.15	0.26
Short-term Muni	0.86	n/a
Intermediate-term Muni	0.97	n/a

Based on data reported by Morningstar, Inc., on 6/30/2000.

8. Comparing Individual Bonds and Bond Mutual Funds

	Individual Bonds	Bond Mutual Funds
Maturity	Set maturity date (up to 30 years).	No set maturity date. Many funds have a maturity range.
Income payments	Defined payments, usually semiannually, sometimes quarterly. Can be monthly if laddered.	Fluctuating monthly payments.
Diversification	To diversify, purchase multiple bonds.	Typically diversified.
Minimum investment	Depends on the type of bond; typically $5,000.	As low as $1,000 initially; $100 for subsequent investments.
Management	Selected by you or your advisor.	Professional management.
Risk	Generally no risk to principal if held to maturity.	Subject to principal risk and credit and call risks.
Commissions	You pay brokerage commissions or a markup (included in the price) on each buy or sell transaction.	You can select funds with no commissions.

	Individual Bonds	Bond Mutual Funds
Management fees and operating expenses	None.	You pay a percentage of invested assets for operating expenses and management of the fund.
Price	Retail investors usually pay more than fund managers when buying bonds, and receive less when selling because of smaller transactions.	Better pricing for bond fund managers because of the larger amount of bonds bought and sold.
Liquidation costs	You pay above costs if you sell before maturity.	None.

Source: *Schwab Center for Investment Research.*

9. Tax Equivalent Yield Table

The following chart demonstrates the potential advantages of tax-free investing. It shows tax-exempt yields and "taxable equivalent yields" for investors who fall into the highest marginal tax brackets in various states.

TAXABLE EQUIVALENT YIELD TABLE*

	Highest Marginal Tax Rates							
	Federal	CA	CT	MA	NJ	NY	NYC	OH
State Rate		9.30%	4.50%	12.00%	6.37%	6.85%	6.85%	7.50%
Combined State and Local Rate	39.60%	45.22%	42.32%	46.85%	43.45%	43.73%	46.43%	44.13%
Tax-Exempt Yields	**Taxable Equivalent Yields**							
	Exempt from Federal Tax Only	**Exempt from Federal, State, and Local Taxes**						
4.00%	6.62%	7.30%	6.93%	7.53%	7.07%	7.11%	7.47%	7.16%
4.50	7.45	8.21	7.80	8.47	7.96	8.00	8.40	8.05
5.00	8.28	9.13	8.67	9.41	8.84	8.89	9.33	8.95
5.50	9.11	10.04	9.54	10.35	9.73	9.77	10.27	9.84
6.00	9.93	10.95	10.40	11.29	10.61	10.66	11.20	10.74
6.50	10.76	11.87	11.27	12.23	11.49	11.55	12.13	11.63
7.00	11.59	12.78	12.14	13.17	12.38	12.44	13.07	12.53
7.50	12.42	13.69	13.00	14.11	13.26	13.33	14.00	13.42
8.00	13.25	14.60	13.87	15.05	14.15	14.22	14.93	14.32

*Taxable Equivalent Yields apply to investors subject to the highest marginal tax brackets. State tax rates given were effective as of October 1999 and are subject to change. The combined federal and state tax rate reflects the deduction of state and local taxes on federal returns. The information provided here should not be construed as tax advice. Please consult your advisor to determine your marginal tax rate and other relevant tax considerations of investing in municipal bonds. Although the information contained in this chart is based on sources that we believe are reliable, Charles Schwab & Co., Inc. assumes no responsibility for its completeness or accuracy. These yields are not intended to represent the yields of any particular investment.

10. Learning More About Financial Advisors

The first step in finding a financial advisor is to compile a list of potential advisors. Word of mouth is one of the best means of doing this. Ask other professionals—your lawyer or accountant, for example. Or ask a friend who you know uses an advisor. You can also contact the following organizations for more information:

- Schwab Advisor Source™
  888-774-3756 or any Schwab branch
  www.schwab.com (click on "Accounts and Services")
- The American College, Student Services (for Chartered Financial Consultants or CFCs)
  270 South Bryn Mawr
  Bryn Mawr, PA 19010
- American Institute of Certified Public Accountants' Personal Financial Planning Division
  1211 Avenue of the Americas
  New York, NY 10036
  888-777-7077
  www.aicpa.org
- Financial Planning Association
  800-322-4237
  www.fpanet.org
- *Money Magazine*
  www.money.com
- National Association of Personal Financial Advisors (NAPFA)
  355 West Dundee Road, Suite 200
  Buffalo Grove, IL 60089
  888-FEE-ONLY (333-6659)
  www.napfa.org

11. The Ins and Outs of Health Insurance

You may be wondering why a book on investing bothers to include information on health insurance. The reason is simple—if you don't know enough about health insurance to make informed and wise decisions, all your investments could be used up in a month if you or someone dependent on you encounters a catastrophic health issue. You know what health-care costs are like these days; a short hospital stay could do some damage to even a sizable portfolio. Good health care protects not only you, but your investments—and your future.

Generally speaking, there are two ways to go in terms of health insurance: managed care and traditional, fee-for-service policies (also called indemnity policies). Managed care typically offers lower cost and fewer choices. You deal with a specific group of doctors, usually at a specific hospital. At a doctor's visit, you typically pay only a co-payment, usually between $5 and $20. Prescriptions are inexpensive as well, and hospitalization and routine care such as checkups, mammograms, and childhood vaccinations are free, which is why managed care rather than fee-for-service is usually more economical for families with young children, where the major medical costs are by far in the preventative care category.

Fee-for-service costs more, but offers more choice. You decide which doctors you see and what hospitals you use. If you feel very strongly about seeing a doctor who does not participate in a managed-care plan, fee-for-service is probably your best choice. But you also pay the bills until they reach the amount of your deductible, and then the insurance company pays, usually around 80%. And you pay the total for costs that aren't covered, which include most kinds of routine care (checkups, mammograms, childhood vaccinations). As you can see, the biggest disadvantage of fee-for-service is its expense. It also requires substantially more paperwork than managed care does.

Now let's go back to managed care. Within that world there are HMOs, POSs, and PPOs:

- ***Health maintenance organizations (HMOs).*** With an HMO, you choose a "primary-care physician" from a list of doctors provided by the HMO. He or she is the doctor you will start with if you have a medical problem, and refer you to any other specialists he or she feels you should see. That specialist must also be a member of the HMO. Without that referral, the cost of your visit will not be covered by the HMO. Referrals can be difficult to get, and may take a few phone calls or an office visit to your primary-care doctor. Also, HMOs can be on the large side, causing some people to feel that they get lost in the shuffle.
- ***Point-of-service HMOs (POSs).*** POSs are a subcategory of HMOs. They aren't as stringent about referrals, meaning that you can see a doctor not authorized by your primary-care physician. But if you do, the HMO will pay less of the cost, perhaps 50% to 80%.
- ***Preferred provider plans (PPOs).*** A PPO is a group of doctors who have formed a sort of group practice. A PPO costs slightly more than an HMO, and it offers more choice. You still have a primary-care physician, but you can see someone in the group or outside of the group without a referral, as long as you're willing to pay.

Choosing a Health-Care Plan

The decision between a managed-care plan and fee-for-service is usually an obvious one, since fee-for-service policies are not usually available through company group plans. In terms of managed care, generally speaking, the lower the cost of premiums and co-payments, the more restricted your choices in terms of doctors and care.

Once you know what your choices are, become familiar with any plan you're considering. Ask around about the level of care that subscribers feel they're receiving, and look at a list of the plan's physicians and see if you can get information on any of those doctors. Read whatever printed material is available from the plan as well, including the fine print. One thing to look for there is the upward limit, meaning the maximum amount that the plan will pay in a year. It's wise to get a high upward limit, at least $1 million, as protection from financial ruin if you or someone in your family becomes seriously ill or injured.

What Happens to Health Insurance if You Leave Your Job?

If you leave an employer through which you've had group coverage, you have the option of continuing to keep that coverage for 18 months after you leave the job, thanks to legislation called COBRA (Consolidated Omnibus Budget Reconciliation Act). This can be a real relief, but bear in mind that continuing through COBRA may not be your best choice. You may be better off finding a new, long-term health insurance plan, rather than going for COBRA during the short term.

12. Medicare and Medigap: What They Will and Won't Cover

Medicare was founded in 1975 as a catastrophic health insurance plan for the elderly. With Medicare, it was hoped that the elderly could take care of themselves physically without ending up in poverty. The plan was that it would be available to everyone, regardless of previous illnesses or health. Benefits were tied to the age 65, at that time just a few years short of life expectancies. Today all Americans are eligible for Medicare at 65, even if they continue to work. There are two sides to Medicare. Under current law, they work like this:

Part A is hospital insurance, and it's free if you or your spouse have paid into Social Security for at least ten years. If you haven't, the premium varies (as of 1997, it was $311 per month[3]), and if you're receiving Social Security, the premium is deducted from your payments. This plan covers all hospitalization expenses for 60 days, after you've paid a substantial deductible before coverage. For the year 2000, that deductible was $776 for a hospital stay of up to 60 days. This sounds good, and it's certainly a help, but there are some drawbacks. First, after 60 days you pay approximately $194 per day for days 61 to 90, and $388 per day for days 91 to 150 (for the year 2000). After 150 days, you pay the entire amount. Second, the deductible you pay isn't an annual fee. It applies to each hospitalization, so if you're hospitalized three times in a year, you're paying that deductible each time.

Part B is medical insurance, with a premium of around $50 a month (deducted from your Social Security payments). Part B is optional, and you'd use it only if you weren't covered by another health plan. It requires an annual deductible of $100, plus co-payments of 20%, or 50% for most outpatient mental health care. It does not cover long-term care (extended care in a nursing home, which we'll discuss later in this Appendix), dental care, prescriptions, eyeglasses, hearing aids, or expenses incurred outside of the United States. Not all doctors participate in Medicare; nonparticipating doctors can charge Medicare an additional amount. (For more information on Medicare, see **www.medicare.gov** or call 800-772-1213 and ask that a handbook be sent to you.)

As you can see, Medicare is a long way from complete health coverage. You cannot count on it for all of your health-care needs, so once you're eligible for Medicare, you'll probably want to supplement it. You can do so with your regular health insurance, through an HMO or PPO, as described above. Or you can use Medigap.

Medigap is a term that's been coined to refer to a number of supplementary insurance plans designed to supplement Medicare. These plans are sold not by the government but by private insurance companies, and they cover some of the things that Medicare doesn't—deductibles and co-insurance under Part B, for example, as well as other services and supplies that Medicare doesn't cover. Currently, the plans are lettered A through J, and they range from the most limited and least expensive coverage to the most comprehensive and expensive.

[3]Jane Bryant Quinn, *Making the Most of Your Money* (Simon & Schuster, 1997).

When you look for a Medigap policy, remember, as with any type of insurance, that the quality of the insurance company is key. Consider only companies with good ratings. You'll need to check with an insurance rating service to do this. You might also check with your current insurance company, a Medicare HMO, and the American Association of Retired Persons (AARP).

13. Disability Insurance

What follows are suggestions about choosing a disability insurance provider and policy.

Choosing a Disability Insurance Provider

If your company's policy is not adequate, or if your company doesn't offer it or you're self-employed, you may want to consider an individual policy. I would encourage you to do two things. First, go for quality. Make sure the insurance providers you consider not only offer disability insurance, but specialize in it. The issues are complex, and the policy you buy will be only as good as the company behind it. And, second, as always, shop around. When you're ready to buy a policy, do your best to find the most reasonable plan that suits your needs. Because disability insurance is on the expensive side, comparison shopping is even more important than usual. If you can't find a policy within your financial reach, you might consider buying what you can for now, and buying a more comprehensive policy when you can afford it.

Choosing a Disability Policy

Make sure any policy you consider meets the following criteria:

- ***It's guaranteed renewable.*** This means that you don't have to qualify each year for your benefits. You don't want to deal with a company that tries to make you qualify each and every year. Once is enough.
- ***It's portable.*** This applies if your coverage is through your employer, and it means that you're still covered if you change employers. Individual policies through employers, rather than traditional group policies, are usually portable.
- ***It has "owner's occupation" coverage.*** This is called "own occ" for short, and it doesn't sound like much, but it's very important. It answers this question: Will I be paid if I can't perform my

current job, or only if I can't do *any* job? There's a big difference there. With owner's occupation coverage (as opposed to "any occupation" or "any occ"), you are paid if you can't do the work you currently do, not just any work (menial labor, for example). The cost of this coverage is considerable, but to my mind it's worth it.

• ***It covers you for illness as well as injury.*** Some policies cover only injury-related disability. Make sure your coverage applies to both illness and injury.

• ***It will cover 60% to 70% of your current income in benefits.*** An adequate policy is one that would cover a minimum of 60% of your gross annual salary, an amount that's probably close to your take-home pay. The higher the coverage, the more expensive the policy. Be aware, however, that some insurers have a limit on the amount you can receive. If your income is high, some insurers may cover you for only 40% of your earnings. There are insurers who offer high maximums.

• ***It has "residual benefits."*** If you can work only part-time, you should be able to receive a portion of your benefits. A policy with residual benefits pays according to how much you can work, so that you're covered if you can work part-time, instead of an all-or-nothing approach. It's a policy that pays according to how much you can work.

• ***It has a waiting period of 3 to 6 months.*** The waiting period, also called the *elimination period,* is the period of time that you have to wait until the insurance company begins paying you. It's typically between three and six months. If your savings are on the small side, a maximum waiting period of three months is wise. If you're better able to live off your investments and savings, lengthening the waiting period is a good way to reduce the cost of your disability insurance. For example, if you have at least six months' income in an emergency fund, you may be all right with a six-month waiting period.

• ***It covers you until age 65 at least.*** Sixty-five is the minimum age you should consider; you may want a policy that covers you for life.

• ***It covers you for disability caused by mental and emotional factors as well as physical ones.*** If you are in a stressful job or industry, you may want to make sure you're covered for disability resulting from stress-related mental and emotional disorders as well as physical disabilities.

14. Durable Power of Attorney for Health Care

A durable power of attorney for health care (DPOAHC) establishes two things: your wishes concerning the medical treatment you receive and the use of life support, and who you want to have the authority to make health-care decisions for you, in the event you are unable to do so.

A durable power of attorney for health care varies from state to state. As an example, in California, you have three general choices:

- I want my life to be prolonged as long as possible, without regard to my condition, my chances for recovery, or the cost of the procedures or recovery.
- I want life-sustaining treatment to be provided unless I am in a coma or persistent/ongoing vegetative state, which two doctors, including my attending physician, reasonably conclude in writing to be irreversible. If my doctors have reached this conclusion, I do not want life-sustaining treatment to be provided or continued.
- I do not want my life to be unnaturally or artificially or forcibly prolonged, unless there is some hope that both my physical and mental health may be restored, and I do not want life-sustaining treatment to be provided or continued if the burdens of the treatment outweigh the expected benefits. I want my agent to consider the relief of suffering and the quality of the possible extension of my life in making decisions concerning life-sustaining treatment. At all times my dignity shall be maintained.

The second part of the document is the *who*. You give someone the authority to take you off of life support if there is no possibility of your living without life support. That person can make other health-care decisions on your behalf as well, if you are unable to do so. This person is called your *agent*, and it's wise to name two additional people to act as co-agents, in the event that your agent can't be reached. Choosing people for this responsibility is a highly individual decision. A spouse may or may not be the best choice. You need to choose people who love you and know you well, but who are also strong enough to follow your wishes. It is critical that you trust their judgment, because while you can try to be specific about what you want, it's always possible that the situation that arises will be one you haven't discussed. It's also important that you and your agent feel similarly about right-to-die issues. Even when you know, without a doubt, that someone does not wish to have their life prolonged by life support, giving the authorization to have them removed from life support is a tough thing to do. So choose wisely. You are truly putting your life in their hands. Once you have chosen someone, be sure to talk with them, and to make sure they are willing to handle this responsibility.

Every state recognizes a DPOAHC, though the forms themselves vary from state to state. You can obtain them at just about any hospital or public health agency. You just have to be certain that the form you're using is valid in your state; one state may not recognize another state's DPOAHC. Once you've filled it in, keep a copy for yourself, then give copies to your doctor, your agent, and your co-agents. You should also send a copy to your HMO or health insurance company and ask that it be part of your medical record. Also remember to update it or do a new form if and when you need to designate a new agent. Don't confuse DPOAHC with a power of attorney or durable power of attorney. Those documents deal with the management and control of your assets; a DPOAHC deals only with health matters. It also differs from a living will, which is not as effective as a DPOAHC. While a living will does give you a way to express your wishes, it does not appoint an agent to act in your behalf. Sometimes a living will and a DPOAHC are incorporated into the same document. In this case, it could be said that the living will/DPOAHC does appoint an agent.

What follows is a sample DPOAHC used in California:

> *I, ______, do hereby designate and appoint ______ as my attorney-in-fact (agent) to make health care decisions for me as authorized in this document.*
>
> *If I become incapable of giving informed consent to health care decisions, I hereby grant to my agent full power and authority to make health care decisions for me, including the right to consent, refuse consent, or withdraw consent to any care, treatment, service, or procedures to maintain, diagnose, or treat a physical or mental condition, and to receive and to consent to the release of medical information, subject to the statement of desires, special provisions, and limitations set out below.*
>
> *I do not want my life to be prolonged, and I do not want life-sustaining treatment to be provided or continued if the burdens of the treatment outweigh the expected benefits. I want my agent to consider the relief of suffering and the*

quality as well as the extent of the possible extension of my life in making decisions concerning life-sustaining treatment.

I understand that this power of attorney will exist for ______ years from the date I execute this document unless I establish a shorter time. If I am unable to make health care decisions for myself when this power of attorney expires, the authority I have granted my agent will continue to exist until the time when I become able to make health care decisions for myself.

I certify my name to this Durable Power of Attorney for Health Care on the ______ day of ______, 20______, at ______, ______.

(Signed) ________________________________

15. Long-Term-Care Insurance

Before you buy long-term-care insurance, you're wise to do some homework in two areas: the insurance company you choose, and the specific policy you're considering.

First, the provider. It can pay to be picky about the insurance company you choose. You have to ask a lot of questions, and be certain you're getting satisfactory answers. As of this writing, the number of insurance companies that sell long-term-care insurance is in the hundreds, and that number is changing constantly. Be sure that any insurance company you consider has a good track record and that it is committed to providing long-term-care insurance. You want to make sure this company has a substantial long-term-care insurance business, and that it's going to be there when you need it, which may be 30 years from now.

As for specific policies, there are a lot of variables, so it's important to compare policies carefully, and to understand exactly what you're getting. For example, you have to make sure that your policy will keep pace with inflation, and that it provides adequate coverage and includes all of the benefits it should. You'll need to do some comparison shopping where premiums are concerned, and you'll need to make sure that the fine print doesn't contain restrictions that cancel out significant benefits.

One key variable has to do with "activities of daily living" (ADLs), which are everyday tasks that insurers use to gauge whether or not a person needs some kind of long-term care. You should look closely at the list of ADLs that any insurer you're considering uses. Commonly included ADLs are that a patient be ambulatory, be able to bathe himself, feed himself, clothe himself, transfer himself (to and from chairs and beds, for example) without help, be continent, and use the toilet. A key consideration in choosing long-term-care insurance is how the policy both defines and measures ADLs. Policies often stipulate that if an individual cannot do two or more ADLs, he or she may be eligible for long-term-care coverage. But the list of ADLs and their definitions vary from policy to policy, so this is a place to pay close attention.

Choosing a Long-Term-Care Policy

As you consider long-term-care policies, make sure you understand the following options:

- ***Comprehensive coverage.*** This means that your coverage is not limited to nursing-home care. To my mind, it's the best choice. Your policy should include all levels of care: skilled, intermediate, custodial, medical, and therapeutic. It should also include coverage for *all* illnesses and injuries, including mental diseases such as Alzheimer's, and it should cover you if you cannot perform at least two tasks from the list of ADLs above. Types of coverage differ among states, so be sure you know what you're being offered. If comprehensive coverage does not include home care, you may want to consider a home-care option as well.
- ***A lifetime benefit period.*** This means you're covered for life, instead of for a specified number of years, and it will probably cost more. Statistically, the average stay in a nursing home is around three years (but almost three times that for Alzheimer's patients), so you may be wise to consider at least a five-year policy. But it's a personal call.
- ***A zero-day elimination period.*** This means how long you have to pay before the insurance company begins paying, typically 30 to 60 days. If you can afford it, zero-day elimination is a good choice. This means the insurance company begins paying as soon as you require long-term care. The longer the elimination period, the lower your premiums. If you choose a longer elimination period, be sure you have the emergency funds to cover that first part of your stay.
- ***An inflation rider.*** This means how much the amount of your daily benefit will increase per year. An inflation rider of 5% compounded annually is common.

• ***A premium waiver.*** This means that you would not have to pay premiums if you started receiving benefits (i.e., if you required long-term care).

• ***Protection for late or missed payments.*** We all know that as we age, our memories tend to become less efficient, even in the absence of such extreme conditions as Alzheimer's. Paying the bills is often one of the things we can forget to do. Make sure that your policy is not automatically canceled if you miss one or a few payments. You can also ask that the provider contact a friend or someone in your family if your policy is in danger of being canceled due to nonpayment.

• ***Coverage is noncancelable.*** This means that the insurance company cannot cancel your policy or raise your rates, which it can do if your policy is only guaranteed renewable.

• ***Whether a hospital stay is required for coverage to start.*** You're wise to make sure your policy does not require a hospital stay for coverage to start. A minority of those in nursing homes were hospitalized before entering.

Before You Buy

As important as long-term-care insurance is, you shouldn't buy it unless you can afford it, so once you get some quotes, make sure you can handle the premiums, not just now but in the future, when you're more likely to need it. It's my opinion that for some people, long-term-care insurance can be crucial enough that it's worth giving up something else for it. But only you can make that decision—and don't go so far as to use your savings to pay your premiums.

Tax Implications of Long-Term-Care Insurance

It's possible that the premiums you pay for long-term-care insurance are deductible as a medical expense. This is true if your medical expenses total 7.5% of your AGI (adjusted gross income), and it is the result of an amendment to the IRS code called the Health Insurance Portability and Accountability Act of 1996, which has applied since January 1, 1997. The tax deduction applies to long-term-care policies purchased before 1997, and to policies purchased in and after 1997 that meet certain criteria. A policy must state whether or not it meets these criteria and is therefore potentially deductible. For more information, you can contact the Health

Insurance Counseling and Advocacy Program, or HICAP (800-434-0222).

16. Life Insurance[4]

This worksheet shows you how to calculate life insurance needs based on your goals and assets.

1. Immediate cash needs at death	**Self/spouse**
Administration expenses—court costs, legal and accounting fees, final expenses, and other miscellaneous costs to settle estate (for a rough estimate, use 5% of the value of your estate)	______
Personal/business debt—any debt for which your estate may be liable (e.g., credit cards, loans, lines of credit)	______
Real estate loans, i.e., any loan secured by real estate (e.g., first and second mortgages, equity lines, contracts for deed)	______
Subtotal—immediate cash needs at death	$______(1)

2. Future cash needs	
Family income (6 times gross annual income) (amount needed to cover daily needs for family)	______
Funds needed to educate your children	______
Spousal retirement fund (optional)	______
Other (special needs, if any)	______
Subtotal—future cash needs	$______(2)
Total cash needs (lines 1 + 2)	$______(3)

[4]This worksheet is provided as a guide to assist you in determining how much insurance you may need. For your unique situation, please consult with an insurance agent or financial advisor.

3. Total assets—what you have now

Investments, savings, and cash	______
Lump-sum employee benefits	______
Other assets	______
Total assets	$______(4)
Total coverage needed = total cash needs (3) – total assets (4)	$______

Choosing an Insurance Company

There are two parts to making a wise decision in terms of buying insurance. First, narrowing your search down to a few good insurance companies; and, second, choosing your policy from among those offered by those companies.

Choosing a good insurance company is crucial, and it can take some time. The main things to consider are the company's financial strength, its stability, and its ratings within the industry. Regardless of the type of insurance you're looking for, any insurance company you consider should have a good track record in the area you're interested in, and a good rating from at least two of the companies listed in Section 17 of this Appendix.

Choosing a Policy

- ***Know what you want.*** Before you start looking, know what you want—the type of insurance, the amount, and the coverage it should include to meet your family's needs.
- ***Check group rates first.*** In general, group rates are lower than individual rates, so if insurance is offered through your employer, look there first. That's where you'll usually find the best rates.
- ***Do some comparison shopping.*** If you can't participate in a group plan, shop around to find the most reasonable coverage you can. This is definitely a time to do some comparison shopping; rates can vary substantially.
- ***Get quotes from at least four companies.*** The easiest way to do this is to use a free price-quoting service. You tell them what you're looking for, and they give you a list of the most reasonable policies that meet your needs. If you're considering changing policies, Consumer Federation of America Insurance Group (202-387-

6121), for a fee of $40, will compare your current policy with your prospective one.

• ***Make sure the policies you compare are offering the same coverage.*** You should compare *deductibles* (how much you pay before the insurance company pays), *premiums* (how much you pay, usually on a regular basis, such as monthly, quarterly, or annually, for the insurance coverage), and *co-payments* (the portion of each claim that you pay). Also find out how long the *elimination period* is (also called the waiting period—the amount of time before you qualify for benefits), and exactly what is included in your coverage and excluded from it. Remember, this is very definitely a time to read the fine print.

• ***To lower premiums, consider raising your deductibles.*** By increasing the amount of your deductibles, you can sometimes lower your premiums significantly.

• ***Shop online.*** Shopping online can often simplify the buying process, and save you time and money. You can get free quotes and answers to your questions immediately, and you can submit your request online when you're ready. In the case of life insurance, it's possible to get the qualifying process started over the phone or online.

• ***Review your policy and rates regularly.*** Once you have term life insurance, remember that it pays to do your homework and to review your insurance rates regularly. Rates change frequently, and it's unlikely that your insurance company will tell you if lower rates are available.

17. Insurance Rating Systems

There are a handful of companies (five as of this writing, which are listed below) whose business it is to rate insurance providers. I encourage you to get these ratings for any insurance provider you're considering, and to consider only insurers who have good ratings (a ranking of 3 or above in the table) from three of the five rating companies, and no mediocre ratings at all.

You can learn the ratings for an insurance provider you're considering in several ways:

• You can contact the rating companies directly. The companies, their phone numbers, and the information you'll get (it varies from company to company) are below. The most commonly used companies are A.M. Best, Standard & Poor's, and Weiss.

Rating Company	Phone	Information Provided
Standard & Poor's ***www.standardandpoors.com***	*212-438-2400*	*Free ratings on up to five insurers*
Fitch ***www.dcrco.com***	*800-853-4824*	*Free ratings on up to three insurers*
Moody's ***www.moodys.com***	*212-553-0377*	*Free ratings on up to three insurers per call*
Weiss Ratings ***www.weissratings.com***	*800-289-9222*	*$7.95 on Web site. A rating by phone is $15, a one-page report is $25, a more detailed report is $45*
A.M. Best ***www.ambest.com***	*908-439-2200, ext. 5742*	*Free ratings on up to three insurers per call*

• You can also find ratings by using a publication called *The Insurance Forum* (P.O. Box 256-J, Ellettsville, IN 47429; 812-876-6502), which puts out a ratings issue giving insurer's ratings from four of the five ratings companies. (A.M. Best does not allow its ratings to be included.) This publication, available at many libraries, contains a wealth of information. In addition to ratings, it tells you what the ratings mean, lists insurance providers suitable for very conservative consumers, and lists insurers to be wary of.

• You can call the insurance provider directly and ask for its rating from each rating company. I'm hesitant to suggest this because providers with less-than-stellar ratings don't always disclose them.

You need one more thing for an insurer's rating to be meaningful: You need to understand the particular rating system that the company uses. Unfortunately, the companies use different systems, so an A+ doesn't mean the same thing from company to company. The rating companies and the rating systems they use follow. The table does not include the lowest ratings. Also, ratings in the same rank are not necessarily equivalent to each other.

Rank Number	A.M. Best	S&P	Moody's	Duff & Phelps	Weiss
1	A++	AAA	Aaa	AAA	A+
2	A+–	AA+	Aa1	AA+	A
3	A	AA	Aa2	AA	A–
4	A–	AA–	Aa3	AA–	B+
5	B++	A+	A1	A+	B
6	B+	A	A2	A	B–
7	B	A–	A3	A–	C+
8	B–	BBB+	Baa1	BBB+	C
9	C++	BBB	Baa2	BBB	C–
10	C+	BBB–	Baa3	BBB–	D+*
11	C	BB+*	Ba1*	BB+*	D

**At this rating and below, The Insurance Forum puts the insurance company on its Watch List.*

18. Some Tax Implications of Charitable Giving

Donated Asset	Advantages	Restrictions
Cash (includes proceeds from life insurance and retirement plans)	Usually fully deductible	Deductions to public charities limited to 50% of your AGI*
	Least complicated choice	Deductions to private foundations limited to 30% of your AGI
	Excess deductions can be carried forward for 5 years	You must itemize your deductions to claim a cash deduction
Appreciated securities	Usually fully deductible at market value if held for more than 1 year	Deduction to public charity limited to 30% of your AGI

*AGI = adjusted gross income.

Donated Asset	Advantages	Restrictions
Appreciated securities *(con't)*	Excess deductions can be carried forward for 5 years	Deduction to private foundation usually limited to 20% of your AGI*
	No capital gains tax for appreciated assets donated to charity	If held for 1 year or less, deduction limited to cost basis
Tangible personal property	Can include almost anything	Deduction limited to 20% to 50% of AGI, depending on recipient and whether property is appreciated
	Usually fully deductible at market value, if held for more than 1 year	If property is unrelated to mission of charity, deduction limited to lesser of cost basis or current fair market value
	Excess deductions can be carried forward for 5 years	
	No capital gains tax for appreciated assets donated to charity	Property may be complicated or costly for charity to dispose of
Your time	Opportunity for personal involvement	May involve sustained commitment of time
	Expenses related to volunteering are deductible	The value of volunteer time is not deductible

*AGI = adjusted gross income.

Tool	Advantages	Restrictions
Direct gift during your lifetime	Immediate benefit for charity	You need to research and choose recipients
	Provides ongoing tax benefits	Deduction subject to AGI* restrictions†
	No associated costs	
Direct gift at death (bequest)	Assets retained during lifetime	Defers support for charities until your death
Donor-advised fund	Contributions usually fully deductible in current year	Deduction subject to AGI restrictions†
	Flexible giving in future years	Fund trustees have final authority over grants
	Low fees and expenses	Less flexible than a trust or private foundation
Pooled income fund	Contributions partially deductible in current year	Deduction subject to AGI restrictions†
	Income for the donor or other noncharitable beneficiary	Income is variable and taxable
	Low fees and expenses	Less flexible than a trust or private foundation
Charitable remainder trust	Contributions partially deductible in current year	Deduction subject to AGI restrictions†
	Income for the donor or other noncharitable beneficiary	Income is generally taxable
	Assets eventually transferred to specified charity	Some types of CRTs cannot accept future donations
		Fees and expenses may be substantial

*AGI = adjusted gross income.
†AGI restrictions: Deduction limited to 20% to 50% of AGI, depending on assets contributed, length of ownership, and recipient organization, but may be carried forward for 5 years.

Tool	Advantages	Restrictions
Charitable lead trust	Generates income for charity	Tax treatment is complex
	Assets returned to donor or other noncharitable beneficiary	Some types cannot accept future donations
		Fees and expenses may be substantial
Your own private foundation	Full control over distributions to charities	Must distribute a minimum percentage of assets annually
	Opportunity to create family legacy	Tax treatment is complex
		Set-up costs and administrative costs may be substantial

Source: Schwab Fund for Charitable Giving.

19. Learning More About Charitable Giving

The following are organizations that provide information on charitable giving and volunteering:

- The Council of Better Business Bureaus (**www.give.org** or 703-276-0100)
- The Council on Foundations (**www.cof.org** or 202-466-6512)
- The Foundation Center (**www.fdncenter.org** or 212-620-4230)
- Philanthropic Research, Inc. (**www.guidestar.org** or 757-229-4631)
- The Schwab Fund for Charitable Giving (**www.schwabcharitable.org** or 800-746-6216)
- Claude Rosenberg's Newtithing™ Group (**www.newtithing.org** or 415-274-2765)

GLOSSARY

1099-DIV form The IRS form from your brokerage or mutual fund that tells you how much income you received during the year.

12(b)-1 fees Annual fees assessed by some mutual funds to cover the costs of marketing and distribution, as a percentage of the fund's total assets. For a fund to be considered no-load, it's 12(b)-1 fee must be .25% or lower.

401(k) plan A defined contribution plan in which your employer takes money directly from your salary and places it in a tax-deferred retirement account, which means that you don't pay taxes on this money until you retire or withdraw it. The decision about how and where the money is invested is usually yours. Employers often match your contributions, sometimes as high as 50 cents on the dollar. The name comes from the number of a paragraph in the IRS code.

403(b) plan Basically a 401(k) plan in the world of charitable and nonprofit organizations, including educational institutions. Your contribution is deducted directly from your salary before taxes, and your employer can contribute. Most employees participating in 403(b)s are allowed to contribute no more than 5% of their annual salary. This name comes from the IRS code.

actively managed mutual fund A mutual fund in which one or more individuals work to outperform the market by handpicking the investments to include in the fund.

after-tax rate of return A rate of return that takes taxes into account—a key factor since taxes are the largest single drag on your investment return.

annual distribution date In a mutual fund, the date that the fund pays capital gains and dividends, typically at the end of the year. Also called the "ex-dividend date."

annual report A financial statement issued each year by a corporation or mutual fund. It lists assets, liabilities, and earnings, as well as some historical information. Each of the company's shareholders receives a copy of the annual report.

asset A property that has monetary value, including personal assets (e.g., house, car, jewelry) and financial assets, such as savings and investments.

asset allocation The process of deciding how to divide your money among the three types of asset classes: stocks, bonds, and cash equivalents. You make this decision based on your tolerance for risk and your time horizon.

asset allocation fund A mutual fund that mirrors a specific asset allocation pie chart and typically includes a mix of stocks, bonds, and cash equivalents to meet a specific growth objective. This type of fund allows you to diversify within investment classes and among them with one investment. Over time, the fund manager reallocates the fund's assets based on changing market conditions, so that your asset allocation remains the same, despite the market's fluctuations.

asset class One of the three major types of investments: stocks, bonds, and cash equivalents.

back-end load A sales charge on a mutual fund that is applied when you sell shares of the fund (as opposed to a front-end load, applied when you buy shares).

beneficiary The person or organization designated to receive the funds or other property from a trust, insurance policy, or retirement account.

blend fund A mutual fund that invests in a combination of funds and includes both growth and value stocks.

blue-chip stock Generally speaking, the stock of a large, well-established company. Blue-chip stocks typically offer less risk because of their solid track records.

bond A type of investment that is similar to an IOU from a corporation or a municipal or federal government. You loan the borrower some money, and in return it promises to repay the full amount on a specific date and pay you interest in the meantime.

bond fund A mutual fund that includes only bonds—typically corporate, municipal, or U.S. government bonds.

bond maturity The lifetime of a bond, concluding when the final payment of that obligation is due.

broad-based growth fund A mutual fund that is specifically aimed at long-term capital growth with minimal risk.

broad-based index fund An index fund based on an index that includes a large portion of the market, rather than being narrowly focused.

capital gain The profit you receive when you sell an investment for more than you paid for it. Capital gains are taxable income and must be reported to the IRS on your tax return.

capital gains distribution A payment you receive when your mutual fund makes a profit by selling some of the securities in its portfolio. Capital gains distributions are usually made annually, often at the end of the calendar year.

capitalization The total stock market value of all shares of a company's stock.

cash-equivalent investment An investment that you can easily convert into cash, such as money market mutual funds, Treasury bills, and certificates of deposit (CDs).

certificate of deposit (CD) A type of investment made with a financial institution, such as a bank or savings and loan. You deposit a specified amount for a specified period of time, at a preset, fixed interest rate. CDs are FDIC-insured.

Certified Financial Planner (CFP) A professional planner who has done the following: met the Certified Financial Planner Board of Standards' requirements in education, experience, and ethical conduct; passed a ten-hour comprehensive examination in investment, tax, estate, retirement, and insurance planning; and agreed to follow a code of ethics. CFP and Certified Financial Planner are federal trademarks owned by the CFP board.

Certified Public Accountant (CPA) A professional who specializes in financial planning. He or she may also have earned a personal financial specialist, or PFS, designation from the American Institute of Certified Public Accountants.

charitable lead trust A trust that enables you to donate assets to a charity and generate income for the charity. The assets are eventually transferred back to you, your family, or another non-charitable beneficiary of your choice.

charitable remainder trust A trust that allows you to donate your assets to charity and then to provide yourself (or your beneficiary) with income. You contribute your assets to the trust, and you receive a tax deduction for the current year, based on the value of the asset less the present value of the future income. Payments from the trust can be fixed or variable, and are generally taxable for the recipient. Assets are transferred to the charity when the trust terminates.

charitable trust A trust that you set up for a qualified charity so that you can leave all or part of your estate to that charity or nonprofit organization. A charitable trust can be a living trust or a testamentary trust. A charitable trust allows you to retain some interest in the assets in the form of either the income stream or the principal. You receive a tax benefit for the portion of the donated gift, allowing you to maximize the tax advantages of your giving.

Chartered Financial Analyst (CFA) A financial analyst who has met certain standards of experience, knowledge, and conduct, as determined by the Institute of Chartered Financial Analysts. The successful candidate must pass three examinations covering economics, security analysis, portfolio management, financial accounting, and standards of conduct.

common stock Securities that represent an ownership interest in a company (as opposed to preferred stock, in which stockholders usually receive preferential treatment). Common stocks are classified in three groups: *blue-chip stocks, growth stocks,* and *small-cap stocks.* (See these terms for more information.)

compounding The growth that results from investment income being reinvested. Compound growth has a snowball effect because both the original investment and the income from that investment are reinvested.

concentrated equity Holding a large amount of one company's stock in your portfolio. A concentrated equity position is usually due to company stock options, but it can also be the result of inherited stock. People use different numbers to define concentrated equity. I consider it to be holding somewhere around 30% of your portfolio in one stock.

Core & Explore™ A model for the stock part of your portfolio in which you include a combination of index and actively managed funds. Broad-based index funds, which are designed to track the performance of a specific section of the market, form the core of your portfolio, and actively managed mutual funds, which are managed by individuals who handpick stocks and try to outperform the market, explore your upside potential.

cost basis What you paid for an investment, as opposed to what it's worth.

defined benefit plan An employer-sponsored retirement plan in which your employer alone funds your retirement plan, and to which you don't contribute. These plans are open only to vested employees, those who have been employed for a certain time, typically between five and ten years. How much you receive when you retire is calculated according to a formula that considers your salary and the length of your employment.

defined contribution plan An employer-sponsored retirement plan in which you, your employer, or both of you contribute to your retirement account. Unlike defined benefit plans, these plans allow you, the employee, to have some say in how and where your money is invested. In some cases, the employee is responsible for all of those decisions. Defined contribution plans are very popular, and include 401(k)s, 403(b)s, and ESOPs, to name a few. You do not have to be vested to benefit from the plan.

direct gift In charitable giving, an outright donation of cash, tangible personal property, or securities to charities during your lifetime, or at the time of your death, through your will.

disability insurance Insurance that protects your income in the event of illness or injury. You purchase it and pay premiums, and the insurance company, if you're injured or ill and therefore unable to work, pays you a portion of your salary. Payments are typically around 60% to 70% of your gross income.

discretionary account A brokerage account in which you, the customer, allow a third party to act on your behalf in buying and selling securities. The third party has discretion as to the choice of securities, prices, and timing, subject to limitations specified in the agreement.

diversification The allocation of money among different types of investments such as stocks, fixed-income investments, and cash equivalents in a portfolio in order to balance your expected returns with your tolerance for risk.

dividend The part of the income earned by a company issuing stock that is distributed to shareholders. You can specify that your dividends be reinvested to buy more shares, or that they be paid to you in cash.

dollar cost averaging Investing the same dollar amount in securities at scheduled intervals over the long term, with the aim being to lower your average cost per share over time.

domestic stock mutual fund One that invests primarily in stocks issued by U.S. companies. These funds are classified according to size and goals. Size is measured by the companies' median market capitalization: *large-cap stock, mid-cap stock,* and *small-cap stock.* The investing goals of mutual funds are classified as *growth, value,* and *blend.* (See the glossary entries for the italicized terms for more information.)

donor-advised fund A type of fund offered by a number of public charities. Contributions to a donor-advised fund are fully deductible (subject to AGI restrictions), and when you give through a donor-advised fund, you aren't liable for capital gains tax when the fund sells any assets that have appreciated. Once you donate assets to a donor-advised fund, those assets are the property of the fund, and are no longer part of your taxable estate. Your contribution is invested and grows tax-free. You can recommend grants from the fund to any qualifying charity.

durable power of attorney for health care (DPOAHC) A legal document that specifies what type of medical treatment and life support you want if you are incapacitated and unable to make the decision yourself. It also allows the person of your choosing to make those decisions for you, guaranteeing that your wishes will be followed.

earnings A company's net income or profit, usually quoted in millions of dollars.

earnings per share, or EPS A company's total earnings for a period (its net income minus preferred dividends) divided by the number of common shares outstanding. For example, a company with earnings of $50 million and 20 million shares outstanding would have an EPS of $2.50. A company's EPS is meaningful when you compare it to earlier EPS numbers for the same company and to similar companies. Your hope is that the company's EPS is increasing.

education IRA (EIRA) A trust or custodial account established to help pay the higher education expenses of a child, grandchild, or other designated beneficiary who is a minor. The EIRA is managed by the person establishing the account (the parent or guardian, for example). Eligible contributions to EIRAs are not deductible. Amounts deposited in the account grow tax-free until distributed, and the child won't owe tax on any withdrawal from the account if the child's qualified higher education expenses at an eligible educational institution for the year equal or exceed the amount of the withdrawal. Contributions are limited to $2,000 each year.

Eligibility to make EIRA contributions depends on the income, not on the relationship to the child. Married taxpayers filing jointly with earnings of $220,000 or less, and single taxpayers with earnings of $110,000 or less, are eligible to contribute to EIRAs. An EIRA may limit the financial aid available to a child.

Employee Stock Ownership Plan See *ESOP.*

employer-sponsored retirement plan A retirement plan offered and sponsored by the company that employs you.

EPS See *earnings per share.*

escheating A situation in which, after your death, your assets go to the state if you have no known relatives and no valid will.

ESOP An acronym for "employee stock ownership plan," a plan in which you acquire your company's stock through a company retirement plan that invests in and pays benefits in the form of company stock instead of cash contributions.

estate plan A document that establishes who will receive your property and possessions after your death. Its most common tools are wills and trusts.

estate tax A transfer tax imposed on the value of property left at death; often called an "inheritance tax" or "death tax."

ex-dividend date See *annual distribution date.*

executor The person named in a will who is responsible for making sure that your wishes are carried out after your death.

expense ratio For mutual funds, the percentage of a fund's average net assets that are used to pay fund expenses. This percentage accounts for management fees, administrative fees, and any 12(b)-1 fees.

FDIC An acronym for the Federal Deposit Insurance Corporation, a U.S. government agency that insures cash deposits, including certificates of deposit, that have been placed in member institutions, for up to $100,000 or more.

fee-based management A way in which you are charged for professional financial help. With fee-based management, you are charged a percentage of the assets in the manager's control, usually around 1% or 2%.

FIFO rule "First in, first out." When you sell shares of a stock or mutual fund, this is the rule the IRS uses that assumes that you're selling the ones you bought first.

fixed-income investment An investment that is similar to an IOU for borrowed money. Most produce a steady stream of income in the form of interest payments. The borrower, called the *issuer,* can be a government—municipal, state, or federal—a corporation, or a bank or savings and loan. In any case, the issuer is borrowing money from investors as a way to raise funds, and the issuer promises to repay the money, plus interest, at a set date, called the *maturity date*. Payments are usually made twice a year, but can be made as a lump sum at maturity. The interest rate is usually fixed at the time the security is issued, and remains constant throughout the life of the loan. You can usually sell fixed-income securities in a secondary market at their current market value, which means that your money isn't locked in until maturity.

foreign funds Mutual funds that invest in developed markets outside the United States.

Form ADV The standard form used by investment advisors to register and update registrations with the Securities and Exchange Commission and the jurisdictions that require advisors to register. The form is also used to comply with SEC Rule 206(4)-4, which obligates investment advisors to disclose material financial and disciplinary information to clients.

front-end load A sales charge on a mutual fund that is applied when you buy shares of the fund (as opposed to a back-end load, applied when you sell shares).

growth fund A mutual fund that invests in common stocks of established and emerging companies with good prospects for sustainable growth.

growth stock The stock of a company that has previously seen rapid growth in revenue or earnings and is expected to see similar growth beyond the short term. Generally speaking, growth stocks pay relatively low dividends and sell at a relatively high price, considering their earnings and book value.

guideline of 230K My guideline about how to estimate how much you'll need once you stop working: For every $1,000 you expect to need each month, you need to have at least $230,000 invested moderately aggressively.

home equity conversion See *reverse mortgage.*

index A group of companies that are considered yardsticks for measuring changes in the economy or in financial markets. The index can measure the whole stock market, or it can measure only a sector of the market, such as technology stocks.

index fund A mutual fund that is designed to track the returns of a specific index. The fund simply moves in tandem with the index it's based on, its gains and losses (minus annual expenses) paralleling those of the index.

Individual Retirement Account See *IRA,* or the entries for specific types of IRAs: *traditional IRA, rollover IRA, education IRA, Roth IRA,* and *SEP-IRA.*

inflation An increase in the cost of living, measured as a percentage and classified according to its severity. Mild inflation occurs when the price level—an average of all prices—rises from 2% to 4%. Moderate inflation refers to an inflation rate of 5% to 9%. Severe inflation (or "double-digit inflation") refers to an inflation rate of 10% or higher. Hyperinflation is out-of-control inflation that ruins a country's economy, in which money loses its value and people turn to barter rather than relying on currency.

international stock fund A mutual fund that invests outside of the United States. International stock funds can include world funds, which invest in securities issued throughout the world including the U.S., or in foreign funds, which invest in developed markets exclusively outside the U.S.

intestate Having made no valid will at death.

IRA (Individual Retirement Account) A self-funded retirement plan (a plan that you, not your employer, establish and fund) that provides tax benefits. There are several different types of IRAs: *traditional IRA, rollover IRA, education IRA, Roth IRA,* and *SEP-IRA.* For more information, see these glossary entries.

irrevocable trust A legal agreement that is permanent and can never be revoked or changed, in which you relinquish ownership of whatever assets you place in the trust, which means they are no longer part of your estate. Properly and carefully drawn, such a trust should not be subject to estate tax.

issuer The corporation, municipality, or government agency that issues a bond or security.

Keogh plan An employer-sponsored retirement plan for a partnership (or for a sole proprietorship for self-employed people). It requires significantly more paperwork than an IRA, and it's more complex to understand and manage. Although it works like an IRA, a Keogh plan can permit self-employed individuals to make higher tax-deductible contributions. Keogh plans must be adopted before the end of the business tax year—usually December 31. Contributions can be made up to the time for filing the employer's federal income tax return, including extensions. If you have eligible employees, you must make contributions for them at the same rate that you use for your own contributions.

laddering A strategy in which you buy bonds (or Treasury notes) with increasing maturities that are staggered so that the interest gives you a steady stream of income.

large-cap stock The stock of a company whose median market capitalization is in the top 5% of the largest 5,000 domestic companies. A large-cap mutual fund is a mutual fund that invests only in large-cap stocks.

limited power of attorney A legal document in which an investor gives a third party, usually an investment manager or financial institution, the authority to trade on his or her behalf, but limits the ability to transfer assets out of the investment account.

liquid investment An investment that can easily be converted to cash.

living trust A trust that becomes effective when you open and fund the trust account. Assets can be placed in the trust as soon as the trust agreement is completed and signed. A living trust can be revocable or irrevocable.

load A commission or sales fee on a mutual fund. A mutual fund without a load is a *no-load* fund.

long-term-care insurance Insurance that covers some or all of the expenses incurred as a result of required long-term care.

lump-sum distribution Receiving an amount of money due (say from a pension plan or divorce) all at once, rather than in periodic payments.

management fees Fees that are charged each year by mutual funds as the compensation for the fund managers. These fees are quoted as a percentage of the fund's average annual assets, and are often called the fund's *operating expense ratio.* Also called "annual fees."

maturity date In a fixed-income investment, the specified date at which the issuer promises to repay the money it has borrowed.

Medigap A term that's been coined to refer to ten insurance plans designed to supplement Medicare. These plans are sold not by the government but by private insurance companies, and they cover some of the things that Medicare doesn't.

mid-cap stock The stock of a company whose median market capitalization is in the 15% following the top 5% of the largest 5,000 domestic companies. A mid-cap mutual fund is a mutual fund that invests only in mid-cap stocks.

Minimum Required Distribution Mandatory withdrawals from a traditional IRA. When you turn 70½, the IRS requires that you begin (if you haven't already done so) withdrawing money from your IRA, even if you are still employed. The IRS calculates how much you withdraw using your life expectancy at the time of distribution. If you do not withdraw this minimum amount, the amount that you didn't withdraw is subject to a 50% excise tax. Minimum required distribution does not apply to Roth IRAs.

money market mutual fund A cash-equivalent investment that invests in short-term obligations from corporations and state or federal governments. Money market funds are designed to maintain a stable $1 share value, but there is no assurance that they will be able to do that.

munis, or municipal bonds Debt securities issued by state and local governments and their agencies. Munis typically pay interest at a fixed rate twice a year, and the issuer promises to return your principal at maturity.

mutual fund A type of investment that pools the money of many investors and buys various securities (such as stocks, bonds, and/or cash equivalents).

mutual fund supermarket A service, provided by a brokerage firm, through which you can choose from hundreds of no-load mutual funds from different fund families, instead of having to go to the individual funds. You can buy and sell funds from different companies through the same brokerage firm without paying any more than you'd pay if you bought the fund directly from the fund company. There is usually no transaction fee. There may or may not be a fee for opening an account.

net asset value, or NAV The market value of a single share of a mutual fund. It is calculated at the end of each business day by adding up the value of all the securities in the fund's portfolio, subtracting expenses, and dividing the sum by the number of shares outstanding. Mutual funds are traded based on their NAVs. Funds with an offer price identical to the NAV are either no-load or they are load funds carrying a contingent deferred sales charge.

net profit The remaining profit on an investment once you've deducted all expenses.

net worth The value of your estate, which you calculate by subtracting what you owe (your liabilities) from what you own (your assets). Your net worth is your estate's taxable value.

no-load (NL) A no-load mutual fund is one that does not carry a sales charge or commission. The initials "NL" in the offer price column of a mutual fund table mean that the fund is no-load, so you can buy and sell the fund at the price listed in the NAV (net asset value) column.

operating expense ratio (OER) A mutual fund's annual expenses (operating expenses, management fees, and 12[b]-1 fees, if any) expressed as a percentage of the fund's average net assets. These expenses are deducted before calculating the fund's NAV.

operating expenses Costs incurred by a mutual fund in its day-to-day operations. Every fund is subject to some degree of operating expenses, which usually include management fees, annual fees, administrative costs, and maintenance fees.

owner occupation coverage, or "occ" In disability insurance, an option that specifies that you will be paid if you can't do the work you currently do, not just any work.

penny stock A stock that sells for $5 or less. Penny stocks typically have no revenue, no income, and no capital. They do not include listed securities, National Market System securities, or mutual fund securities, even when they are priced under $5.

P/E ratio, or price/earnings ratio A measurement that represents the relationship between the price of a company's stock and its earnings for the past year. To get a company's P/E, divide its current price by its earnings per share (EPS) for the past year. Stock P/Es can vary tremendously, from as low as .5 to over 100. A stock's P/E is an indicator of the market's expectations about that stock. A higher P/E means higher expectations for the company's growth in earnings.

permanent life insurance Life insurance that is in effect until the death of the policyholder. Also called "whole life insurance."

pooled income fund In charitable giving, a type of fund in which contributions of many donors are pooled in an investment vehicle that gives income to the donor or any other noncharitable beneficiary. You contribute assets to a pooled income fund, and you receive a tax deduction for the current year (subject to AGI restrictions), based on the value of your donation less the present value of the future income.

portfolio The combined holding of stock, bond, and cash-equivalent investments held by an individual investor, a mutual fund, or a financial institution.

portfolio manager The person in charge of managing a mutual fund's holding.

pour-over will A simple legal document that states that anything you may have neglected to place in your trust during your lifetime should be placed in it at your death. While assets passing under a pour-over will are generally subject to probate, transfers of a small amount may be excluded from this procedure. This amount varies from state to state.

preferred stock A class of stock that has a claim on the company's earnings before payment is made on the common stock if the company declares a dividend. Preferred stockholders sometimes receive preferential treatment.

pre-tax rate of return The return you're currently getting on your investments. This rate of return represents how much money you're making, but it doesn't take taxes into account, which an after-tax rate of return does.

principal The amount of money that is financed, borrowed, or invested. For a bond, the face value, payable at maturity.

probate The legal process, supervised by the state, that is used to value your estate, settle any debts, pay estate and other taxes, and make an orderly distribution or transfer of title of your assets to your heirs.

professional investment manager A person who, for a fee, offers professional advice on the development of an investment plan, and buys and sells securities on behalf of the customer to implement that plan. A professional investment manager may hold qualifications such as Certified Financial Planner, Registered Investment Adviser, and/or Registered Broker.

prospectus A legal statement that describes the objectives of a specific investment. Every mutual fund is required to publish a prospectus and to give investors a copy free of charge. The prospectus lists the fund's goals, restrictions, advisors, and fees. You should read it carefully before you invest.

real rate of return See *after-tax rate of return.*

rebalancing your portfolio Changing the way in which your investments are allocated among asset classes.

redemption fee A fee charged by some mutual funds when shares are sold, usually within a short period of time. The fund's prospectus will provide details.

registered representative An employee or partner in a brokerage firm who is registered to handle customer accounts. A registered representative must pass an examination administered by the National Association of Securities Dealers.

retirement plan distribution A withdrawal of funds from a retirement plan.

reverse mortgage Also called a "home-equity conversion," a type of loan in which a lender loans you money against the value of your house, allowing you to tap the equity in your home. The amount you can borrow depends on your age, the age of your spouse, the amount of equity you have in your home, and the plan you're interested in.

revocable trust A legal agreement that can be revoked or changed as long as you're alive. It becomes irrevocable at your death. The assets in the trust remain in your control and ownership until your death.

rollover IRA A tax-free transfer of assets from one qualified plan to another. Also called a "conduit IRA." If you change jobs, retire, or get a divorce settlement that includes a distribution from a company retirement plan, you can "roll it over" into an IRA to preserve your capital and keep it growing free of current-year taxes. Your distribution will be subject to an automatic 20% withholding for income tax unless your old employer rolls it over directly from your current plan into the new plan. To roll your distribution over directly, your check or electronic transfer must be made payable to the sponsor of your IRA (or the trustee of your new employer's retirement plan for your benefit).

If your old employer made your distribution directly to you, you must deposit the funds into a rollover IRA (or your new employer's retirement plan) within 60 days from the date of the distribution to avoid current-tax liabilities. If your assets are not transferred within the 60-day limit, they become current income for tax purposes and in most cases carry a 10% additional penalty if you are under 59½ years old. Your employer will be required to withhold 20% of your payout, so you will only get 80%. In order to avoid paying taxes on the 20%, you will need to make it up out of other funds and roll over all the rest of your distribution into an IRA. You can then request a refund of the withheld taxes, but this is an undesirable approach.

Roth IRA A type of retirement plan that is structured to provide benefits to a broad segment of the population. The Roth IRA was first available for the 1998 tax year. For those who qualify, a Roth IRA offers more flexibility than a traditional IRA. Earnings can accumulate tax-free as long as the account is open, and there are more ways to withdraw funds without penalty. Whether or not you are eligible to contribute to a Roth IRA depends largely on income. In very general terms, it's designed for single investors whose annual income is less than $110,000, and for married investors (filing jointly) whose combined annual income is less than $160,000. If you already have a traditional IRA, it may be possible to convert it to a Roth IRA.

SARSEP (salary reduction SEP) An employer-sponsored salary reduction plan available to companies with 25 or fewer employees. SARSEPs are similar to 401(k) plans in that they have the same annual contribution limits, but they do not allow for plan loans. As of January 1, 1997, new SARSEP plans may not be opened.

self-funded retirement plan A retirement plan (such as an IRA) that you establish and fund yourself, rather than doing so through your company.

SEP-IRA An acronym meaning Simplified Employee Pension. A SEP-IRA is an alternative for those who are self-employed or own a small business with employees. It is easy to administer and maintain; the employer contributes to the plan but does not administer it. You can fund a SEP-IRA each tax year, although annual contributions are not required. Contributions may be made until your tax filing deadline, including extensions. The plan allows you to contribute up to 15% or $24,000, whichever is less. The withdrawal rules are the same as for a traditional IRA.

SEPP An acronym for "Substantially Equal Periodic Payments." Under legislation passed by the federal government in 1986, to withdraw money before you reach the age of 59½, you can set up a schedule of regular equal payments that will last for your life expectancy (if you're single) or the joint life expectancy of you and your spouse (if you're married). The IRS calculates the amount of the payments using life expectancy tables and a presumed interest rate. The payments must continue for five years or until you reach the age of 59½, whichever is longer. Once you've received the payment for that length of time, you can give up the payment plan and take withdrawals in any amount you want, without penalty.

short-term redemption fees Fees that apply to mutual fund redemptions made within 180 days of the purchase date. These fees are usually around 0.75% of the principal.

small-cap stock The stock of a company with a relatively small total market value, meaning a median market capitalization in the lower 80% of the largest 5,000 domestic companies. Small-cap stocks potentially offer increased growth and higher returns, but they are often more volatile and therefore riskier. A small-cap mutual fund is a mutual fund that invests only in small-cap stocks.

Standard & Poor's 500 (S&P 500) A well-known index comprising New York Stock Exchange (NYSE)-listed companies as well as a few American Stock Exchange (AMEX)-listed and over-the-counter stocks. The S&P 500 accounts for about 70% of the market value of the NYSE. The index is based on the eight-member selection committee's opinion of the country's largest companies, according to market capitalization.

stock An investment that represents the ownership of shares in a company.

STRIPs An acronym for "separate trading of registered interest and principal" securities. STRIPs are Treasury zero-coupon bonds, which are bonds that don't pay interest until maturity. You purchase STRIPs from a brokerage firm.

Taxpayer Relief Act of 1997 Legislation that allows penalty-free withdrawals from an IRA before the age of 59½ for first-time home purchases (up to $10,000) and qualified higher-education expenses.

term life insurance A type of life insurance that is in effect for a specified period, usually a 5-, 10-, 15-, 20-, or 30-year term.

testamentary trust A trust that becomes effective at your death through the probate of your will. This is when the assets are transferred to the trust. A testamentary trust is required to go through probate. When probate is complete, assets are distributed to the trust, and your trustee takes control.

traditional IRA An IRA to which you can now contribute $3,000 a year if you qualify, which you do if you or your spouse is employed. Married couples who file jointly may contribute up to $3,000 to each spouse's IRA for a total of $6,000 annually, even if one is a nonworking spouse, provided combined contributions do not exceed combined compensation. That money then grows tax-free until you withdraw it, which you can do without penalty after the age of 59½. You have complete control over what you invest your money in.

Treasury bills or T-bills Short-term, highly liquid U.S. Treasury securities available in maturities from three months to one year, with a minimum investment of $10,000.

trust A legal arrangement in which one person (the trustor) holds legal title to property for the benefit of another person or institution (the beneficiary). To be valid in most states, a trust must meet certain basic requirements. For example, it should contain a specified purpose (e.g., the management of distribution of assets) and specifically identified property, it should indicate one or more easily verifiable beneficiaries, it should make provisions for a trustee to manage your property for the benefit of your beneficiaries, and it should spell out the terms under which the trust will terminate.

trustee The person or institution who manages property according to the instructions in the trust agreement.

two-life pension (joint and survivor) option An option in a pension plan that specifies that you want your pension to cover you as well as your spouse. This will cause the amount of your pension checks to be less, but it means that your spouse will continue to receive payments after your death.

U.S. Treasury notes Securities that are debt obligations of the U.S. government, issued through the Department of the Treasury and backed by the full faith and credit of the U.S. government. They are considered virtually free of the risk of default.

value fund A mutual fund that invests in companies whose assets are considered undervalued, or in companies that have turnaround opportunities, with lower price-to-earnings ratios.

whole life insurance See *permanent life insurance.*

will A legally binding document directing the disposition of one's property, which is not operative until death and can be revoked up to the time of death or until there is a loss of mental capacity to make a valid will.

worker's compensation Payments that replace income lost due to injury if and only if you are injured while performing your job.

world fund A mutual fund that invests in securities issued throughout the world, including the U.S.

zero coupon bonds, or zeros Bonds that do not pay interest until maturity. They are sold at a discount from their face value, and their value increases as they near maturity. Your return comes from the appreciation. There are three types of zeros: corporate, municipal, and Treasuries.

INDEX

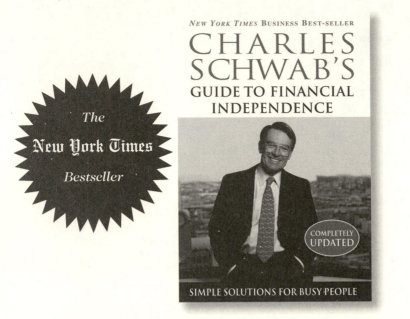